BEHAVIOR CONTROL

Also by Perry London

THE CHILDREN'S HYPNOTIC SUSCEPTIBILITY
SCALE (1963)

THE MODES AND MORALS OF PSYCHOTHERAPY (1964)

FOUNDATIONS OF ABNORMAL PSYCHOLOGY
(with David Rosenhan, 1968)

THEORY AND RESEARCH IN ABNORMAL PSYCHOLOGY
(with David Rosenhan, 1969)

Behavior Control

PERRY LONDON

Harper & Row, Publishers

1817

NEW YORK,
EVANSTON,
AND LONDON

FIRST EDITION

LIBRARY OF CONGRESS CATALOG CARD NUMBER: 69–15316

To my mother, Rose London, who lovingly freed me,
early in life, from gratuitous controls

Contents

Contents

Acknowledgments

During its more than four-year gestation, dozens of colleagues, students, assistants, secretaries, friends, and relatives have helped to write this book. They have braved tedium and fatigue to search a huge technical literature for the facts on which it is based, typed and retyped the many drafts that seemed necessary to make their presentation clear, and criticized parts of the manuscript or its themes, sometimes suggesting major additions to the book and often saving it from disastrous errors of fact or logic.

For technical assistance, I must thank Terry Barak, Patricia Gibson, Linda Joslyn, James P. Robinson, Marilyn Rutgers, Kenneth Schaefler, and Steven Willard, at the University of Southern California, and the 1968 seminar of clinical psychology students at the Instituto Psicologico of Puerto Rico.

For clerical help, I am grateful to Judy Hayashi, Nancyanne Nash, Nancy Naves, and Patricia Poinsett, at USC, and to Sylvia Horowitz, Judy London, Miriam London, and Dvora Pope, at the Hebrew University of Jerusalem.

For critical comments, I am indebted to Alfred Blumstein, of the Institute for Defense Analyses, Leslie M. Cooper, of Brigham Young University, Lynn Curtis and Patricia Gurne, both of the National Commission on the Causes and Prevention of Violence,

Norman Matlin, of the Instituto Psicologico de Puerto Rico, Eugene J. Webb, of Stanford University, and William Klein, Israel and Amia Lieblich, and Jane Lowenstein-Cohen, all of the Hebrew University. Vivian London was helpful throughout, and Miriam London saved me from carelessly reporting that lightning follows thunder.

During much of the work, I have been supported by a Public Health Service Research Scientist Development Award (#K3-MH-31,209) from the National Institute of Mental Health. Seymour Fox, Dean of the School of Education at the Hebrew University generously provided facilities at the University, which were of enormous value in enabling me to complete the book.

PART I

The Shaping of Man

The Advent of Behavior Control

The whole history of human development has engaged man in an
endless struggle for control. The record of his ascent from brutish-
ness is kept in the simple tools by which he enlarged his size and
strength and stretched his grasp to control the physical environment in which he lived. The rise of civilizations, and their fall,
reflect still more capacity to master things and people. The history
of religion and its institutions, from Hindu yogis to Greek gym-
nasts and from Hebrew ecstatics to British Methodists, is a history
of efforts to control the self, mind and body, or to regulate the
cosmos and the flesh by means of spirit.

Control of individuals has not been easy though, especially control of their inner lives, where hope and will reside. And though
man has been the constant object of his own inquiry, he still knows
less about his own behavior than about most other things he has
explored. But he is learning quickly and improving faster still, so
that his present knowledge has already fashioned a rude technology of behavior control, and he will soon have learned enough
to make it massive and refined.

Behavior control is the ability to get someone to do one's
bidding. From antiquity until almost now, the only common
means for doing this have been coercion by force and threat of

force and persuasion by inspiration and education, but these techniques have been mostly gross or tedious in their application and clumsy or unsure in their effects. All this is changing now, and means are being found, in all the crafts and sciences of man, society, and life, that will soon make possible precise control over much of people's individual actions, thoughts, emotions, moods, and wills. Never in human history has this occurred before, except as fantasy. Even now, most of the scientists, technicians, teachers, doctors, engineers, and other specialists in the learned professions have not yet looked upon the tools that they have made or use as parts of a technology for controlling behavior. Still less have they designed grand strategies, singly or together, for "taking over" the lives of individuals or society. Even so, when the facts of today's behavioral technology are assembled and put in context, as is intended here, some people may be surprised at the extent to which it is now possible to manipulate people systematically. And it is petty compared to what will soon be possible.

The techniques of psychotherapy, for instance, widely practiced and accepted as means of curing psychological disorders, are also methods of controlling people. They can be used systematically to influence values and attitudes, if not overt behavior, toward conventional norms of conduct, or to release feelings of great intensity, whose expression can change the course of people's lives. Such things are done routinely in traditional psychotherapy. Behavioral psychologists, at the same time, are inventing even more sophisticated techniques for treating personal disorders ranging from stuttering to schizophrenia. They are learning to attack specific aspects of individual behavior with increasing precision, "burning out" traumatic fears by creating an internal explosion of anxiety; restraining chronic lusts like homosexuality, and the incontinences of habit, from alcoholism to enuresis, by means of electrically aided "training" devices; or conditioning human emotions and the body's involuntary functions to respond faithfully to the manipulation of critical signals by a behavior-control expert. But these, perhaps better known right now than other things going on, are the weakest of the control techniques that are developing. The biochemical and neurological substrata of behavior are being mined at even greater speeds, and the technology that results from these discoveries ranges from the surgical control temper to "the pill," with its attendant effect on the sexual mores of our society.

The chemicals and the electronic hardware of behavior-control technology are proliferating even faster and more powerfully than are psychological tools. The host of tranquilizing and energizing drugs already on the market represents the bare infancy of an industry that will soon produce drugs much more precisely capable of steering people's moods and emotions and, soon thereafter, of affecting important parts of their intellects, such as memory. Electronic miniaturization and improvements in surgery increasingly exploit discoveries of the exact locations in the brain where various behavioral functions are managed; skillful invasion of these sites permits interference with the functions; radio remote controls over epileptic seizures, sexual desire, and speech patterns are already operational. Few people yet have thought much on the long-range prospects of such technology.

While all these new developments affecting individuals are proceeding, computer technology increasingly automates production, reducing the work force; it discovers better and better data-processing methods, making it easier all the time to track and predict virtually any kind of mass behavior trend; this makes it easier, in turn, to forecast, then control, the individuals who make up the mass.

In some ways, this development is certainly a good thing. Some of its blessings may be the elimination of mental illness, crime, and even war, and the prospect of achieving these goals by scientifically controlling behavior is appealing. But the same arts which can be used to restrict such evils might serve to stifle good behavior, too, and if the refined management of individual behavior represses freedom or destroys initiative, then the cost of having it may exceed the profit to be gained. The enormous risks involved make it urgent for intelligent people of good will, especially the scientists and technologists who are most responsible for inventing and testing the techniques of control, to plan, carefully and considerately, how to do their work with the least threat to human freedom and the most promise of promoting mankind's welfare. Without such planning, their amoral infant may become a freak or a monster, for it is already born, if often still unrecognized or unnamed, and it will certainly mature, no matter who protests.

The technical conquest of the external environment is already so advanced that its frontiers of exploration have moved to outer space and to the ocean's depths. The rest of this century will see breakthroughs in biology and in behavior science that parallel the great discoveries of physics in the last two centuries and more.

Each wave of theoretical advance from pure research anticipates a spurt of growth in engineering, for each makes possible a new technology, which sires, in turn, new offspring of its own. Electronics thus begets television and computers and compact hardware and spaceships; genetics and biochemistry beget efficient animal husbandry and contraceptive pills and tranquilizing drugs; and so on, in any field one chooses to observe. It is plain to anyone who troubles to look that once the potential for a particular technological development is clear, the actual technology follows, sometimes sooner, sometimes later, but without fail. The technology of behavior control, then, is bound to grow more elegant from strides now being made in the biological and behavioral sciences. And its future pace will, if anything, accelerate. Already, technology decides most of the course of human affairs, and biology most of what remains. Wealth and poverty, happiness and misery, even life and death, are decreed by the fantastic powers that electricity and chemistry and even the primitive mechanics of the flush toilet ordain. To murder masses swiftly or sustain multitudes in famine or heal epidemic plagues or prevent millions from being born only to starve demands technologies of gases (for Zyklon B or for refrigeration), of fungi, of hormonic chemistry—all things already here.

In the face of all this, given all that our species knows and has already done with knowledge, and all it seems about to do with it, the questions of how well man can steer himself and for how long are more open than politicians and social "actionists" and scientists and seers like to consider. But everybody knows how badly he can steer, how quickly he can err in plan and action, and how decisive the results can be in misery and in death.

All the people fixers therefore, knowledgeable or not, already share a common social purpose: to mobilize, repair, and program man to best equip him to control the world he has set in motion. This means not only to direct his overt acts, which force can do alone, but to influence his internal states as well, and to guide his motives and intentions by whatever means. Psychologists, psychiatrists, and other mental-health practitioners have been in the business of individual behavior control for a long time, via psychotherapy; but it has been such a slow and sometimes useless means of influence that they have not been forced or felt the need to see it as an effort toward that end. In consequence, they are not always any readier for this technology, which they must sometime understand, accept, and master, than is anybody else. There are some good reasons in the intellectual history of the West for this situation, but it is still a bad, even dangerous position to be in. Like it or not, these mental hygienists are human engineers.

Human engineering differs, hopefully, from any other kind, by ethical restrictions on its contents and efficiency, which must be far more stringent for experiments on people than on harder and less precious substances. Also, the theoretical limits of control may be much narrower for human behavior than for other stuff. Even so, important as such restrictions and limits may be, the development of a refined technology of behavior control in modern society is as inevitable as the maintenance of all our other technologies is certain, for all technologies are ultimately corollaries of each other. And the nature of the refinements will make real what has hitherto been mostly a fantasy of the ignorant—control of the mind. As 1984 draws near, it appears that George Orwell's fears for Western democracy may have been too pessimistic, or at least premature, but it is also clear that his conceits of the technology by which tyranny could impress its will upon men's minds were much too modest. By that time, the means at hand will be more sophisticated and efficient than Orwell ever dreamed, and they will be in at least modest use, as they have already begun to be, not by the will of tyrants but by the invitation of all of us, for we have been schooled to readiness for all these things and will demand their benign use regardless of their potential risk. The capacity for control will continuously grow, evolving from benevolence.

The Psychological Readiness for Behavior Technology

Once the scientific stage is set for new engineering projects, the major deterrents to their progress are economic and psychological. In the United States at present there do not seem to be serious economic deterrents to anything, so these need not be considered here. Psychological deterrents are another matter, but even though some of those exist, there seems to be a general readiness for behavior technology. Three important reasons for this readiness are: first, there is a great need for resolutions of the kinds of problems which can be addressed by a technology of behavior control; second, there is a ready-made and widely accepted rationale for it in the logic of pragmatism; and third, we are already well acclimated to technical change and its consequences.

The Need

Whatever the hypothetical dangers of an efficient behavior technology may be, the real social evils sustained by abstention from it are severe. There are problems of motivation and incentive, as with high school dropouts and unskilled workers; problems of social organization and responsibility, as with demonstrators, protesters, rioters, and police, with delinquents and criminals, with businessmen who destroy forests and pollute waterways, and with plain litterbugs; problems of attitude and prejudice, as with enemies of Negro civil rights or with employers who reject Catholics and Jews. All these problems abound, and to be solved, they must finally be reduced to the level of changing individual behavior. Some of the needed solutions can, of course, be legislated, and for those, the problem of changing individual behavior applies only to people who defy the law. But for many of these problems no direct legislation is possible, and other answers to them must be sought. Behavior-control technology offers one avenue of approach to this purpose.

The Rationale

A technology is nothing but a systematic way of doing something, and as long as you are sure you want to do it, you will almost certainly approve of somebody's figuring out the most efficient way possible. The stronger your own motive to get it done, moreover, the more leeway you may give him to risk some damage in order to do it well. We let dentists drill our teeth because preserving them is worth the pain, and, with whatever trepidation, we let surgeons cut our hearts open, balancing the risk of living sickly against that of dying quickly. We do this because our motive to live well is great and the promise of the surgeon's technology combines with the depth of our need to overcome restraint. Most of us are even more generous when the risks involved are damage to others and the promised gains our own, and the more so when we are not ourselves the wielders of the instruments that do the job. This pragmatic disposition may have served in ancient times to justify the stipends paid to priests by decent folk who never could have brought themselves to throw live babies into Moloch's fires or to call upon the gods in person with the dripping hearts of human victims. In modern times, it sets the stage for the entire march of technology which, for any given case, can always be rationalized as producing some greater good by its presence or permitting some evil by its absence.

Too many motives of too many people in our society are now united for the purpose of sustaining technological development to permit much carping or complaint against it to take effect. William James's philosophy of pragmatism has won the day in spades; for most of us the practical value of any new thing outweighs the sentimental yearning of a few for something lost.

The Adaptation

The blessings of technology inevitably change our lives in many critical ways, some of which we notice, like the speed and ease of travel, and some of which we take for granted, like the ubiquity of electric power. But whether we notice them or not, there is little choice of effects left open to us once we accept some technical cause as proper. And even our noticing depends mostly on how new the changes are.

We like to think of ourselves as creatures of our own free wills, so we spend little time in everyday life observing the many ways in which we are used by the technology we use. But hardly anyone will fail to answer the telephone when it rings, regardless of how annoyed he is by its intrusion; and almost no one folds, spindles, or mutilates computerized pay checks even if it is very bothersome to carry them as directed. These are only small irritations, of course, and the benefits of telephones and computers make them worth bearing many times over. The point is not that they are small or large but that taken together they profoundly influence our lives. They often do so for the good, but we are so thoroughly acclimated to technological change in any case that the only difference in our tolerance for changes, good or bad, may rest in how quickly they are assimilated into our lives.

Most of the profound changes that occur in a man's life, like growing and aging, happen slowly enough so he can adapt to them before he even has to notice them. This is true for the multitude of men as well, so great changes sometimes come about in society or in the physical environment as imperceptibly as in the individual. When the last of the million-year-old redwood groves are hacked away to make space for freeways to be built, no one who has not seen them before will need to see them, least of all those who ride the high road later on, never even knowing trees were ever there. So too when the San Francisco Bay is slowly filled with junk, it will not be missed a hundred years later by those who cross it without knowing there was ever water there. Those who have known only the yellow murk above Los Angeles' hills need never reminisce about the times when all the air was clear for miles around.

As long as change comes slowly enough, and quietly, and mingles any poisons that it bears with compensating pleasures (or at times just with relief), it can take hold. Nature will not cry out, offended—nor will men. She, and they, will simply change whichever way they must to meet the new conditions that impose on them. The notion that an outraged Nature will rebel against banal invasion is poetic but untrue. It is untrue of men as well, and more and more becoming dangerous to believe.

Sources of Delay in the Development of Behavior Technology

The argument thus far: A technology of behavior control is, at this point in history, scientifically inevitable, socially necessary, and psychologically prepared for. But its development has inadvertently been somewhat delayed and inhibited until now and will be actively contested in the future. The control capacities already in existence are not being used full blast and are still not even known to most of the professional people who could use them. And as they are becoming known, some important resistance to their use is becoming evident.

The first and certainly the most important source of delay has been the lack until quite recently of technical means for controlling behavior in any but the very grossest fashion. The means available have been generally limited to fairly crude educational techniques and to the threat of force.

Second, most people in positions of power throughout history have not needed very refined methods of individual control. The majority of men have always lived under tyrannical conditions, where people were easily expended and replaced. And when life itself is cheap, power seekers need not trouble themselves much to learn the subtleties of control. Political control, which is traditionally the kind of greatest interest, has always been sustained primarily by force. Even law, the most important means of rational control that human genius has produced, has had much of its impetus only because it was backed by the threat of force.

Historically, the only way to control people, other than by coercion, has been to promise them rewards for doing what was wanted of them. Most rulers have been content to try to harvest power by shrewdly husbanding these two alternatives before their followers and victims. How many kings have died in bed, or still in power, is unknown.

Despite their seeming practicality, traditional coercive controls were generally the least desirable for political purposes as well as for individual ones, and modern behavior technology has relatively little to contribute to man's long-standing oversophistication in the brutal use of force on individuals. But refined means of social control and subtle means of individual control are very much the objects of such a system. It is particularly the possibility of discovering very subtle methods of coercion, in which people can be made to want to do what the controller wants them to, or to act at his behest without knowing it, that gives rise to contemporary resistance to behavioral technology.

Technical limitations aside, future resistance to behavior technology may revolve entirely around its moral implications. Two main lines of moral argument on this topic are already clear and will probably dominate discussions of the subject for a long time. They may be conveniently labeled the "existential," or "humanist," argument and the "argument from ethical tradition."

The existential argument is apt to be the most popular intellectual base of opposition to behavior technology for quite a while. It says in effect that deliberate control of human behavior is immoral because it dehumanizes man. Anything that reduces an individual's ability to make choices (whether he wants to make choices or not) is objectionable precisely because it does so; the exercise of choice is the heart of morality, which in turn is one essence of humanity. Since the imposition of control is the very antithesis of choice, it *ipso facto* dehumanizes, and since man is morally obligated, above all else, to exercise his human attributes, he should not support an enterprise dedicated to their subversion.

The existentialist position typically makes it clear that being human means something quite different from being an animal. In a *Commentary* article, Leslie Farber, former president of the Washington, D.C., Society of Existential Psychiatrists, attacks one increasingly popular, if still primitive, technology of behavior control:

. . . I would attribute the moral obtuseness of Action therapists to the occupational fact that they have been so long closeted with laboratory animals and . . . too bewitched by the ingenuity of their experiments with these animals. . . . I would agree that, unlike morality, behavior—objective, visible, measurable behavior—is bodily conduct we share with animals. But the moral imagination to consider such matters as good and evil, including of course the behavior associated with these human realities, is not a capacity we share with animals. To treat an animal as though he possessed this capacity is merely silly, but to treat a human being as though he were only his behavior is, I am afraid, wicked.

The term "behavior" is used narrowly here to mean "bodily conduct we share with animals," and the idea that man is more than his behavior is evidently intended to add the "moral imagination," which is ours alone, into the formula for being human. It seems reasonable to distinguish ourselves from other species on this basis and, to that extent, to say that morality is of the essence of humanity. To whatever extent it reduces moral involvement, the argument runs, behavior control is wicked; it makes of man a mere animal.

Another way of stating the humanist argument is to say that by making man equivalent to his behavior, or to his animal attributes, you are denying his freedom. Freedom, in this sense, or self-fulfillment, is an extension of the concept of choice, and it is assumed to be the broad possession of individual men, extending to most aspects of their relationships to the world. In essence, this position rejects the idea that there are limits to the capacities of individuals to fulfill themselves or express themselves and that the laws that govern the conduct of other physical bodies must have equal governing powers over man as well. The very possibility of deliberate behavior control frightens the adherents of this view because it implies that man's freedom is very limited.

The argument from ethical tradition is also a source of resistance to behavior technology, but more in the sense of conservative restraint and concern than of outright objection or opposition. Some major principles in the ethical tradition of the liberal West are particularly challenged by the potentialities of behavior-control technology. Culled from the ancient political and religious experience of the Mediterranean basin and refined and annealed in Europe until the American and French Revolutions made formal doctrine of them, three of the most vital ones are: the rule of *noncoercion,* which says that people should not be forced to do what others want but should be free to refuse them; the rule of *explication,* which is that people should not be seduced into compliance but should be told what is wanted of them; and, corollary to the first two, the rule of *self-direction,* which is that people should be free to decide for themselves how they want to guide their lives.

None of these rules can operate in a completely unrestricted way if social organizations of even the simplest kind are to persist, but they are all vital to an ethical tradition which we still revere and accept as a model of conduct. No matter how complicated society becomes, these rules, which amount to an operational definition of freedom in human intercourse, retain their value. But value depends on meaning, and the traditional meanings of these terms are potentially subverted by the facts of behavior technology.

It is easy to understand coercion, for example, in a civilization whose weapons are bows and arrows—or even atomic bombs. It means assault, with jail or pain or death resulting. But what about a kind of surgery to prevent, let us say, recidivist crimes of violence by dismantling the physiological machinery within the nervous system that incites aggressive acts? Or perhaps a pill to erase memory, to wipe out the toxic nest of fancied injuries that shrill for violent vengeance? Or hypnotic training, or conditioning, or some splendidly effective psychotherapy whose object and effect is to teach people to abhor violence? Are these truly coercive? Traditionally, coercion means making people do things against their will, but that takes for granted that "will" is itself somehow inviolable. The techniques in question here aim to change will, not to rape it; their initiation may be coercive, but their effect is seductive.

But seduction is not much easier to evaluate than is coercion as the means at hand for doing it grow steadily more elegant. The practical ethics of explication were always problematic, because some things which need to be taught, like character education, are simply better learned obliquely, by imitating others and by incentives to "be good" than by exhortation or explanation. Behavior-control technology adds to the old problem simply by increasing the available machinery for influencing people against their will, or indifferently to it. It is the seduction of will that is finally at stake, not the explication of purpose.

But the essence of will is self-direction, and the direction of self-direction in all our lives is, in many ways, a direct result of the opportunities and restrictions that technology bestows. Once it allows easy control over individual behavior, it is virtually impossible not to meddle with its Faustian implications. Thus the pill puts the finishing touches on a moral revolution already heavily endorsed for fifty years by the automobile. An even cheaper drug makes possible the easy emulation of mystical experience—and the entire field is barely opened up.

It is clear that will is as manipulable as are many of our actions. What is not clear is how to re-evaluate the ethics of behavior control that have guided our civilization until now, based as they are on the idea of will, with its ultimate seating in the idea of soul. This is not a merely academic question, because, as a practical result of behavior technology, the effects of errors in social planning will become less random and more sweeping than ever before in human history.

Controlling Behavior Control

There are still some people who, observing the enormous variability of human beings, and the enormous contemporary ferment in the social and behavior sciences, believe that any significant technology of behavior control is a thing which will only come to pass in the distant future, if at all, because too little is now known of human nature. Perhaps nothing could be less the case. The degree of control possible is enormous. It will always be limited by genetically based differences between individuals, of course, but even these are increasingly subject to manipulation by the biochemists and the surgeons. At all events, an applied science of human behavior becomes possible as soon as enough relevant facts are assembled for some studied purpose of prediction and control to be achieved. No more of human nature need be known than satisfies this purpose. Even an applied behavior science with utopian aims does not require limitless knowledge or vision of its own objectives in order to be engineered. It does require *some* knowledge of human nature, a great deal of planning, a commitment to some foreseeable goals and to some self-regulating scheme for achieving or abandoning them, and some imagination for the wider ripples in the world's affairs that planned interventions accidentally bring. The more that is known, the better, because knowledge is the key to control and accident its bane. But it is a mistake in this connection to be entrapped by the professorial caveat, "We do not know enough to act," which is just true enough often enough to paralyze the good-willed muddled.

In fact, knowledge of the facts, sense knowledge, always waits on history. Precision for deciding how to act can only be a colloquy of probabilities, whose relevance, once calculated, must be tested to be known. The refusal even to calculate (to think to test) is a self-indulgent kind of cowardice incognito, which calls itself conservative restraint.

There is probably little point today, if there ever was one, in debating at length whether or not behavior-control technology is feasible or should generally be attempted or avoided. In general, no such choice is any longer possible. What remains is to determine the characteristics of this technology, the rules for implementing control, and the purposes which it should serve. This is no small matter. We can no longer choose whether or not to explore the secrets of nuclear particles either, but that does not make it clear that we must drop atom bombs on each other.

Behavior scientists had better start thinking about this now because few other people are in equally good positions to do so. Physicists did not devote themselves much to the implications of atomic physics until after they had found the means to blow up the world—and their worried deliberations since then have not been terribly productive or useful to the politicians who must implement these things. Behavior science is still only on the verge of powerful control technology. It has not yet accomplished it so thoroughly that it must be quickly taken out of scientific hands, though it is too important to be left entirely in them. Suppose there is no atom holocaust. What kind of world must we make, knowing we must make one?

The judgment of history becomes easier to forecast all the time in this connection, for we come closer all the time to shaping it, not just reading it. More and more, like W. C. Fields, it proclaims, "Never give a sucker an even break."

Aldous Huxley foresaw this problem with great clarity in *Brave New World, Brave New World Revisited,* and *Ape and Essence,* and science-fiction writers have been discussing it for years. Behavior scientists must enter the discussion now, however, and help others enter it as well; it is their responsibility more than anybody else's, for they are the designers and may become the engineers of control, whether they like it or not. The future, already upon us, must be controlled.

2

The Emergence of Control Technology

A catalogue of all the ancient ways that men have used to control
each other would show that there were many and that some of
them were effective. Even so, they do not amount to much as *technology,* for that term implies a system, a planned pattern of control,
with effects that are precise as well as powerful.

Even the old dreams of occult power over men, like the natural
means at hand, were gross and absolute. They generally took two
forms. In one, mental projections of people were transmuted into
supernatural beings with supernatural powers. In the other, ordinary people could command similar powers by the purchase of
suitable goods and services or the mastery of appropriate skills.

In old fairy tales, which often reflect folk fears and aspirations,
and religious myths, which always reflect folk beliefs, ghosts,
angels, and genii could be manipulated magically to use their
powers for the aggrandizement of the human clients who commanded them. More recent legends have come closer to the truth
of what is possible. The last few centuries have seen a progression
of ever more naturalistic fancy in this regard, from the story of the
golem, in sixteenth-century Prague, to Frankenstein's monster in
the last century, down to zombies, hardware robots, and androids
in this one. The last two received the final seal of public approval in
America in 1966, in the form of a television comedy series for
family consumption. Lovable monsters made it earlier on family

18

television, and a few years earlier still among teenagers in the form of bizarre rock-and-roll records, comedy greeting cards, and similar paraphernalia, and tongue-in-cheek monster movies like *I Was a Teen-age Werewolf.*

The legends of these beings often portray them as creations of man, less than human only because their substance is inspired by men, not because they lack man's capabilities. (This suits our convention that God alone inspires the breath of life.) Mrs. Shelley and the spinners of tales of zombies go so far, indeed, as to compose their critters from people parts.

The second form of magical power seeking, more naturalistic than trying either to negotiate with supernatural beings or to manufacture them, involved efforts to gain power directly by the magical use of incantations and formulas together with a wide assortment of chemical adjuncts, which usually included some obnoxious compounds to be administered under propitiously vile circumstances. A lively traffic in love potions and power pills, from which much of today's pharmacopoeia derived, was always extant, along with some drugs for healing. This was handled primarily by priests, shamans, sorcerers, lunatics, and common folk whose aspirations were ordinarily limited to a particular murder, seduction, or profit. Through most of history, and in most places, witches and witch hunters have worked the same side of the street, trafficking in the same assumption that limitless powers are available to people who can take advantage of the right magic.

These ancient dreams of power have always differed so much from the facts of power, however, that practical power seekers rarely troubled much to discover concrete means of individual control in occult lore. Then as now, they could not afford to invest too much in dubious and often fraudulent ventures for controlling single individuals when what they needed were gross and brutal controls over masses of individuals to satisfy a very small number of goals: (1) governing, (2) preventing (or fostering) insurrection or resistance to conquest, and (3) promoting religious institutions. Practical aspirants for the control of society could never wait upon the means for controlling *individuals,* however helpful it would have been to have them.

All behavior control is, of course, the control of individuals. Perhaps the only sensible distinction between social and individual controls is that social controls are ostensibly impersonal; laws, for example, are addressed to whole classes of people by some controlling body. However, this impersonal aspect of laws impresses none of the people who are individually affected by them, either as agents or as victims, and the term "social control" is probably useful finally as a merely dialectic convenience for indicating that many people are involved. At all events, the great power seekers of history have been concerned primarily with man in multitude, not singly, and it is the breadth, not the depth, of their aspirations and effects which has brought their names through time.

Traditional Behavior Controls

The main control techniques that lent success to their employers have always been psychological. The primitive exceptions, in which governors work by murder, torture, and jail, and priests work by drugs and exorcisms, are relatively rare and mostly have had only transitory worth. All the common controls in use until now have evolved from chance discoveries of the power that lay in the manipulation of habit and conviction and in the appeal to fear and desire. The last is the most important of these. It is more from believing they have something to gain than from fearing they have everything to lose that subordinates sustain the power of chieftains over the long run.

The classical psychological techniques of control are separately illustrated in the three main social functions which have required it, government, religion, and insurrection. Examining these, as they have consistently operated throughout history, makes it easier to understand the nature and evolution of control technology.

Government

Much as explicated in the United States Constitution, all governments work through the interaction of legislative, judicial, and executive functions and functionaries. Regardless of how these functions are distributed among different people, and regardless of who it is that demands an accounting from them (the main thing that distinguishes democratic from tyrannical governments), the mechanisms of operation are fairly distinct: legislative and adjudicative entities exercise control through discourse and decree, and executive bodies control by coercion and reward. The purpose of coercion and reward is, of course, to enforce legislation and adjudication, but it is still important to distinguish them because the results of legislative discourse often require no enforcement whatsoever from any formal governmental bodies. Psychologically, at least, law is observed by most people because it is promulgated, not because it is enforceable. The habits of obedience may be instilled early in life by the experience of reward and punishment, but they operate with relative autonomy in the daily lives of most adults.

Religion

Two techniques of control are central to organized religion. The first, and most important, is the performance of ritual acts (including prayer), the second is preaching. A ritual act is characterized by its symbolic nature, that is, by the fact that its control function is indirect. One may sacrifice food to the gods to gain their favor without believing that they eat, for example, or bless them without believing that they tally their adulation. Preaching is characterized by its inspirational nature, by the fact that its purpose is not simply to transmit information but also to elicit a certain response, generally emotion-laden, from its listeners.

Insurrection

The problem of control in insurrection is how to arouse people individually and in mobs against an existing organization. The only difference between individual and mob action is that arousing a crowd has a catalytic effect on the individual in it, which destroys his sense of personal and separate responsibility for his behavior. Participation is an experience in which the individual maintains a sense of self-consciousness, even though he may be doing exactly what everyone else around him is doing. It acts as a preservative or prophylactic against immersion, which is the spirit of selflessness that defines a mob. The crowd is the catalyst for transmuting the sense of participation into the feeling of immersion.

Insurrectionists are especially interested in promoting mob action because the inherent dangers of rebellion make it very difficult to arouse people individually to action. The discursive methods of established governments cool the blood and hinder the swift and violent strokes the insurrectionist requires. So, to stir the crowd into a mob, he willy-nilly applies the primitive behavior-control mechanisms of religion to his affairs. Preaching is his primary tool for this purpose. His sermons may incidentally give people information that would stimulate some action from them, but information as such is secondary to the main purpose, which is to arouse emotions that catalyze the message so that its impact on action is strengthened. It is the emotional overtone, not the ostensible information, that contains the main message of preaching, and it is in turn the catalytic character of the emotional arousal that makes preaching an instrument of control.

Control Through Catalysts

The catalytic character of a device is what makes it, for our purpose, a significant means of control. In chemistry, a catalyst is a substance which speeds the interaction between other substances but is not itself affected much in the process. It is an agent, so to speak, for other chemical processes to which it is largely irrelevant. Extended outside chemistry, a catalyst may be seen as any medium which speeds the confluence of events, a phenomenal brokerage in which transactions are quickened without distorting their intent or character. On the face of it, the services of a catalyst are entirely irrelevant to what actually can transpire, just as the services of travel agents have no apparent effect upon the schedules of the planes or ships they book or on their prices. But examining catalytic agents of control as media through which reactions between events take place shows that this is not necessarily the case. The medium may not merely speed up what would happen anyway without itself being affected; it may dictate what finally occurs and itself be changed by the occurrence. Water is the medium through which ships pass, but without it they could not move at all, and their design would have to be altered to make them negotiable in air or on land. And passing through water, ships cut a wake which disturbs or changes what goes on within the medium itself, shifting the waves or the courses of fish or the movements of other boats. A medium may have more than a passive connection to the events it contains. This is not to argue, as does Marshall McLuhan about communications media, that "the medium is the message," which, by and large, I think, could not be true. It does say, however, that a crowd of people, which is the medium for the creation of a mob, is not incidental or irrelevant to it. Even though the sense of immersion, or the loss of self-consciousness, is what defines membership in a mob, and not the fact that a person is physically close to a lot of other people, still, if the crowd did not exist, it might be very difficult to produce the same sense of immersion in that individual at that time. The problem of finding equally powerful but more economical media has always plagued religious missionaries and political insurgents, because most of the action they desire from individuals can neither be produced nor sustained by a mob.

The use of catalysts for behavioral effects is widespread and long known in human society, and even accepted unself-consciously for many purposes. Psychological catalysts of behavior have so long been taken for granted that the problem of their misuse has been incorporated into law as "the exercise of undue influence." Chemical behavior catalysts, equally familiar since history began, have not all been limited to fanciful and useless love potions, invisibility drugs, or preservatives of youth. Some of them have worked very well, like drugs that change states of consciousness. Use of these may be intrinsic to civilization, with very advanced and very impoverished societies using them more than others. Alcoholic compounds are used far in lead of all other awareness-changing drugs, and their use has generally been accepted and assimilated into every aspect of the formal organization of society. Fasting, flagellation, dancing, and other Dionysian rites are also among the many drastic changes in body processes and behavior which people have always used deliberately to change their sensory and intellectual experience from the dreary commonplace to some exalted novelty. The point of all of this, from our perspective, is that the behavior, or drug, in question is recommended and indulged not for its own sake but as an instrument for gratifications extending beyond the media themselves. Marijuana does not get smoked for flavor nor alcohol guzzled for taste. The media are the keys to new experience, nothing more.

Ritual functions as a medium in exactly the same way; it is, by definition, the catalytic agent for functional events: The performance of rain dancers is a medium to invoke the gods, who in turn send the showers; the vicarage of priests is a medium of communication with God, to facilitate, not to replace it.

One of the most powerful control methods ever developed is the ritualistic use of words in the form of slogans and oaths. Slogans are sometimes doubly boosted by the music of national anthems, patriotic hymns, and marching songs. Music is often used effectively as a catalyst for increasing the emotional impact of situations, particularly as background for emotional or suspenseful situations in movie, radio, and television dramas. A less familiar but easily recognized catalytic control device is the use of irrelevant acts or words to catalyze the message so its content will be more deeply imbedded. Hitler's torchlight ceremonies made brilliant use of this method to create and unite a mob. The pageantry was deliberately designed and executed to provide an emotional mystique of such power that by the time Hitler actually began talking it made no difference at all what he said. The near-hysterical masses were already his adoring slaves. A subtler and more powerful event of this kind is illustrated by the Mau Mau oath, which, by its obscenely terrifying form, served to control people individually. The ritual that attended the words of the oath had no relation to them. It was gratuitously frightening and foreign, cloaking its words in mystery which, if not exalting them, still embellished their power.

The Sequence of Technological Development

The raw materials for behavior control are catalytic agents, but the basis for technology is a plan or system for exploiting them. The pattern of development for behavior-control technology, as for any other, is one in which these raw materials are first used casually, perhaps even by accident, then systematically but without a grand design, then deliberately. As this happens, their effects, at first vague, become increasingly precise.

The earliest historical precursors of behavior technology were probably institutions created for control functions. The organization of religion into priesthoods may have been the first event of this kind, beginning as men increasingly came to believe it was possible to propitiate the gods of nature, which means to control their behavior. In that case, some special people would be justified in abandoning more obviously productive work in order to devote themselves to such propitiatory functions. The evolution of those functions into priestly rites is nothing less than the evolution of a machinery for control, involving mystery, alcohol (wine), sacrificial or other ritual objects, oracles, and formulas. Technology begins as this machinery gets differentially and deliberately applied to individuals, because the recognition of individual differences leads to a need for precision in the means for dealing with those differences.

True technology is not only deliberate but precise. It demands four capacities: (1) to produce a specific *variety* of effects, (2) to control the *intensity* of effects, (3) to specify the *domain* of effects, and (4) to control the *duration* of effects. With respect to behavior, none of these capabilities has really been within our grasp until very recently, and it will still be a long time, maybe eternally long, until they are entirely so. But once it is recognized that these abilities are the prerequisites of control technology, it becomes possible for people to treat the whole problem as one of engineering and manufacturing and thus to envision its boundaries with a measure of clarity that both speeds and controls its development.

The thing that augurs most for the fruition of a true technology of behavior control in this era of blossoming biochemistry is the fact that gross control has long existed without recourse to externally produced chemicals or their like. Skilled manipulators have intuitively recognized for ages that behavior is itself the ideal catalyst of behavior. If one can correctly understand how to arouse people's emotions or to get responses from them which subsequently trap their emotions, he can get them to behave in other ways as he desires, regardless of the expense to their own interests. He can persuade them to go to war against all sense and reason, as Nasser has done in Egypt, or to betray their kith and kin for vague and meaningless applause, as Stalin did in Russia, Hitler in Germany, and Mao Tse-tung in China. Or he can get them to give their lives without regret to water trees whose fruit will not be borne a thousand years beyond, as Jesus did, and as few others dared.

The mechanics of behavioral catalysis were not so much chosen throughout history as chanced upon, usually by some accidental projection by the controller of his own emotions. Sometimes, of course, he also had control of the tools of destruction, as did Napoleon or Julius Caesar or Alexander, but not always. Buddha had no henchmen, nor did Jesus. What they did have was sympathy, the power to share emotion with others, so that their own feelings could be attached by other people to their words. Sympathy has always been the most powerful of behavior control devices, since it is intense and makes refined communication and understanding superfluous. The most powerful of sympathetic expressions is love, because in love, sympathy catalyzes the gratification of an independently intense drive—sex. Compliance is reinforced by pleasure. Hate is a powerful form of sympathy as well, because complicity with others in its gratification relieves guilt. So it is that demagogues have always evoked the best and worst in men, conjugating with their most powerful emotions, seducing their intellects, and profiting from their acts.

But sympathy is not an efficient mover of behavior, even if it is the most powerful mover, in an age when psychology and biochemistry promise to reveal the mechanics upon which human behavior is mounted. Sympathy finally works its effects only in a context of good will, which translates politically into either docility or support. At best, sympathy never brings a precise response, which explains the periodic downfall of Don Juans and politicians both, despite their often vast experience and exemplary craft and skill.

Informational and Coercive Controls

For the first time in history, science promises a pure control technology, which has no contents and no aims but to control. Its origins are medical, not political, and its originators are more interested in its curative than in its creative applications. They want to attack disease, not society.

They have found two main ways of doing this. The first is by controlling the information processed by our senses so that our own mentalities will guide us in some desired direction. The second is by controlling the physical mechanisms which underlie our senses, so that we will respond as desired regardless of the information transmitted to us. Control by information is very familiar to everybody, because it includes most of the communication and persuasion methods that people in our civilization have always regarded as legitimate, ranging from propaganda to education. It also includes more esoteric methods, however, like psychotherapy, hypnosis, and conditioning techniques. Control of physical mechanisms is done mainly by drugs and by surgery. Drugs are not usually thought of as behavior-control devices but are commonly used as such. Even the humble aspirin is a behavior controller, in some respects, and the not-so-humble sleeping pill a great deal more so. Surgery, especially with the refinements of control which electronic miniaturization and modern brain mapping permit, is hardly known at all in this connection (and must seem ominous to some), but it has been used in simple form for many years and is ready now to be used in much more complex ways.

Because they work directly on bodily processes, I have called drug and surgical controls "coercive." This does not so much mean that their use leaves its victim no choice of how to act as it means that since they work directly on body processes, their physical effect is fairly certain. In similar vein, since educational, persuasive, and other methods of communication do not impose so directly on body processes, but rather on the messages sent to the sense organs, I have named them "information" controls. The real distinction is not quite so obvious or complete as the names imply, however, and it is important not to be misled by the idea that they are completely different.

As we saw in Chapter 1, and will see again, the meaning of coercion is not always clear. Insofar as it concerns negating someone's will, it is easy to see that this can be done as well by controlling the information available to him as by controlling his body. The most primitive kind of coercive control actually works through information of a sort rather than physical manipulation, namely, by the threat of pain or other hardship. And to the contrary, physical manipulations such as drugs may be contrived to help withstand coercion or to allow more choices than might have been possible formerly. In medicine and war, all this is so well known that it is beyond dispute. Anesthetics give latitude about whether to undertake surgery; and spies and soldiers, knowing they can kill themselves by poison instantly on capture, are emboldened to do more than fear of torture or betrayal might otherwise allow.

The real difference between informational control and coercive control is that the former does not deliberately attack the physical structure or the organism in order to do its work, while the latter does. This is not a distinction of intent or of effect as far as the behavior in question is concerned, only one of technique. Nobody tries to control behavior without wanting to control it, and it is therefore fair to suppose that most decisions to be made about which kind of technique should be used in which situation are themselves technical decisions, revolving around questions of economy, certainty of effects, and the knowledge and skill of the manipulators.

Even from the narrowest technical perspective, moreover, the difference between information and coercion is not always clear and cannot be honored too much without a hopeless resurrection of the now sterile philosophical question of the relationship between mind and body. This limitation is best illustrated by the placebo effect in medicine.

"Placebo" is Latin for "I shall please." The term became an honorable part of medical pharmacopoeia centuries ago when some physicians discovered that some patients for whom there were no suitable medicines would neither go away nor pay their bills unless the doctor "did something" for them, like prescribing an herb with an impressive Latin name. It has the same modern meaning: an inert or irrelevant chemical given to a patient who is told that it is a potent medicine. For the most part, such chemicals do nothing to the patient's metabolism or pathology, which makes them useful for comparisons with drugs that are supposed to work. Some placebos do produce significant metabolic changes, however, called "placebo effects," which are usually explained as "the result of suggestion" and, as such, might be considered an informational means of control. But the suggestion which is actually made is that a particular drug, which the patient thinks has some more elegant chemical properties than those of sugar, chalk, or aspirin, will serve to relieve a particular ailment—and the marvel of placebo treatments is that they often do work, which is to say that physical relief occurs! The only reason anybody might hesitate to call such treatment a physical manipulation is because he cannot specify exactly what mechanisms of nerve, gland, or sinew are involved. But it is clear, even so, that a physical change of some sort has come about by the interaction of an informational and chemical assault. A precise understanding of this interaction might make the distinction of control techniques entirely superfluous, but the understanding has not yet been achieved.

The distinction might be more or less superfluous even now

were it not for the conventions we have already established about the properties of different means of control and the ignorance of most of us about the marvelous and intricate means of control potentially at hand. Such ethical questions must be considered at length. But they only become significant after it is clear that alternative control methods are available and that some more or less precise effects can be associated with each alternative. There are no meaningful ethics of impotence; that is, there can be no meaningful debate about the ethics of methods that do not work. In this sense, ethical problems are the offspring of technological innovations.

Once a control device works, the ethical problems surrounding its use have nothing to do with whether it is informational or coercive in type, but only whether it shall be restricted to certain populations and ordained or banned by certain authorities under certain conditions. Until now, unfortunately, most of us have been schooled to understand only the extremes of casual information and force of arms as acceptable means of exerting control over others. Our civilization has legitimated education and warfare, mostly by force of habit, and we are prepared to regard any subtler influence as hypocrisy or perfidy. There is probably a good reason for this foolish failure to countenance the many ways that man can be controlled, but whether it cloaks itself in the pretentious liberalism that falsely claims to permit anybody to do what he pleases or in the reactionary fury that detests the slightest hint of freedom among men to deviate from any norms, the foolishness produces the same consequence—an ignorance (and fear) of the real character of human beings and of its exploitability.

Man is an immensely plastic creature, and his plasticity, propelled by prodigious intelligence and tool-like hands, has set him to the arrogance of believing there is no end to his variety. He fancied once that he was at the center of all things, which literally spun about his planet home. Retreating from that pose, he still imagined that he was unique in species, the special product of a special creation. And when the evolution of human understanding convinced him finally of the evolution of the human species, his pride retreated once again, this time into the subtlest of conceits which he maintains today—that he is personally unique and set apart, more than a fleshy cog in an insane galactic wheel, more than a random sentience in a random medley of atomic pinball games. And he has taken this to mean that in some way he can identify, he is unbounded, unpossessed, and at liberty, not in politics alone, which is the common gift of decent men to themselves, but in some inner self which, mortal or not, has some inviolability.

He cannot believe that this inner self lies in his body parts, which are visible from man to man and much alike to see. So there is nothing left on which to proclaim it but on the stuff of his activity—his behavior. This, if nothing else, he says, is ultimately his.

From this philosophy, or desperate wish, to be more accurate, evolves an ethos of behavior in which it is all right to teach somebody what you want because he might comply, or to kill him or worse because he won't, provided only that you do not exact obedience that is neither forced nor offered, which would undercut the precious myth of *will*. For to do so, especially by demonstrating a refined and variable control over man's needs and his desires, let alone his acts, would be to recognize, if not declare, that the mechanics of his self are different from those of his other organs only in complexity, that they too are the stuff of tissue and anatomy, of nerve and gland, that can be mapped, manipulated, and maneuvered by another's will. Nothing could proclaim more loudly man's mechanical nature than an instruction manual for working his machinery.

For some people, such a recognition is anathema because it forces them to face the fact that they believe in an incorporeal self, a confrontation especially painful to people who deny traditional religious creeds of immortality or, worse still, mock them. But even people who have no inner religious conflicts may be concerned that this bold mechanism will make harsh use of human liberty in politics, by denying, as it does, any absolute basis in human nature for human freedom. To oppose this, they put forth an ethic of relationships which orders violations of freedom in descending rank, with plain coercion as the most severe, plain information least, and all the stages of threat, persuasion, and manipulation in between of varying amounts of immorality.

This scheme has merit, and it is in terms of it that the present taxonomy is made, not as an apology for a code or creed which can no longer be sustained, but as a framework for an ethical system which can be constructed from knowledge of man's true nature and capacity. There is some difference between control by information and control by coercion, by and large, though finally there is not enough that separates them to justify an antimechanistic moral code or so much identity between them as to make any moral discourse foolish. Spelling out their details, differences, and implications is the task of the next chapters.

PART II

The Tools of Mastery

3

Control by Information (1): Psychotherapy

Since Eve and the Serpent first began their fateful talk, the transmission of selected information has remained the most important means by which people have manipulated each other. It probably always will be. Education, prayer, rhetoric, propaganda, demagoguery, romantic seduction, and advertising are all typical efforts to this end, though they are only a fraction of the whole. All of them are forerunners of the technology of control by information, and some have grown sophisticated enough even to be considered bona fide parts of that technology. Most of this chapter and the next will concern the three refinements of information technology currently used most widely for individual behavior control: psychotherapy, hypnosis, and conditioning. Like most methods of information control, these techniques do not yet involve very elaborate use of hardware; in the future, however, machinery will greatly augment informational control, so some attention is also paid to electronic communication devices, computers, and other gadgetry potentially useful for this purpose.

The Character and Classes of Information

Every kind of information and every medium for communicating it is potentially useful as an instrument of control, so there is no need to look into all of them in order to understand the main principles or methods involved. But it is important to know the main classes of information and the main media for transmitting it in order to assess their powers and flaws, their meanings, values, and dangers. "Information" is not limited here only to words and not transmitted only by speech or writing. It includes sights and sounds, dreams and feelings, and, in fact, all things that can be communicated to the senses and many that are communicated below the level of the senses. Anything that acts as a signal from some kind of sender to some kind of receiver is information. Indeed, chemicals, electrical impulses, and some other physical entities which we shall be looking on primarily as coercive devices can all qualify technically as information in the sense that they can all function as signals.

As understood here, information controls are techniques that can be applied with "no hands," so to speak; that is, methods that do not require or depend on gross tampering with physiology in order to take effect. Although presenting information to the senses may affect physiological processes throughout the body, it does so in such subtle ways, compared with surgery, drugs, or radiation, that we usually think of sensory and perceptual processes as if they were in a class by themselves. Such thinking is reflected, to some degree, in the mistaken common notion that there exist such things as purely "mental" processes. Even so, what we commonly look upon as the stuff of the mind, like thoughts, images, and sensations, is chiefly what is meant here by information.

From the long view which history affords, all technologies develop in a sequence of increasingly precise capabilities, which makes it convenient to present them in a more or less historical order. Information-control technology begins with verbal information, the most familiar clay of human experience with communica-

tion, and passes from infancy to childhood with insight psychotherapy and its corollaries. Greater precision and more mature
skills in information control are afforded by action therapies,
which rely less on verbal formulations than does insight therapy.
These therapies open the door to a second generation of information-control technology, in which hypnosis and conditioning are
used to produce changes in behavior and attitudes that may or may
not involve the personal problems of traditional psychotherapy.
These techniques capitalize on other processes than language;
hypnosis ostensibly relies on imagery; and conditioning, on non-
verbal sensory signals. More important, they can be aimed at
mental processes which are ordinarily considered involuntary, they
may be usable with relatively great speed, and they are applicable
to many settings outside the laboratory or clinic. Some dramatic
behavior-control phenomena of political, religious, and cultural
interest have been explained as special cases of hypnosis and/or
conditioning; these include brainwashing, religious conversion, and
voodoo-type vicarious murder.

A third generation of informational behavior controls comes
with the use of sophisticated hardware to present or elicit information. Computer therapy illustrates the former, and computer data
banks and electronic bugging devices illustrate the latter. Both are
still in embryonic stages of development, but they will soon
become important tools of behavior control and will present important problems accordingly.

Verbal Information

Words are the most widely dispensed and, for most purposes,
the cheapest and most efficiently packaged kind of information.
Language thus serves as a prototype for all kinds of informational
control. Since language is sometimes imprecise, however, and
often ineffective, many people are misled into thinking that words,
and informational controls in general, are not really control devices at all. Every lawyer, shrew, and gigolo knows better.

The most widely recognized effort at control by verbal information is probably advertising, a publicly accepted form of propaganda designed to control acquisitive behavior in situations where people have some choice, as in the toothpaste they buy or the politician they elect. Like television and other communications media, however, advertising is generally addressed to masses of people rather than to specific individuals and so will not concern us here. Most attempts at verbal control of individuals are denoted by labels like "persuasion" or "suggestion," which imply that the controller does not use force to get his way. When a controller's goal is not apparent to the subject of control, or when his skill at overcoming resistance is great, his techniques are subtitled "seduction" by intellectuals and "salesmanship" by most other people. Success by any of these methods, moreover, is usually labeled influence rather than control, implying that the subject had some responsibility for the behavior which was asked of him.

The arts of persuasion were probably about as well developed in the age of the biblical patriarchs as they are today, but they have never pretended to be a true technology, despite the existence of an enormous modern literature, often very technical, on how to sell everything from manufactured products to one's own personality. There are formal education facilities, moreover, to study every aspect of commerce (the business of selling things) in colleges and graduate schools of many major universities, which also reflects some technological promise. If advertising fails to qualify as an individual behavior-control method because it deals with people on a statistical basis—that is, because it tries to influence masses of unnamed individuals—then the individual salesman, by the same standard, is the apotheosis of the verbal behavior controller. Nevertheless, he has failed to claim the title in any formal way. No doctorates are given in hustling.*

---

* This cultural lag seems to stem from a combination of sociological and religious sources. Some people in the business of science (or letters or art) disdain the idea that there is a science of business (or letters or art), and a lingering ethos of otherworldliness makes it seem slightly obscene, even for business schools, to have doctorates, dissertations, and diplomas in salesmanship.

Psychotherapy: The Prototype
of Information-Control Technology

The first true technology of individual behavior control through verbal information was probably psychotherapy, especially the multitude of systems and subsystems called insight therapy, which aims to help people solve personal problems primarily by special ways of talking to them and listening to them talk. One or another form of psychotherapy is probably familiar to educated Americans either directly in relation to problems or in derivative versions such as sensitivity training or personal encounter groups.

Psychotherapy is a technologically primitive means of behavior control compared to what will come after it, but it is significant in its own right because of the breadth of its applications, if not their power, and because it embodies virtually all the ethical problems which conscientious students of behavior control must encounter. There are literally millions of people undergoing psychotherapy at any time in the United States alone, and millions more probably would be if it were up to many psychotherapists, educators, clergymen, parents, or their enemies to decide. There are *several dozen* formal psychotherapeutic systems or schools presided over by official mental-health experts like psychiatrists, psychologists, and social workers. There are many more semiofficial or unofficial variants of psychotherapy conducted by clergymen; marital counselors; guidance, counseling, or personnel officers in high schools, colleges, and businesses; family doctors; and laymen whose personal experiences have qualified them for the work, like the leaders of Alcoholics Anonymous, Synanon, and other voluntary organizations with special therapeutic missions. The catalogue thus far, which is not exaggerated, contains none of the host of psychotherapies which involve "the game" without "the name," such as sensitivity training or personal encounter groups—but these are no less important than are psychoanalytic consultations in controlling behavior.

Without counting subprofessional mental-health workers, like hospital volunteers or mental-health counseling aides, let alone all-purpose charlatans, astrologers, tea-leaf readers, kindly old ladies who sell apples on the street, or the hypno-quackery advertisers in big-city newspapers, it is plain that an entire industry is engaged in psychotherapeutic practice. Its techniques, therefore, are not merely abstract discourses on influencing human beings but practical plans for doing so, promoted and supported by several full-blown professions, by associations for promoting its use, by manuals of practice, by journals of the trade, and by codes of fair exchange between practitioners and their customers. What is more, its operation is often protected by legislation and by custom and nurtured by enormous public and private funds, which go into its further development and into the discovery of new ways it can be applied to individual troubles, hopefully for the satisfaction of social needs. Considering the huge amounts of public concern, energy, and funds expended on the search for means to cope with behavior problems in one form or another, and thus with behavior control, by one name or another, psychotherapy is an important force to be reckoned with.

Even were its scope less broad, psychotherapy would still be an important prototype of informational behavior-control technology because of its noncoercive character. All psychotherapies are merely special cases of the many kinds of situations in which some rational, persuasive, and nonviolent means are needed for controlling individual behavior or for teaching responsible agents of society how to do so. Part of its value as an area of study is that it involves the development of controls under conditions of maximum disadvantage to any controlling agency. "The therapist," as Neal Miller of Rockefeller University puts it, "does not have direct control over the important rewards and punishments in the patient's environment." Neither coercion by police power nor continuous charge over rewards and punishments, such as parents have, are ordinarily available to a psychotherapist; this turns his operations into relatively pure attempts to influence with only limited resources, the chief of which is language. It is not cynical, therefore, to say that the systematic persuasion methods which are psychotherapy are salesmanship elevated to the level of technology.

Because it relies on this most complex medium—the "higher processes" of language and symbol (sometimes considered the only uniquely human attributes)—psychotherapy is also a straightforward extension of education which, in the ethical perspective of our age, is regarded as the antithesis of control through coercion. And because it addresses individuals directly, it may be the closest thing extant to an agency for individual control that also satisfies the modern morality of freedom and individual choice.

Much of its social significance, indeed, results from the fact that everything that has been said so far about the psychotherapy industry could also be said about education. This sometimes unnerves physicians, who would like to consider therapy a branch of medicine, and psychologists, who tend to regard it as an altogether unique enterprise. Actually, psychotherapy can always be properly regarded as a special case of educational treatment, though it is more often seen as a separate discipline which is not exactly the practice of medicine, not quite the same as teaching, more than just giving advice, and less than religious revivalism— but still a way of changing people's lives by means of information.

The Objects of Psychotherapy

All forms of psychotherapy aim to control behavior which, by one standard or another, is considered mentally deranged, diseased, disturbed, or otherwise disordered. For this reason, psychotherapists commonly refer to their methods as techniques of treatment rather than control. Such terminology makes no difference to their operations.

The variety of problems for which people seek psychotherapeutic help, in any case, is simply enormous. It includes virtually every kind of individual human complaint. They range, at one extreme, from difficulties in relation to society, other people, objects, or skills. At the other, they include complaints about oneself, one's inner life, mood, feelings, aspirations, ideals, or even physical ailments. Any number of complaints may be combined at one time in one person, moreover, and all of them appropriately brought to a psychotherapist. There are also many different ways of cataloguing the problems for which people seek therapy. Some of them revolve around the social character of the problem in question, categorizing people on the basis of their social competence or of how much they deviate from social norms. Others classify problems according to how they arose, such as by particular processes of learning or habit formation or during particular stages of child development. Still others list problems according to their philosophic implications in people's lives, such as whether they involve narrow behavioral troubles or broad existential crises. And there are other classifications, too, for example, the apparent severity of symptoms, their degree of physiological relevance, the amount of anxiety involved, and so on.

What all psychotherapeutic problems share, and perhaps the only thing they share, is that they are all *behavior* problems in the broadest sense—that is, they are all problems of action, emotion, and attitude, rather than problems of purely physiological functioning. The most common psychotherapeutic problems involve some aspect of the victim's behavior which seems to be out of control, either from his own point of view or from that of some other presumably responsible people. The inability to refrain from drinking too much or from taking certain kinds of drugs; to restrain sexual impulses or to express them; to concentrate on schoolwork; to stop ruminating over trivia; to learn to read properly; not to wet the bed at night; to free oneself from an overdependent attachment to parents; to assert one's rights; to refrain from antisocial aggression or to express appropriate hostility; to get along with one's wife or to seek a well-earned divorce; to be free of groundless anxiety; to quell irrational fears of remote, unlikely, or harmless events; to be able to feel good; to shake oneself free of despondency or to come down from an endless, manic "high"; to keep physical equanimity in the face of stresses which raise fits of asthmatic strangulation or scale one's skin or cover it with hives or knot one's stomach into ulcerous aches; to move one's limbs, paralyzed by no known trauma of nerve or sinew; to shake loose the delusion that one is being watched or persecuted or chosen, or the strange sensation that one's body is dissolving or decomposing or that one's sex is changing as he watches helplessly or that one's ability to reach out to others by speech or glance or even touch decays until he stands alone in catatonic stupor, despairing of repair and murderously angry in his silence—all these, and many others that need not be tallied here, are the common province of the psychotherapeutic arts. And the goal of therapy in every case is to restore control of the disordered behavior to the patient or to eliminate it from the repertory of his behaviors by exerting a complex series of controls over him so that, either way, he will not be troubled by it any more.

How well these goals are met is often quite another tale, not always ending happily. This fact, in turn, creates a constant need to find and test new ways to control the great diversity of human impulses, inhibitions, and bedevilments. Different kinds of psychotherapy try to meet this need.

The Psychotherapeutic Systems

Not only is the variety of psychotherapeutic problems vast, but the profusion of schools, systems, and orientations purporting to tackle them is also great, probably exceeding fifty, if everything that calls itself a school is taken at face value. Even so, the variety of treatment operations and the specific things to which they are applied are manageably fewer. Viewed this way, the many schools reduce, for most purposes, to two types: insight therapies and action therapies.

Many people still confuse the general term "psychotherapy" with "psychoanalysis," that special form of it which is the prototype of insight therapy. Psychoanalysis became subject to a variety of heresies, mostly at the hands of Freud's students, shortly after the turn of the century, when he discovered the technique. A number of important offshoots of psychoanalysis were promulgated from about 1910 until shortly after World War II. Some of these variant therapies are still related to psychoanalysis by name, such as the analytical psychology of C. G. Jung. Some others, with no evident origins in psychoanalysis, are also descendants of it, such as the will therapy of Otto Rank or the client-centered therapy of Carl Rogers. All of these, plus some others, are familiarly called "insight therapy."

The influence of therapies derived from psychoanalysis has been so great in America that many people are still unacquainted with the therapy systems that have arisen from the "conditioning" studies of Ivan Pavlov in Russia and the "learning" research of E. L. Thorndike in the United States, both working at the same time that Freud was formulating psychoanalytic theory in Vienna. Pavlov and Thorndike were both laboratory scientists rather than clinical practitioners, which is one reason that their work was not translated into clinical situations for some years. By now, however, two generations of scientists have added novelties and refinements to their early findings, and the psychotherapy systems derived from Pavlov's and Thorndike's studies are arousing increasing interest in universities, clinics, schools, and hospitals everywhere. I have named these methods action therapy, to contrast them with insight therapy. Their most familiar trade name, however, is "behavior therapy," after the "behaviorism" of John B. Watson.

Insight and action therapies overlap considerably in application. In both, people may be seen one at a time, in small groups, or in a combination of the two. Similarly, both systems may use a wide variety of adjunct or auxiliary methods like dramatic acting (called "psychodrama"), hypnosis, or drugs such as LSD. They cannot be distinguished any more easily by their details of organization than by the fees their proponents charge. To the casual observer, a psychoanalytic therapy session (insight) might look about the same as a desensitization session (action).

The chief differences between insight and action therapies are found, first, in their respective technical activities and, second, in their somewhat different objectives and effects. One system aims to foster the patient's insight or understanding into the problem-relevant aspect of his life; the other tries to produce some definite change in his actions. The actual operations of each system tend to be so consistent that they permit almost any school of psychotherapy to be classified and labeled according to its leaning in either the insight or action direction of technical activity.

For historical and economic reasons, as well as for theoretical ones, the therapy systems are competitors. Each tries to be simultaneously comprehensive and rigorous, treating everything and explaining everything. Neither aim is achieved very well because the extremes of each position reflect an oversimplified view of human behavior; translated into the clinical arena, this oversimplification requires psychotherapists to be continuously ready to cheat on their systems or on their intellects if they want to work very well and explain to themselves what they are doing. Devout partisans of both modalities tend to describe their own scheme by its theoretical underpinning and the other by its practical deficiencies, but neither of these is usually quite accurate. The main difference between them is that insight therapy addresses what David McClelland, of Harvard University, calls "internal behavior systems" (motives, feelings, attitudes), using techniques intended to expand consciousness, while action therapy addresses "symptom clusters" or "external behavior syndromes" (the overt problems presented for treatment) by methods designed to affect them directly. Action therapists thus tend to be preoccupied with the specifics of stimulation, response, and reinforcement. Insight therapists are more concerned with the inner lives of their patients. Neither method offers an altogether certain means of healing anybody, but each has developed a plausible "first-stage" technology which anticipates some of the future character of individual control through information. The specifics therefore require some description.

Insight Therapy

The basic idea that guides all insight therapies (though subject to many variations and polemics of interpretation, expansion, and detail) is that *motives dictate behavior;* this means that disordered behavior is the result of peculiarities inside the individual. To treat such disorders successfully, it is argued, the therapist must seek out the inner states that underlie the surface difficulties and, by bringing them to light, loosen the bond between them and the disordered behavior they produce. Stated differently, the therapist tries to lead the patient to some insight into the relationship between his motivations and his behavior, on the assumption that this insight will give him greater control over them than he previously had.

Insight means understanding. All the techniques of insight therapy try to lead the patient to greater understanding of himself, particularly those aspects of himself which have not been fully conscious or which he has been unable previously to face in a direct and forthright manner. As the patient himself sees it, he is trying to find out why he acts and feels the way he does, expecting that the discovery will free him of the troubles that brought him to therapy in the first place.

In the course of the inquiry, which sometimes takes hundreds of hours spread over several years, he will probably explore not only the reasons for his original problem, but his feelings and experiences of inhibition, anxiety, guilt, hostility, anger, pleasure, competence, self-esteem, lust, sorrow, love, jealousy, and dependency in all his important interpersonal relationships and many less important ones; and he may experience these same feelings in the therapy session itself and in relation to the psychotherapist. With luck, patience, and effort, he may get rid of his symptoms, too, but he will gain self-understanding in any case.

Understanding the basis of one's own behavior, of course, makes that behavior more meaningful; thus insight therapy comes to be regarded by most of its adherents as a technique which not only frees the patient of disabling symptoms but which also, by seeking the meaning of his acts, helps to make his whole life more meaningful. This characteristic of insight therapy gives it its greatest appeal in modern times, especially in the form of existential psychotherapy, which maintains its popularity unblemished, while its actual potency as a means of reducing troubling symptoms is increasingly challenged, doubted, and denied.

Techniques of Insight Therapy

The way that insight therapy works upon behavior is essentially a systematization of the Socratic teaching method, in which a person's (student's, patient's, subject's) ideas, attitudes, and feelings are probed, challenged, and queried (by the teacher, doctor, manipulator) until they are either confirmed, reformulated, or rejected. Called "maieutics" by Platonic philosophers, the method supposedly draws out of a person only things that are already within him; this would mean that any conclusions he comes to are ultimately under his own control and, therefore, are his own responsibility.

This reasoning pervades all insight therapy; details of technique vary in many respects among brands, but they share, as a primary rule, the dictum that the patient himself must assume responsibility for virtually all the subject matter of the therapy sessions. In general, the onus rests on him to initiate discourse and to conduct it, with the therapist there to guide the stream of the patient's consciousness, not to interfere with it. Everything the therapist does, in fact, is supposed to encourage and reinforce the patient's exploration of himself, not to put new contents in his life. Not only does the insight therapist avoid pressing his own opinions on the patient, therefore, but in general he also avoids significant disclosures about himself. This anonymity further forces the patient to be responsible for himself; otherwise, by knowing too much about the therapist's personal life, he might pattern his own behavior after this potential model. In its purest forms, insight therapy is more a guided dialogue of the patient with himself than a substantive discussion with another person. Its Platonic ideal is to Know Oneself, and its Neoplatonic credo is that in process of doing so, the truths one learns will make him free of the troubles he brought with him into treatment.

It may sound as if, in the ideal case, the insight therapist does nothing but sit passively and the patient gets well by talking to himself, or to a sympathetic-looking lump. This is not true. But Carl Rogers, in his major work, *Client-Centered Therapy,* actually does report one such case, in which a girl came to therapy a few times and said very little to a therapist, who, in turn, said little, albeit sympathetically; eventually she declared that her problems were worked out so that she no longer needed to see him. Objective information from others indicated she was right. Similar reports have come from a counseling program originated by Westinghouse Corporation for its employees; several people said they felt better after talking things out to a counselor who did little but grunt sympathetically. And the abundance of jokes (and complaints) about therapists who fall asleep during sessions (along with some serious papers on the subject, which should be jokes), also illustrates the relatively passive, tentative, or restrained behavior of insight therapists in their consulting rooms. The drama of insight therapy is not sustained by its animated dialogue; at its best, it may be visible only to the mind's eye of the patient who experiences it.

The influence of the insight therapist comes from the subtle methods he uses to guide the patient through therapy. Subtlety is at once the greatest asset and liability of insight treatment. When it works, it may produce profound and lasting changes in the patient —of feelings, attitudes, values, and activity—for which he feels solely responsible. When it fails, he may have wasted his time, energy, and money—and it often fails because its very gentleness makes no impression or because, by giving the patient his own reins, it makes wrong impressions on his life. At all events, three specific techniques are used most in insight therapy; we may conveniently label them *association, interpretation,* and *relationship.* Their respective purposes are to facilitate the disclosure of problems, the channeling of attention, and the reformulation of behavior.

Some kinds of insight therapy, such as client-centered therapy, do not have special techniques for getting people to disclose their secrets, problems, or peculiarities; here, the therapist simply listens to whatever they have to say and tries to work with whatever information about themselves they volunteer. In most psychoanalytic therapies, however (which are probably the dominant strain), one or another association technique tends to be widely used to get people to disclose themselves. Sometimes the method may be as simple as the therapist's asking questions about whatever he thinks is important or, when the patient has said something of possible interest, asking him, "What does that bring to mind?" In some therapies, such as Jungian analysis, the therapist has the patient write down dreams or compose fantasies or fairy tales as gateways to his inner self; Freud called dreams "the royal road to the Unconscious." Though they all serve much the same purpose, however, none of these procedures is quite so formal as free association.

"Free association" is the main psychoanalytic method for uncovering unconscious motives. The analyst tells the patient to utter everything that comes into his mind without exception; he then sits back, usually out of sight, and waits. It is quite difficult to free-associate. Merely keeping track of all one's thoughts is hard; revealing them to another person is even harder. One purpose of using the analytic couch is to relax the patient so he can free-associate more easily. The analyst may occasionally make remarks to stimulate the patient's associations, but the responsibility for gaining skill at free-associating rests with the patient. The same thing that makes it hard to learn to free-associate makes it valuable for discovering hidden thoughts. Unlike ordinary discourse, in which the speaker is obligated to keep to his train of thought and to move logically from item to item, in psychoanalysis, the very chain of thoughts that would usually be suppressed as irrelevant or embarrassing or improper is most useful and germane. One reason it is useful is because thoughts occur in associative chains, the more conscious ones coming first and those that are more repressed coming later. Free association permits one to move gradually from the more open to the more hidden, uncovering ideas, affects, and experiences that are anxiety-laden and unavailable to consciousness.

But free association is useful also because it violates ordinary conversation manners. By encouraging what Donald Ford and Hugh Urban call the "urge to utter" in the patient, he is led to value and to explore his ideas and feelings.

As the patient develops skill at associating or as his problems become otherwise clear, the therapist increasingly offers *interpretations* of what is happening. Sometimes these are interpretations of the contents which the patient has communicated, sometimes of feelings he has exposed but not explicated, sometimes of things he has not revealed but which the therapist infers. One kind of interpretive remark, called "reflection," is the main device of client-centered therapy. In reflection, the therapist restates what the patient has said in a way that exposes the feelings which underlie the statement and communicates understanding and acceptance of them. This has the effect of reinforcing the patient in the pursuit of his own ideas and associations and in taking responsibility for the therapeutic discourse. Interpretations which are not reflective may also have the same effect: by timing his interpretations so that they do not go beyond what a patient is prepared to understand and accept, the therapist communicates that he is "following" his patient and thereby encourages him to continue his self-initiated exploration.

It is through interpretations that the insight therapist has the most opportunity to affect the patient's behavior, because it is here that he has the most latitude to direct the patient's thinking. The patient chooses his own problem, so to speak, and to some extent his own associative material, but only the therapist chooses the interpretations he makes of them. Whether those interpretations support or challenge the patient's behavior patterns, his acceptance of them reflects, to that extent, his acquiescence to the therapist's controlling influence.

The extent to which the patient is likely to buy the therapist's interpretations, with whatever that implies for his behavior, probably depends more on their personal relationship than on any other single factor, including the wisdom or accuracy of the interpretation. The importance of the therapeutic relationship is widely recognized by insight therapists, who ostensibly use it as a means of promoting further self-understanding rather than of promoting their interpretations. The classic device for producing a warm, friendly atmosphere in all psychotherapy is simply listening sympathetically to what the patient says. Action therapists identify sympathetic listening as one of many techniques called "reinforcement withdrawal," but its operations and effects are the same by any name. It boosts people's tendency to reveal themselves to the therapist and to change because of him. If someone expects to be derided, criticized, or condemned for exposing his thoughts, feelings, or experiences, for example, he becomes anxious and clams up. If he does reveal himself, however, and no such unpleasant result occurs, the anxiety diminishes or disappears (is extinguished) and he feels more free to open up to his listener. John Dollard and Neal Miller, then of Yale University, have pointed out that this kind of reinforcement withdrawal is a common technique of insight therapy. By simply listening to his patient without reacting negatively to what he says, the therapist avoids reinforcing the patient's anxieties about self-revelation and willy-nilly makes it easier for him to talk.

Sympathetic listening has a strong seductive effect on people in ordinary life situations as well as in psychotherapy. If it is difficult for someone to talk to people, then the more need he feels to do so and the more he expects an unsympathetic response if he does, the more likely it is that actually unloading to an unexpectedly sympathetic listener will produce in him strong feelings of gratitude and even affection toward that person. The shrewd listener, if he chooses, may then exploit those positive feelings to get money, sex, or other largesse from his grateful "client"—and may say, in so doing, that he has not actually "done anything" to the other person. The intuitive recognition of this principle is one of the main things that sends professional confidence men after *lonely* victims who have nobody to talk to. Indeed, the ability to systematically elicit trusting and affectionate reactions is what makes them confidence men. In this connection, James H. Bryan, of Northwestern University, and I found, in an extensive interview study of American call girls, that an important motive of some girls to attach themselves to procurers, give them all the money they earn, and stay hopelessly and futilely "in love" with them despite the general shabby treatment received at their hands is that they provide a sympathetic ear. A pimp is, if nothing else, "somebody to talk to," especially for a girl who fears to discuss her work publicly, and especially in the cold and lonely hours before dawn. For many people, loneliness mostly means "not having somebody to talk to."

Most psychotherapists use sympathetic listening as a general means of fostering a good relationship with patients, but psychoanalysts make more precise use of it, in combination with their deliberate anonymity, to produce transference reactions. "Transference" is the experience of projecting onto the analyst the attributes of other people who are important in one's life and then feeling the same emotions toward him which the other people arouse. A patient may come to believe, for example, that the psychoanalyst is just like his cruel father, and then begin to feel furious and fearful toward him just as he feels toward his father. Transference occurs to some extent in any intimate personal relationship, but psychoanalysis makes deliberate and ingenious use of it to help the patient expose feelings that have been frightening him and impairing his relationships with others. Once exposed, they can be analyzed and the transference resolved.

The therapist's personal anonymity helps promote the transference reaction by withholding information which would give the patient a realistic basis for evaluating and responding to him. Since the patient knows little about the analyst's life or what he is really like, the things he attributes to the analyst and the emotions he has toward him must be taken from his experience with other people. One reason Freud began sitting out of sight of his patients was to minimize the influence of his own expressive gestures and reactions on them (he also found it wearing to have to look-at and be-looked-at for many hours every day).

The Consequences and Conundrums
of Control by Insight

Insight therapy has been subjected to many criticisms on both technical and moral grounds. In terms of its status as behavior-control technology, these reduce to two complementary arguments. The first says that it is an ineffective means of controlling behavior; the second that, where it does work, its effects are obtained immorally, either by seducing the patient away from his original purposes or seductively changing his purposes to fit his peculiarities. Both arguments have some merit.

Insight therapy is clearly a poor means of symptom control; after almost seventy years of use, there are still few indications that uncovering motives and expanding of self-understanding really confer much therapeutic power over most troubling symptoms. Studies of therapy's effectiveness have proved equivocal, by and large. A few report fair results; others show little evidence that therapy "works" in the sense of removing symptoms. The fact that intelligent, educated, sophisticated people tend to stay in therapy for a long time anyway suggests that it works in some other sense which is not measured by most research into its effectiveness. It is here that the morality of insight therapy is challenged.

By assuming that problems of motive underlie the symptoms that bring people into psychotherapy, the insight therapist inevitably tries to move the patient toward a concern with his motivations. But it was concern with symptoms, more than with motives, that brought him to treatment in the first place. If it then turns out that the treatment of motivation fails to cure the symptom, the therapist finds himself seductively selling a somewhat different product than the patient intended to buy—understanding instead of relief.

While seduction for this purpose may be reproachable, the product may still be worthwhile, supporting the claim that insight therapy helps to resolve people's existential dilemmas even when it fails to cure their symptoms. Many patients who enter therapy at first wishing only to be free of their symptomatic difficulties later discover that "the quest for meaning," or what James Bugental calls the "search for authenticity," is really more important in their lives. In such cases, the patient is now in the position of saying that though the symptom has not been treated, he is no longer troubled by it. Here, therapy has changed the patient's needs to suit the symptom instead of curing the symptom to suit the patient's needs.

There is often little else that it can do, for the very nature of insight therapy, let alone the scientific and moral rationales of its practitioners, makes it function as a very general, nonspecific means of behavior control, which tends either to radically alter people's life styles or to leave them unaffected. A person is much more likely to change his career as a result of insight therapy than to lose a nervous tic, more likely to move away from home, shift his political position, or alter his religious convictions as a result of psychoanalysis than to give up phobias, smoking, homosexuality, or compulsive hand washing.

One patient, who entered therapy because he was afraid to drive on Los Angeles freeways, after one year of treatment divorced his wife, successfully changed careers, and radically altered some important patterns of social relationships—but still could not drive on the freeways. He considered his therapy successful, even though it never satisfied his initial purpose.

Both the assumptions and methods of insight therapy make it most effective only on broad targets. Its first assumption is that the only proper locus of behavior control is the patient himself, which means that the only proper behavior control is self-control. Second, it assumes that self-control results from expanding consciousness; and third, that consciousness can be expanded by verbal means. All the techniques of insight therapies serve these ends, at once promoting the patient's search of himself and avoiding any sharing of responsibility with the therapist for what he finds. Free association and reflection both leave the patient in control of his own activity; the therapist, by maintaining anonymity and interpreting the transference, avoids exercising undue influence on him. "Undue influence" means anything the therapist does that dictates what the patient should do, even if doing it might help cure his symptoms. The source of control is more important to the insight therapist than is the act of control. If it cannot be vested in the patient himself, he believes, then it cannot legitimately be achieved at all. And strict adherence to the ground rules of the system not only makes therapy depend entirely on consciousness-expanding methods, but demands in turn that these must work through consciousness alone, pure and unadorned, without external props such as drugs. The aim is not simply to treat the patient, but to do so without *manipulating* him.

Regarding manipulation as immoral gives insight therapists some defense against some critics. If they are selling something the patient did not originally intend to buy—self-understanding instead of symptom relief—they are still selling something of value in its own right; and the patient himself is responsible for whether or not he wants to take it. If uncovering motives does not always relieve symptoms, it is still wrong to remove symptoms by indecent means, even though they work. Finally, the quest for meaning is more important than the lust for contentment, and if the patient deliberately and meaningfully changes himself to live with his symptom, one cannot gainsay the therapy on that account. If a man loses his ability to make money, talks to a therapist because of it, and discovers that his life is made more meaningful by a new career that can never make him rich, it is naïve (or worse) to say that the treatment failed. The only control which insight therapists promote, by their lights, is self-control.

Most observers of insight therapy, on the other hand, would say that it does not work quite so purely as it pretends and that insight therapists use far more influence on their patients than they realize. There is some evidence to that effect in research reports that patients tend to identify with their therapists, gradually developing similar personal values.

It is no wonder that they should. For no matter how tentatively he approaches the patient, nor how pure his motives *not* to control or dominate, the insight therapist cannot help but address what he himself considers the most salient material presented to him. Eventually, the patient's ideas of salience must largely correspond to his or the interaction cannot continue. What is more, the inherent imbalance in the relationship, where one person is always helping and the other receiving help, makes the patient look up to the therapist as a potential authority, model, or inspiration, no matter how little he knows of the therapist's outside life. Almost inevitably, he knows plenty about the therapist's attitudes toward the things that count most in his own life, and it is those attitudes that he is most likely to absorb.

This says, in short, that control in insight therapy works by a combination of subtle suasion and benign neutrality; the one turns the patient's attention to whatever the therapist thinks important, the other encourages him to adopt whatever attitude he thinks the therapist has. All this happens without the therapist's trying to exert control; were he to try, he might have more powerful or precise effects than he usually does.

Whether or not they wish to control their patients, at all events, insight therapists must take some responsibility for relieving symptoms as long as they hang out shingles telling symptom-ridden people to come to them for help. And it is this responsibility which their gentle techniques will not support, and with respect to which they are ill-defended, regardless how much either therapists or patients think of them. Without a good technology for symptom relief or a disclaimer of the ability to provide it, the moralistic refusal to manipulate becomes the ultimate manipulation because it is patently irrelevant grounds for keeping somebody in therapy. Suppose a doctor treated appendicitis by feeding patients bananas and, when they died, defended himself by saying it would have been wrong to feed them apples! Insight therapists are thoroughly in the business of controlling behavior, like it or not, but the stringent restrictions of their theories on their activities prevents this control from being exercised over symptoms. Allegiance to those theories leaves them useful agents of control in other respects, perhaps even in more important ones, but it paralyzes or invalidates their symptom-curing role.

It is over symptom relief in particular that action therapies have registered a legitimate complaint against insight methods. Making this their sole criterion of therapeutic success, they have built a strong competitive system, leading to a new dimension of control through information.

Action Therapy

In technical procedures, action therapies fall toward the opposite pole from the insight therapies. Instead of concentrating chiefly on the motives that produced a person's symptoms, they tend to focus treatment on the symptoms proper without much concern over their origins or meaning. Instead of seating responsibility for treatment with the patient, they place it entirely with the therapist. Instead of focusing on the patient's existential concerns, they attend only to his functioning and to how his symptoms interfere with it. Instead of handling therapy as a means of aiding self-understanding, they view it as a *planned* attack on disorder in which it hardly matters whether any insight comes about. Most symptoms, they believe, are really habit patterns which, according to Hans Eysenck, the distinguished British psychologist who coined the term "behavior therapy," are learned "through a process of conditioning and capable of being extinguished through several techniques of demonstrated effectiveness in the laboratory. . . . Treatment is directed entirely to the symptoms, as distinguished from psychotherapy with its stress on hypothetical underlying complexes and disease processes."

Two of the leading expositors of action therapy are Joseph Wolpe and Arnold Lazarus, both currently at Temple University and both practitioners as well as researchers. They similarly define the field as the use of "experimentally established principles of learning" for overcoming "persistent maladaptive habits." In fact, action therapies are less critically tied to scientific theories or laboratory studies of learning than their expositors would like to believe. Even so, they are broadly based on some established principles of learning that serve as useful guidelines for planning specific therapeutic efforts. Like most practical therapists, actionists are more concerned about the value of their methods for treating people than about the scientific status or origins of those methods.

Behavior is behavior, and action therapy, as a competing system, is used for the same sets of behavior as insight therapy, differing in how it works and in what it accomplishes, not in what it attempts. Their different perspectives on human nature and psychological theory are less important than their technical differences, which reduce to a single issue: the ability to exert *precise* control over *specific* behavior problems. Action therapies assail the insight therapies as imprecise, which means lacking control power. They make relief of symptoms the main criterion for therapeutic success because it is the most visible index of ability to control behavior. By its efforts at precision, action therapy begins to meet the criteria of a true technology. What is gained or lost by having one depends on what it can do and where it leads.

Techniques of Action Therapy

There is no overstating the cardinal rule of all action therapy technique: be specific. All its methods, therefore, depend upon the same clear sequence of operations. First, define the problem precisely; next, calculate a specific way to attack it; then, do what you planned; finally, see how it worked. The problems, symptoms, or troubles (as you please) to be defined, and the ins and outs of evaluating how the treatments worked, are the same for all kinds of therapy; the actionist's specific ways of attacking them are less familiar to most people. Two of the main ones, "counterconditioning" and "extinction," are used chiefly to relieve extreme fears (phobias), anxiety, and sexual problems. A third, called "behavior shaping," or "*operant* methods," is used mostly for training desired habit patterns or skills. All of them claim pronounced effectiveness, and sometimes in very short order, like a single treatment session.

Counterconditioning means replacing one feeling or behavior with another that is antithetical to it. In treatment, this generally means replacing a useless or bad feeling with a constructive or pleasurable one. The helpless anxiety of a milquetoastish employee is turned into justified, constructive anger at an unreasonable supervisor. The relentless desire to guzzle whisky is converted to nausea at the sight of it. The obsessive preoccupation of a college sophomore over what other people think of her is exchanged for a calmly realistic recognition of what difference it makes in different situations.

There are several ways to do counterconditioning; most of them are associated with the contemporary work of Joseph Wolpe, but they originate, as he points out, in treatments reported as early as 1924.

Sexual impotence can be helped by "discriminative training," which is used almost exclusively for such problems. It consists basically of teaching a patient to recognize which sexual encounters are likely to be frightening and disabling, to tell them apart from those likely to be gratifying, and to adapt his behavior to his understanding. As Wolpe describes it, the patient is taught to attempt sexual relations *only* when "he has an unmistakable, positive desire to do so, for otherwise he may very well consolidate, or even extend, his sexual inhibition." He is taught to seek out people with whom he can be aroused in

a desirable way . . . and when in the company of one of them, to "let himself go" as freely as the circumstances allow. . . . If he is able to act according to plan, he experiences a gradual increase in sexual responsiveness to the kind of situation of which he has made use . . . [and] the range of situations in which lovemaking may occur is thus progressively extended as the anxiety potentials of stimuli diminish. . . .

For people who are easily intimidated and exploited by others, a very common complaint of psychotherapy patients, "assertive training" is the method of choice. In it, the patient is taught when and how to respond to others with (verbal) aggression, practices doing so in the therapy sessions, and applies his training in real life, reviewing and rehearsing appropriate aggression with the therapist's coaching. Assertion is not only used to teach aggression; Wolpe also uses it to facilitate "the outward expression of friendly, affectionate, and other nonanxious feelings" and for "gaining control of an interpersonal relationship by means subtler than overt assertiveness." For the latter, he takes Stephen Potter's

Gamesmanship as a worthy text and recommends Potter's works unhesitatingly "to patients who seem likely to profit from reading them."

Like all counterconditioning methods, assertive training is based on the assumption that anxiety inhibits self-expression. Practicing assertion inhibits anxiety, which gives the patient greater latitude to express himself in his dealings with others.

The reduction of general, or "free-floating," anxiety is done by "conditioned avoidance" methods. Wolpe describes one, rarely used in practice, which works by subjecting the patient repeatedly to a harmless but painful electric shock. Before shocking him, the therapist tells the patient that if he finds the shock excessive, he can terminate it by saying "calm." Continued over many trials, the word "calm" becomes associated with (conditioned to) pain reduction so that merely thinking or saying it has a soothing effect. Presumably, this conditioning generalizes beyond the consulting room, so that whenever the patient is confronted with intense anxiety, he can reduce it by saying "calm."

Conditioned avoidance can also be used to reduce the pleasure of behavior patterns that patients wish to get rid of. To free a man of homosexual desires, for example, the electric shock is connected with pictures of nude males. Each time the patient is aroused by a picture, he is shocked, till eventually the pleasure of the picture is destroyed by coupling it with pain. The resulting "unlust" generalizes to real-life situations where he faces homosexual stimulation.

Extinction methods work by making head-on attacks on problems rather than by replacing old feelings with new ones. In practice, three techniques are recommended. Where the symptom is pleasant or gratifying to its perpetrator, as is common in the behavior problems of children, remove the reward; this is called "reinforcement withdrawal." Where the problem is anxiety, as in phobias, eliminate the fear, either by gently manipulating the patient's imagination with "systematic desensitization," or by "burning out" his capacity for neurotic anxiety with "implosive therapy."

The treatment of bedtime temper tantrums illustrates reinforcement withdrawal. When children have such tantrums, typically, they scream and rage after their parents have left the room; this brings the parents back and permits the children to stay up longer, which reinforces (rewards) their having yelled in the first place. But if the parents put the child to sleep in a leisurely fashion, leave the room, and do not return when he rages, he will gradually give up the tantrum. C. D. Williams, writing in the *Journal of Abnormal and Social Psychology,* charted changes in crying during one such treatment. On the first night of his parents' "cold turkey" treatment, the little boy in question screamed for forty-five minutes before falling asleep. On the second, he went to sleep immediately, cried for ten minutes on the third, and so forth till, by the tenth night, he neither whimpered nor cried but even smiled when his parents bade him goodnight and left the room.

The most widely used, tested, and evidently successful single technique of action therapy is systematic desensitization. Originally developed by Joseph Wolpe, desensitization is a method of using imagination to dissolve anxiety, especially in phobias. It works as follows: The patient and therapist jointly compose a list of things that arouse anxiety, ranking them from least to most frightening. The patient is trained, sometimes with hypnosis, to relax deeply; then, the therapist describes the lowest ranking item on the list and asks him to imagine it vividly. If he can do so without getting upset, he is given a description of the next item and told to imagine it. When any image starts to make the patient tense, he signals the therapist, who then backs up to an earlier one. This goes on from session to session until the most frightening item finally fails to disturb the patient's relaxed state in the session and, from the evidence at hand, he is no longer troubled by the real-life fears outside of it.

Implosive therapy serves the same purpose as desensitization, but it looks dramatically different. Instead of letting the tantrum, phobia, or whatever wear itself out, this method tries to create an internal explosion (implosion) of anxiety, frightening the patient as much as possible without letting any actual harm come to him. As in desensitization, the therapist and patient decide what things are more and less anxiety-arousing, and the therapist then gets the patient to imagine them. Unlike desensitization, however, the implosive therapist starts at the top of the list, with the most frightening items; he describes them as intensively and fearsomely as he can, trying to terrify rather than soothe the patient. The principle involved is a kind of elegant distortion of the adage "Sticks and stones may break my bones, but words will never hurt me." Since phobic anxiety is, by definition, "neurotic"—that is, unrealistic—its repeated experience from mere words, where its dread consequences go unrealized, causes its extinction. Treatment is completed when the therapist can no longer frighten the patient with his scary stories. Implosive therapy was devised by Thomas Stampfl less than ten years ago and is just beginning to be widely known in psychotherapy literature.

The fact that desensitization and implosion are both used on the same types of problems and that both seem to work very well is hard to explain, since they appear to be diametric opposites, the one soothing, the other terrifying. Which is really a better technique for whom, or whether it matters, is a moot point.

Critics of implosive therapy sometimes fear that, in the hands of a sufficiently dramatic practitioner, patients may be frightened into heart attacks or into being "overwhelmed with anxiety"—that is, scared out of their wits. No such event has yet been reported, perhaps because implosive therapists are not good enough at their own game or because frightening words really don't hurt as much as people fear they will.

An increasingly popular variant of consulting-room extinction methods has therapists assigning homework to patients or going with them to confront the things that frighten them, riding together in elevators, airplanes, or subways, or giving them other live practice with experiences that help overcome their fears. In one such case, extreme claustrophobia was cured by having the patient practice staying alone in a tiny room, locked from the outside, while bound hand and foot in a zippered sleeping bag. As everyone knows who has learned any dangerous skills, people adapt to frightening circumstances if they are exposed enough to them without being hurt.

Behavior shaping is derived from the work of B. F. Skinner, who, though not a psychotherapist, has devised important training methods with promising applications to psychotherapy. Behavior shaping is used for chronic conditions which require complex changes in activity. This includes not only many symptoms of neuroses and psychoses, but behavior problems as narrow as stuttering, at one extreme, and as broad as juvenile delinquency, school failure, and general social adjustment at the other.

Two simple principles form the basis for all behavior-shaping operations. First, the principle of reinforcement, common to all action therapies, which says that an organism will learn to repeat an act for which it is rewarded and to avoid one for which it is ignored or punished. The second principle, that of learning by "successive approximation," says that complicated behavior patterns, especially "skillful" ones, are learned gradually, in small steps that come closer and closer to an optimal level of performance.

To make practical use of these principles, the therapist must know what his patient finds rewarding or unpleasant. He must have enough control over the environment so that he can provide or withhold these rewards at will, increasing them when the desired behavior increases and withholding them when undesirable behavior appears. He might also, of course, use punishment to control undesirable behavior. But punishment, unless applied with great skill, often has unexpected effects. The Skinnerian therapist, therefore, commonly works only with reward and need, manipulating the one to satisfy the other.

The technique requires more ingenuity and inventiveness than do any other action therapies and may take longer to work. Some impressive results have nevertheless been achieved by behavior shaping. At the University of Virginia, Bachrach, Erwin, and Mohr were able to induce a person with anorexia nervosa (a form of depression in which food is refused) to eat and gain weight, by controlling the availability of things she found rewarding, like listening to music and chitchatting with people. Willard Mainord, at the University of Louisville, and others have used behavior-shaping methods for therapeutic groups and therapeutic hospital wards. Still others have used them to teach parents and teachers how to manage behavior problems in children. Since each unit of behavior that can be taught by behavior shaping tends to be very small, however, the method has not yet proved as effective with chronic psychotics as was originally hoped. But even here it is more promising than not. Ivar Lovaas and his collaborators at the University of California at Los Angeles have had more success in teaching schizophrenic children different intellectual and social skills than have most other workers; they have done so with supposedly hopeless cases; and they have notably succeeded in teaching nonprofessionals to perform the same therapeutic functions that Lovaas's senior team members can do—which gives behavior-shaping methods tremendous economic promise. Their profound importance for behavior control in general will become even plainer when we examine them further as aspects of conditioning.

Action therapies are easier to evaluate as control systems than are insight therapies because they are more explicitly designed to function as such. The techniques of action take for granted that the proper locus of behavior control belongs with the therapist. He must decide what needs to be done to help (change) the patient, and he is obliged to direct the doing. His job is to give the patient not self-control but symptom relief, which can be done by many different means, only one of which is verbal; whatever works without damaging the patient is acceptable. The expansion of consciousness is usually irrelevant, occasionally harmful, and rarely valuable for this purpose.

Skill at manipulation, anathema to insight therapy, is the moral prize beyond purchase of the actionists, whose title to exercise control is as certain to them as their responsibility for healing is clear. To them, successful manipulation is not merely a useful tactic but a moral imperative which they must satisfy to have the right to offer help at all. Therapeutic intervention in the patient's life is the goal and *raison d'être* for their activity. The ability to do so successfully demonstrates their technological promise, makes of action therapies much more than merely optimistic cook books for cooling people's anxieties or reshaping their appetites or making them happy, and anticipates the moral quandaries that all behavior technologies will sometime face.

Action therapy is not a rudely empirical enterprise with no theoretical foundations, but its emphasis on finding practical applications makes theory sometimes seem an afterthought. Advocates of action have no more mortgage than do insight therapists on the belief in cause-and-effect relationships, for example; their practical use of the idea, however, leads them to plan their therapeutic work more precisely and to judge it by standards that can be understood by everyone. In so doing, they sometimes overlook or oversimplify complexities of human nature and experience, inadvertently fictionalizing them. But these fictions are more valuable for therapeutic use than most of those available until now, for action therapies have been comparatively much more successful with many problems than insight treatments have been.

The most important fact that separates the action therapies irrevocably from all their predecessors, regardless of how much Adler, Jung, Freud, Rogers, Sullivan, and all the rest dispute among themselves, is that the actionists have firmly linked the things they do to those they undertake to treat. One technique is best for sex, they say, another for tantrums; this for timidity and that for terror; and a third for aggression or stuttering or quietly burbling insanity. And once this claim can be put forth with any measure of its truth in evidence, then a technology has been founded, regardless of how limited it may be. This has happened in the case of action therapies not because their methods have been devised from novel theories, which they have not, or because the methods themselves are very novel, which they are not, or because they are so successful, which they sometimes are and sometimes aren't—but because they have transcended, in their multiplicity, what was hitherto the common coin of all psychotherapies, the use of language as the singular medium of communication and control.

The Common Coin of Psychotherapies

The growth of action therapy does not imply that insight therapies have no practical value, but only that they are less specifically applicable to clear-cut, narrow symptoms. In that sense, they are less precise, ergo, less technologically advanced. Depending on the particular ax to be ground or psychic snake oil to be sold, "specificity" can be used to defend or to attack either therapy system by deducing, for example, that the more trivial a problem is, the more useful action therapy would be to it, or that the vaguer a problem is, the more one can use insight therapy to solve it. In fact, specificity does make action therapy neat and scientific, but at the cost of possible pertinence to some important psychological problems. Generality, pervasiveness, or diffusion, all do lend importance to what insight therapy attempts, but at the cost of some effectiveness.

These differences are useful ones because different people really do have different kinds of problems, because some of them really are more specific than others, and because the importance of a problem has nothing to do with its complexity. Simple phobias are simple problems scientifically, but they can thoroughly disrupt a person's life; his title to treatment and the importance of its success do not depend on how easy it may be to provide. The pertinence of any kind of therapy depends on the kinds of troubles people have. For narrow problems like phobias, compulsions, and the many personal irritants which can all be considered habits, pure action therapies are in order. For the broad existential problems which people associate more with general happiness than with sensual gratification, and with life goals as opposed to impulse aims, some kind of insight therapy must be used. Existential problems, voiced more by people in the upper strata of society than by the deprived, apparently cannot be attacked as overt behavior disorders but only as internal ones, at times reflected more in attitudes than acts. Between these types fall many of the modal problems faced by modern man, in which functions and feedback are somehow dissonant—that is, where people's actions and attitudes are in conflict, so that the individual lives at odds with himself and often with the social system. Psychopathy and deviance come largely under this heading, and neither action nor insight therapies, in any simple form, seem able to address them very well. A number of offshoot methods try to with varying degrees of precision and success.

Until recently, psychotherapy of all kinds has been largely a consulting-room affair, in which efforts at behavior control have been limited mostly to discursive means, with the discourses often long and tortured in making their points. The chief instrument of therapy, in other words, was speech; the chief means of behavior control was verbal information.

This has generally been more true of insight than of action therapists, though both have tended to give short shrift to the actual verbal character of their activities. Carl Rogers, for example, says that the changes in a client's feelings and perceptions of himself and others, which are the crux of therapy, do not happen "as the result of verbal interchange" but are "due to an experience in a relationship." Wolpe makes no precise statements in this connection, but, clearly, from his point of view, the therapist's verbal activity is meant to direct the action between stimulus and response connections, and the content of the words themselves is of only secondary importance. Like a crap game at a church social, as most therapists might see it, the hymn singing is up front, but the action is in the back room. Insight therapists, predisposed to argue that most mental problems and their cures revolve around the emotional character of interpersonal relationships, may come to think that feelings and not verbal content are the crucial elements in therapy. Action therapists, sometimes thrilled to find that human beings can learn what pigeons, rats, and goldfish can, may be so taken with the gross parallels between species that they forget the gross differences implied by the fact that other animals lack man's capacity for language.

Even so, action therapy has the technical advantage over insight of making simpler use of language; it promotes only one language system, while insight therapy encourages two kinds of simultaneous internal discourse. Insight promotes consciousness and the consciousness of consciousness—that is, self-consciousness; action therapy supports only consciousness. For most everyday purposes, it is better to be conscious than self-conscious; it is ordinarily more valuable to think of the solution to a problem than to be aware that you are doing so; being self-conscious by itself does not contribute much to solving most problems, whether of arithmetic or intrapsychic conflict. Contrary to Ecclesiastes, on the other hand, there is no evidence that increasing knowledge really does increase pain, nor is there much good reason to think, accordingly, that the absence of self-awareness makes anyone's life better; it probably does not make problem solving easier or more efficient, and it is almost certainly less satisfying, reinforcing, and motivating than is the recognition of one's own personality or ego or self in his accomplishments. The value of self-consciousness, in any case, has so far only been advocated, but not demonstrated, by insight therapists. The relatively low success rates of insight therapists may, in fact, reflect their unwarranted preoccupation with self-preoccupation, just as the higher success rates of action therapists may largely demonstrate the simple virtues of working on the right problem. If so, the differences between the therapies as language systems are not necessarily critical for controlling behavior. Insofar as language has effects on behavior, insight therapists might get the same ones as actionists simply by aiming their discussions more accurately toward the right problems. This is just about what Wolpe thinks is happening when they do accomplish anything.

The promotion of self-consciousness in insight therapy is not only a matter of technique, however, as are the uses of consciousness by actionists, but also an expression of the fundamental differences between them as meaning systems. Some versions of the insight position promulgate self-consciousness as an ideology, opposing it to the mechanism of actionists, which they find despicable; others, more reconciled to mechanistic doctrine, see it as an expression of the cerebral—that is, the computer, or executive —functions of human machinery, which endows its parts with the capacity to work efficiently and, more critically, with choice, so it can act as if it, and man with it, were free.

The philosophic differences between the systems, however, are ultimately less important to the people most affected by them than to their practitioners. Therapy patients, as individuals, do not usually care much whether they are "things" or "people" in the abstract, so long as their anxieties get eased and their capabilities, desires, and functions are sustained. The main effect of their concern with meaning has been that insight therapists construct or borrow moral schemes for people to use in deciding if they are leading meaningful lives and that they develop new techniques for expanding self-awareness. The latter are sometimes so different from the conventions of scientific therapeutics in our society that it is impossible to evaluate them in those terms. Some have distinctly religious overtones, often Oriental ones, like yoga studies, transcendental meditation, and the intense perusal of mystical religious lore, especially of Hassidism. Some are more hedonistic exercises, like the body-awareness classes of California's Esalen Institute or the growing institution of nude group therapy. And some of them, like marathon group therapy, are neither salvationist nor sexy, but use well-known principles to break down individual ability to resist suggestions in order to promote the norms or mores of the group or therapist.

These consciousness-expanding methods all develop more or less haphazardly, based usually on a morality that says self-awareness is desirable rather than on a technology that makes it rewarding (to the patient; the therapists do fine). And all identify themselves, if anything, as nontechnologies. It is probably correct to view them as self-contained forms of insight therapy, aimed at sharpening the individual's knowledge of his inner self for its own sake rather than at the manipulation of his acts or mood to solve some concrete problems in his life.

In a society where religion is no longer able to provide such institutional experiences for people, and where the conditions of living are too crowded and noisy for them to occur unplanned, such self-contained therapeutics may be of great value for individuals and have great impact on society. But they are not part of the mainstream development of behavior technology. Inevitably, that becomes identified as an outgrowth of action therapy, which sees its methods as instruments rather than objectives and which makes use of whatever comes to hand to change behavior—like hypnosis and conditioning, methods without purposes, which, by virtue of that fact, examplify a second stage in the technology of informational controls.

4

Control by Information (2):
Hypnosis, Conditioning, and
Electronic Tools

The two most distinct informational control methods in popular
use, *hypnosis* and *conditioning,* are historically the respective sires
of insight and action therapies, not their derivatives. Hypnosis has
been known and used, in one or another form, since very ancient
times. It began to gain scientific recognition (condemnation, to be
precise) during the American Revolution, when Benjamin Frank-
lin helped a French Royal Commission disparage the healing
powers of "mesmerism" and dismantle the booming business of
Franz Anton Mesmer. The subject led a precarious public life for
the next century. It was renamed "neurohypnotism" by England's
James Braid because of its superficial resemblance to sleep, was
variously used and rejected by a great assortment of European hospitals, surgeons, and psychiatrists, and was first adopted and then
abandoned by Freud at the end of the century in favor of the
psychoanalytic method he had deduced from it. Conditioning
methods have also long been used for such purposes as animal
training, but they had no formal names, advocates, or industries
concerned with them before Pavlov and Thorndike, also at the

71

turn of this century. Pavlov coined the term "conditioning" to describe a particular learning process, but it has since come to refer to many kinds of teaching or learning.

Neither hypnosis nor conditioning are popularly as well understood as psychotherapy, but both are very important for behavior-control technology. In their methods, their aims, and their implications, if not quite in their achievements, they aim for higher standards of technological precision than do other means of informational control.

Behavior Control by Hypnosis

Despite a long history and vast anecdotal literature, there is less scientific knowledge about hypnosis than there are exorbitant claims for its power over human behavior. Early research on hypnosis was sporadic and sometimes poorly carried out. Current work on it in the United States is still done by a very few individuals and laboratories; Russian scientists have had a more consistent interest in hypnosis than have Americans ever since Pavlov's disciples began trying to relate higher mental processes to the conditioning of simple behavior, but they do not seem to have learned very much about it. (They have done considerably better with conditioning studies.) Americans have done better in many respects, but crucial scientific questions about the phenomenon remain unanswered.

The proliferation of hypnotic lore has not been deterred by this fact. More claims have probably been made for the power of hypnosis in manipulating individuals than for any other technique in history. There may not be a single aspect of human behavior untouched by somebody's claim that it could be changed significantly, for better or for worse, by some hypnotic means. Listing them all would be boring and uninstructive, but they can easily be classified.

The broadest, most ominous, and generally most fictitious stories about hypnotic behavior control allege that people can be turned into automatons by this means, completely subject to the whim and will of the hypnotist and unable to judge the moral quality of his demands or, in any case, to refrain from obeying them. Worse than that, the victim cannot even prevent his being hypnotized; it can be done against his will or without his knowledge, can be done to individuals or masses, even without the physical presence of the hypnotist (such as over radio or television), and can be perpetuated or renewed periodically by signals or posthypnotic suggestions which will make the victim hypnotize himself. Such notions are not only the stuff of plays, novels, and detective stories. Many educated people, to this day, believe that Rasputin controlled the last Czarina of Russia by hypnotic means, and there have been court trials for murder and seduction in which the criminal acts were ostensibly committed under the irresistible sway of hypnotic suggestions.

Less extravagant but still provocative claims for hypnosis say that it can be used to control intellectual functions; to manipulate emotions, attitudes, and motivation; to alter body processes; to change physical performance capacities; and to treat all sorts of mental and physical ailments. According to these claims, it can be used to increase or reduce memory or to recover lost memories; to speed up learning; to provoke dreams and hallucinations; to make people oblivious of their real surroundings; to reduce resistance to interrogation and the revelation of secrets; to induce emotional states or to heighten them; to change attitudes toward race, religion, or politics; to increase motivation so that people become capable of abnormal feats of strength, endurance, or coordination or feel profoundly committed to undertakings they would otherwise soon abandon; to increase their physical ability to resist the stress of heat or cold or fatigue or pain; to change their heart rate, blood pressure, or the electrical activity of their skin or brain; to raise blisters on their skin by mere suggestion; to anesthetize them so that major operations can be performed without chemicals; to remove warts; to cure asthma; and much, much more. Strangely, there is some real evidence in support of all these claims!

All the things mentioned above have actually been done using hypnosis; most of them have been described many times in the clinical literature on the subject; and a few have been verified by careful laboratory experiments. There are recorded cases of athletes having been hypnotized before major contests to improve performance; there are some laboratory studies evidently substantiating such procedures; and there are upright and serious organizations like the National Institutes of Health, the National Science Foundation, the USAF Aerospace Medical Laboratories, and the U.S. Office of Education which support research on the use of hypnosis as a medical, educational, and military tool. With all of this, the power of hypnosis as an instrument of behavior control is all too easily overrated. The variety of documented hypnotic effects is remarkable all right, but they are also remarkably uncertain from one subject to another. They can rarely, if ever, be produced without the intent, consent, and cooperation of the subject, if then; and when they do occur, they are not always the result of hypnosis itself, but may be a by-product of the situation. Mass hypnosis is certainly possible, even common, as anybody knows who has watched stage hypnotists perform; it can certainly be accomplished via radio or television—but not everybody will be hypnotized, even if he wants to be; almost no one will be hypnotized unless he is paying attention and actively cooperating with the hypnotic suggestions; and, even then, no one is likely to become robotized, automated, or otherwise helplessly irresponsible for what he does. Hypnosis has some significant and potent effects, but they are not come by cheaply easily, or dependably.

Hypnotic Control of Cognition

Several mental functions are manipulable by means of hypnosis, sometimes with useful practical results: learning, memory, and imagination can all be affected. Hypnosis has been known to aid learning by improving concentration, and by relieving anxiety, well known as an inhibitor of concentration and learning ability. In some cases, a technique called "time distortion" is used to facilitate mental rehearsal; with it, the subject imagines he is living through hours, days, months, or years in what the clock marks as a few seconds or minutes, and he can practice music, foreign languages, or other skills with presumably improved efficiency.

Hypnotized people often undergo unusual tricks of memory, called "amnesia" (loss of memory) and "hypermnesia" (increased memory). Amnesia sometimes occurs spontaneously, after a hypnotic session, but it is more often suggested by the hypnotist. Posthypnotic suggestions are also commonly accompanied by the suggestion to forget that they were given. The ability to request amnesia enables the hypnotist to elicit disturbing material during the session and to put it "under wraps" again afterward.

Hypermnesia does not seem to occur spontaneously; it is used as an aid to learning and to help people to recover lost memories. In many cases, hypnotic hypermnesia has been used by police and lawyers to get witnesses of crimes or accidents to recall details they were previously unable to produce. This method has worked best in cases where the potential witness is suffering some kind of traumatic loss of memory.

Hypnosis generally has a relaxing effect on people, both physically and mentally, which tends to lower their psychological defenses. This relaxation effect may be one reason that learning and memory sometimes improve in this state; tension and anxiety do not have their usual distracting influence. At all events, the combination of lowered defenses and hypermnesia sometimes makes hypnosis a useful tool for the interrogation of spies or prisoners of war as well as of witnesses.

The elicitation of hallucinations and imagery is the core of most hypnotic manipulations. Many people become unusually capable of having vivid hallucinatory experiences when hypnotized, can entertain unconventional, *outré* ideas on suggestion, and can sometimes project themselves so completely into a suggested scene that they believe themselves part of it. This capacity is used to produce "age regression," in which the subject re-experiences some event of his earlier life, often with "revivification," the intense experience of repressed emotions from the past. Hallucinations may also be induced by having the subject fantasize that he is watching a movie screen while a critical scene from his life unfolds on it; he can simply observe and report what he watches rather than tax his memory and emotions to recollect. Or the hypnotist can suggest that upon some such signal as the snapping of fingers, the count of five, or the tap of a pencil, the subject will find himself growing smaller and younger till he is only "x" years old, in his childhood house, maybe attending his birthday party, wetting his pants, or lusting after his mother. Stage hypnotists use this method to get people to act roles in public that they are ordinarily too embarrassed to play.

Hypnotic Control of Emotion and Motivation

Among the more dramatic effects of hypnosis are the emotional changes which sometimes occur in response to suggestion. These run the whole gamut of feelings and expressions: people laugh at no obvious jokes, grieve over no apparent deaths, are furious at no visible enemy, or fearful of no apparent danger, or sexually aroused by no evident partner—all upon demand. Stage hypnotists routinely, and thoughtlessly, put subjects through such emotional paces for the entertainment of their audiences; psychotherapists do it for the edification of their patients. Emotional outbursts also occur spontaneously in hypnosis, but not nearly as often, probably, as they are elicited by hypnotists. There are several clinical reports of people aroused to murderous fury or extreme sexual excitement during hypnosis who, as a result, assaulted the hypnotist or someone else present in the room. There is also a fascinating experimental literature on the elicitation of antisocial behavior during hypnosis, in which people have thrown acid in somebody's face, picked up live poisonous snakes, and other pleasantries, in response to hypnotic instructions to that effect. Some brilliant studies by Martin T. Orne and his colleagues, now at the University of Pennsylvania, suggest that this kind of behavior is not a direct outcome of hypnosis but rather of the reasonable, if tacit, expectation of virtually all subjects in psychological experiments that the scientists who solicit their participation will protect them against doing or suffering harm, even if their instructions seem not to. Whether or not Dr. Orne is correct (some capable experimenters disagree with him), the fact remains that hypnosis *is* the kind of situation in which people sometimes obey crazy or dangerous-sounding suggestions such as these.

Although the short-range drama is less, the long-range potential of hypnosis as a tool for raising motivation is even more significant than its use in arousing emotion. There is some evidence that hypnosis has a kind of booster effect on instructions, so that people's normal desire to perform well in difficult situations is further intensified if they are exhorted to do well while hypnotized. At Stanford's Laboratory of Hypnosis Research, Robert Slotnick, Robert Liebert, and Ernest R. Hilgard, its director, found these hypnotic exhortations still more effective if experimental subjects were emotionally involved and committed to the experiment, a result confirmed in a subsequent experiment by Kenneth Schaeffler and myself at the University of Southern California.

Hypnotic Control of Performance and Physiology

Perhaps because of the effects of hypnosis on motivation, subjects seem at times stimulated to dramatic increments of strength, endurance, muscle coordination, or sustained attention for long periods. Military planners and trainers of athletes have long been interested in hypnosis primarily in this connection. In addition, aerospace scientists have been interested in hypnosis as a tool for stress resistance, to help pilots or astronauts continue functioning in the face of equipment failures or other problems which might suddenly subject them to extremes of heat, cold, pain, or fear. In a preliminary study some years ago at Wright-Patterson Air Force Base in Ohio, college students were trained hypnotically to resist extreme heat for up to an hour, while continuously working at a "vigilance" task, by devoting part of their consciousness to more comfortable things. A typical report of one student, after leaving the "hot box," where physiological recordings showed that he was slowly being "cooked" by the 140-degree heat, was that he thought about his experiences as a life guard at a swimming pool and felt cool and comfortable throughout the session. Michael Ogle, I. P. Unikel, and I found a similar result in a variation of that study at the University of Illinois.

Physiological resistance to stress is ultimately more important than merely feeling good while one slowly roasts or freezes to death; there is some evidence that hypnosis affects body functions as well as subjective feelings. C. V. Kissen, A. T. Reifler, and V. H. Thaler, all of the Biophysiological Stress Section of Wright-Patterson's Aerospace Medical Laboratories, found that hypnosis helped diminish the debilitating effects of freezing temperatures on heartbeat and shivering, among other things. Ronald McDevitt and I enlarged upon their study somewhat and trained our California subjects in autohypnosis instead of having them hypnotized by others before their "cold box" sessions; we found more variable, but generally similar, results.

There have been many studies of the influence of hypnosis on physiological processes. While the experiments are not always good and the results often equivocal, some clear-cut evidence exists that hypnosis influences a number of functions, some of them quite astonishing. According to Gordon L. Paul, at the University of Illinois, an exhaustive review of studies of skin blisters allegedly produced by hypnotic suggestion forced him to the conclusion that the phenomenon was genuine, even though he was able to invalidate or disavow most reports to that effect. Also, there are any number of well-documented reports of hypnotic anesthesia in medicine and dentistry as well as in the laboratory, and at least one color movie has been made of major surgery in which a patient's thyroid gland was removed while she was anesthetized by hypnosis alone. Finally, hypnosis is used, sometimes very successfully, to reduce the symptoms of some serious ailments, ranging from allergies to epilepsy.

Hypnosis in Psychotherapy

Hypnosis has never been the special property of action therapists, but unlike insight therapists, they are not made nervous by admitting that they use it. Orthodox psychoanalysts have had nothing to do with it since Freud observed that symptoms removed by authoritarian means, which he thought were involved in hypnosis, later returned or were replaced by other, sometimes worse symptoms. Though the bulk of evidence does not support his observation, the fear of "symptom return" still persists among some insight therapists, for whom hypnosis is still under a ban. A few psychoanalysts, however, especially some with strong research leanings, like Margaret Brenman of the Menninger Foundation and Merton Gill of San Francisco, have given it considerable clinical and scientific study and have written on its therapeutic value. Hypno-analysis, so called, is simply psychoanalysis that uses hypnosis to help reveal unconscious motivations, arouse and resolve transference, and aid the associative process.

The hypnotic effects that are useful in psychotherapy have all been implied or stipulated above. The most important ones are the lowering of mental defenses, which gives people access to their hidden thoughts and feelings, and the raising of the capacity to experience and tolerate hallucinations. The former helps people to free-associate more easily than usual, to talk less inhibitedly, to dredge up memories more adeptly, and to disclose their inner selves less reluctantly. The latter enables the therapist to help the patient uncover hidden material, face old fears and other feelings as if they were being experienced for the first time, rehearse new situations with the conviction that they are real, project himself into the roles of other people, watch his own actions as if he were a total stranger observing himself objectively, perhaps for the first time—and to cover up the whole mess at the end of the session should it look like too great a burden for the patient to consciously handle on his own. With hypnotic suggestions, the therapist can get the patient to write "automatically," without conscious design or plan; he can have him distort perception of time; he can have myriad images flash in and out of mind, or make emotions rise, play out, and disappear in seconds more. He can get patients to communicate, at times, the dynamics of their own physical syptoms, explaining the unconscious sources of their headaches or paralyses as if they always knew what troubled them and only lacked opportunity to tell. Instead of commanding symptoms to disappear, thus risking their return, he can sometimes get patients to transfer them to another part of the body where they will be less troublesome to the body's routines and society's demands. One hypnotherapist I knew persuaded a patient with a dangerous bladder retention problem to urinate freely as needed, but to develop a twitch in the little finger of one hand, just to have a physical symptom for his hidden mental woe. In another case, a psychiatrist reported how he had persuaded a schizophrenic girl, obsessed with ghostly shadows following her, to deposit all of the ghosts in his coat closet between therapy sessions, and the rest of the time to go her way about the world like everybody else. Reports like these are legion, and many of them are known to be true. Even the Royal Commission that "did in" Mesmer two centuries ago admitted that his cures were real, discounting them only because they were achieved "merely" by suggestion.

The Status of Control by Hypnosis

The reason that hypnotic effects occur is less clear than the fact that they really do. It is critical, nevertheless, for evaluating hypnosis as a behavior-control technique. To whatever extent these effects are by-products of relaxation, or of the expectations which subjects or patients have of scientists or doctors (as many of them may be), hypnosis itself is irrelevant to the manipulations performed: any equally impressive interpersonal situation or any mumbo jumbo equivalent to the usual hypnotic induction patter might do as well to produce the same effects. In that event, we ought to study the persuasiveness of hypnotists rather than the potency of hypnosis. Some hypnotists, indeed, are sure that hypnotic effects result from their skill at inducing trances or maintaining rapport with subjects; but while it is true that hypnotists vary in persistence and perhaps in suggestive ability, there is no good evidence that hypnotic effects depend much on that skill.

What they do depend on is evidently so subtle, complicated, and poorly understood as to make hypnotic behavior control a thoroughly undependable general instrument, despite its great value in individual cases for some specific purposes. The most careful experimental work demonstrates, typically, such a great variety of individual responses to hypnotic manipulations that precise schemes for behavior control by this means could not be laid until much more is learned about it than is now known. It is true, for example, that learning, memory, emotion, body processes, and the rest are dramatically manipulable in some people by hypnosis; but the same methods which have profound effects on one person have none at all on another. One subject is totally amnesic, per suggestion; another remembers everything, including the suggestion to forget; a third remembers some things, but not others, when total amnesia has been suggested; a fourth remembers precisely what he was supposed to forget and is amnesic for everything else. And on and on, with virtually every facet of this puzzling phenomenon.

The most important factor presently known to affect responsiveness to hypnosis is the susceptibility of the subject to being hypnotized in the first place. Susceptibility does not mean willingness or gullibility, but is the capacity to accept unconventional instructions for experiencing uncommon subjective states of consciousness.* It is fairly well established as a consistent personality trait, like intelligence and moodiness. Even susceptibility to hypnosis does not allow any simple prediction about where hypnosis will or will not work. Most hypnotherapists, for example, agree that the utility of hypnosis in psychotherapy usually *does not* depend on the patient's susceptibility. What is more, there are some experiments which show that hypnosis sometimes has more powerful effects on people who are low in susceptibility than on those who are highly hypnotizable. Nobody really knows what hypnotic susceptibility is or, for that matter, what hypnosis is. The scientific convention is to call it "an altered state of awareness,"

---

* Cynics may observe that this definition is somewhat circular; it seems to say that hypnotic susceptibility is the ability to be hypnotized. In this, they are correct. More elaborate definitions could only make this fact more obvious. I am sorry.

but the phrase is not very descriptive of anything that helps understand it. In 1967, Joseph Hart, Morris Leibovitz, and I discovered some large differences between the waking brain-wave patterns of women who were extremely susceptible to hypnosis and those quite unsusceptible to it. Gary Galbraith and Leslie M. Cooper joined us in a follow-up study which showed clearly that the more susceptible people are to hypnosis, the higher their general level of brain-wave activity is. This means that hypnotic susceptibility is a function of brain physiology, not of hypnotists' skills or the character of hypnotic suggestions. But what that means in turn for behavior control by hypnosis is not yet clear.

What is most clear, on the other hand, and is most important to behavior control, is that hypnosis involves verified and replicable phenomena (if somewhat untamed), in which *some people's behavior becomes highly manipulable, especially via imagery*. In hypnosis, they can produce, on demand, such profound responses to hallucinatory suggestions that, under other circumstances, they might be considered deranged. And despite considerable theorizing and experimental investigation to the contrary, the work of Martin T. Orne and his colleagues shows conclusively that these effects cannot all be explained away as offshoots of the hypnotic situation or as elegant forms of play-acting. To all intents and purposes, hypnotic hallucinations may be as real subjectively as the tragic hallucinations of insanity, tempered only by their transitory appearance on demand and their tailoring to the situations in which they are aroused.

Hypnosis departs from the *semantic exchange* which is the traditional instrument of information control used in psychotherapy; it makes deliberate capital of the imagery which people can conjure up without any discussion whatsoever. It is important to behavior-control technology, moreover, despite its undependability because it uses very definite methods for arousing, intensifying, and producing action in relation to that imagery. The action that hypnotists produce, in large part, is mental, involving changes in ideas, perceptions, and memories rather than *direct* changes in muscular or glandular functions. In terms of treatment, this makes hypnosis a "next generation" of insight therapy in particular. Insofar as it is able, by suggestions of impersonality and amnesia, to inhibit the inhibitions that people normally feel about confronting their secret selves, it is insight therapy without self-consciousness and without the most inhibiting and civilizing corollary of self-consciousness, the sense of responsibility.

The "mental" character of hypnosis also makes it appear to be the opposite of conditioning, which is an evolutionary spin-off of the spinal reflex, a system of parleying primitive muscle and gland action into fancy behavior. Hypnosis begins its effects in the higher brain centers, where it is induced by means of speech; it starts at the mind and works downward. In that sense, desensitization and implosive therapy are both akin to hypnosis: they aim at the mind directly, primarily by verbal means, and they use the images conjured by the therapist as catalysts for manipulating the emotional responses of the patient. But they are also conditioning methods, producing the same effects by the same means on human beings as on cats and rats. They thus represent a bridge between hypnosis and conditioning, which may be more closely related processes physiologically than is now known.

Conditioning and Behavior Control

So many people have been subjected so many times to the tale of Pavlov's drooling dogs, if not of Thorndike's angry alley cats, that they would prefer to hear no more about conditioning. Conditioning methods are so important to behavior control, however, and a knowledge of their mechanics is so indispensable to seeing why, that it seems worth the risk of boring some readers with what they already know. Conditioning methods are hypothetically useful for learning to do or to stop doing almost anything. By that very fact, they are also among the most vital means for controlling behavior. They are the basis of all habits, all skills, and in some people's estimation, all learning. Some scholars think they also underlie such esoteric and ominous events as psychosomatic illness, voodoo death, religious conversion, brainwashing, and hypnosis, let alone psychotherapy, where we have already seen some applications of conditioning procedures (and jargon) in action methods. The extent to which people can be manipulated by conditioning techniques is not thoroughly understood, but it is among the most widely studied and controversial topics in applied and in theoretical psychology.

Conditioning has a less lurid popular history than hypnosis only because it is less venerable, more technical, and better understood—not because it is less powerful. Novelists, playwrights, and newspaper reporters have had less time to glamorize it and perhaps less interest in doing so upon finding out how complex and boring its technical details can be. All things considered, however, they have not done badly, in science fiction and utopian novels over the past generation, and especially since the end of the Korean War. At that time, news about Chinese treatment of American prisoners gave rise to stories of how skillful malevolence with conditioning methods was used to wash out *esprit de corps,* American political ideology, and national loyalty from the minds of our soldiers. The fact that much of the relevant technical literature is in Russian only reinforced the credibility of this idea.

It is certainly not true, at the present time, that very complex behavior can be controlled by any unadorned conditioning methods. There are essentially only two kinds of conditioning procedures, neither of them very good for washing out brains or turning people into robots: the one, used to control voluntary behavior, works by strictly voluntary means; and the other, which can be used to control involuntary activity, cannot be used at present to produce very complex behavior changes at all. Those it does produce, moreover, sometimes require such a cumbersome laboratory apparatus, and must be applied under conditions of such difficulty and for such a long time, that casual observers might think the book is not worth the candle, especially in comparison with the cheap and rapid "no hands" approach of hypnosis. Such an easy conclusion would miss the main significance of conditioning, however, for its effects, even exerted on only small pieces of behavior, are often as dramatic as those of hypnosis, are generally much more dependable, and tend to last much longer, sometimes seeming irreversible. Conditioning methods involve more precise operations, more specific steps, and more exact measurements, both of their effectiveness and of the conditions under which they can be used. Conditioning, in short, is a more reliable technology than hypnosis, using more "lab" and less "lore" to produce simple, reliable effects which can be joined with other behavior-control devices and expanded and elaborated into complex and refined ways of coping with complicated human activity.

A large body of scientific literature shows plainly that conditioning methods can be used to control several types of voluntary and involuntary activity, affecting thinking, language, imagination, emotion, motivation, habits, and skills. People can be conditioned to blush or otherwise react emotionally to meaningless words or phrases; to respond impassively to outrageous epithets; to hallucinate to signals; to feel fear, revulsion, embarrassment, or arousal upon demand; to feel cold when they are being warmed or warm when being chilled; to become ill when lights are flashed; to narrow or enlarge their blood vessels or the pupils of their eyes; to feel like urinating with an empty bladder or not feel the need with a full one; to establish habits and mannerisms they had never known before; and to break free forever from lifelong patterns of activity they thought could never be forgotten.

The part of the above list which sounds much like the effects of hypnosis can be accomplished much more dependably than can any parallel hypnotic effects. And those parts which require much training mostly cannot be done at all by hypnotic means. Far more than hypnosis, therefore, and for far better reason, the study of conditioning theories, methods, and applications has received enormous financial and professional support from all manner of public and private funding agencies.

The conditioning methods are respectively called "classical" and "instrumental"; the latter was first described by E. L. Thorndike in 1898, the former by Ivan Pavlov in 1903. There are a number of important technical distinctions between them, but the critical difference in terms of behavior control is that classical conditioning serves to control internal, often involuntary behavioral events, like emotion, mood, or sensation, and the functioning of smooth muscles such as the stomach, blood vessels, and (partly) heart; instrumental conditioning, on the other hand, involves the systematic control of voluntary behavior, which includes the teaching of social and intellectual skills and of voluntary motor and muscle activity. Both methods can be used to influence some aspects of thinking and attitudes. They may also be combined with each other and with adjuncts like drugs, surgery, and electronic communications and computing equipment. These combinations may make it possible to use conditioning to teach virtually any attitude, from authoritarianism to xenophobia, any skill, or any emotional disposition. The actual accomplishments of conditioning methods, even in their most sophisticated forms, have not yet brought this theoretical possibility to fruition, but the potential for doing so is more evident than are any limitations on it.

Conditioning Involuntary Behavior

Classical conditioning is actually a special form of instruction in the use of signals, by means of which one learns to expect forthcoming events by attending to forecasting signs, somewhat like learning to expect thunder upon seeing lightning. The difference between classical conditioning and other kinds of signal learning, however, is that the events being forecast are all inside the subject's body, and the signs which foretell them are all arbitrary. The signals in classical conditioning are parts of a code; they have no intrinsic meaning of their own but represent whatever the code's inventor wishes, according to whatever rules he establishes for their interpretation. When Pavlov's hungry dog began salivating right after the bell rang, in the original classical conditioning experiment, for example, there was nothing about a bell in particular which signaled forthcoming meat powder any better than a chime, a light, or a drumbeat might have done. It was the arbitrary association with meat that lent meaning to the bell, so that it became the code or signal that food was forthcoming. This same process of association is also used to teach people arbitrary connections between their own body processes and some otherwise chance external events. Used systematically, these procedures can control human emotions and other important physical functions.

The simplest instance of such control occurs regularly in everyday life, usually by accident: a child who is barked at, chased, or bitten by a dog rapidly learns to fear dogs, just as children who have been burned dread fires, and so forth. In all such cases, a single painful experience with a harmful or frightening object conditions its victim to feel fearful emotions every time it faces the object in the future. Only one such encounter with a dog makes the child fear all dogs, even if they are some distance away, even if they do not bark, and even if they are caged and harmless. It is no surprise to experienced parents, moreover, to find that the child also subsequently fears *pictures* of amiable, colorful, and altogether well-intentioned doggies, despite his clear intellectual knowledge that the picture cannot harm him. His emotions have been conditioned sufficiently to overwhelm his intellect.

There is no basic difference between fear that is conditioned by accident or by intent. Anybody who wants to make a child fear the fire can easily do so by sticking his finger in it or, less cruelly, by frightening him when his attention is fixed on a flame. The same principle applies to inducing fears in adults, though it may take a little more work. George Orwell, in *1984*, has the agents of Big Brother terrify the novel's protagonist by confronting him with a device which lets starved rats eat a victim's eyes out. There is no need to actually hurt him; the vicarious experience does as well.

The second level of emotional conditioning is called "semantic generalization," which means producing conditioned responses to words when these responses have previously been made only to objects or to other words. Thus, the child conditioned to fear dogs may also learn to fear the word "dog."

The most powerful response comes from conditioning them to emotional reactions, but words can be attached to other physical processes as well. More than thirty years ago, Gregory Razran, of New York's Queens College, conditioned people to *salivate* to words like "style" or "urn" much as the famous dog learned to salivate to the bell; then he got them to transfer their response and salivate to synonyms like "fashion" and "vase" as well. Such a generalized response is ordinarily weaker than the original one, and as some experiments have shown, the subject's intellect may play an important role in producing it. The point, nevertheless, is that it is possible systematically to give words, and thus presumably language, emotional connotations that are totally unrelated to their rational properties or meanings.

Since time out of mind, demagogues have used their intuitive understanding of the emotional power of words without knowing anything about classical conditioning, let alone about semantic generalization. Love of God, of country, of tribe, of party, or of principle; fear, distrust, and contempt for strangers, minorities, majorities, races, religions, doggies, and harmless little garter snakes—all have been taught, in every human society, by classical conditioning, in which words take their connotations from the emotions aroused in connection with their use. Hate peddlers, warmongers, evangelists, and politicians "on the make" all use the same essential technique for what is, structurally, the same purpose: to arouse the emotions of their choice to the otherwise irrelevant verbal signals at their command. Pavlov's bell is the catalyst described in Chapter 2.

Demagoguery is not the only means for attaching emotional connotations to words. Teachers, parents, and other esteemed adults condition sentiments in children less noticeably by coupling words like "Negro," "Jew," "Catholic," or "cop" with quiet sneers, frowns, scowls, or other gestures of contempt. The difference between descriptive and derogatory meanings of these terms comes from the common experiences people have had with them, not from their intrinsic properties; ugly connotations are derivatives of the ugly expressions and intonations that went with adult usage.

All classical conditioning of words, like all classical conditioning, is by nature irrational. What we mean by the "rational" use of language is that its entire message comes from the denotations of the words—that is, from their content. When the message to be communicated is an emotion, and the word only a signal for it, as is the case here, then the word acts to control behavior but not to rationalize it.

Emotions are not the only internal processes that can be conditioned to words or ideas and thus controlled by them. Involuntary processes like the constriction and dilation of blood vessels or the contractions of the stomach can also be controlled by "interoceptive conditioning," a method dramatically demonstrated many times, especially by Russian psychophysiologists. In one experiment, people were given information that their stomachs were being warmed though nothing was actually being done to them, and they reacted physiologically with stomach muscle dilations; told that their stomachs were being cooled, they reacted in appropriately opposite fashion, with stomach constrictions. In other experiments, people were trained to react physiologically in one way to a series of blue lights flashed in a certain order; they were next taught the same reaction pattern to red lights administered in a different sequence. Then lights of both colors were presented in random sequence; the result was that the subjects became ill, sometimes vomiting, having sensory distortions, and complaining of headaches. Other experiments on other visceral functions have demonstrated similar results. The natural equivalents of these laboratory demonstrations are seen in psychosomatic illness and in even more common changes in bodily functions, ranging from diarrhea to yawning, which are connected with a great variety of verbal and other informational stimulation. There is every reason to think the basic procedures involved are applicable to virtually every organ of the body and any expression of mood and emotion, with all the therapeutic possibilities that implies. Classical conditioning methods have already received practical application, in the techniques of counterconditioning, to the treatment of anxiety and undesirable sexual impulses. Similar methods have been used with varying success to treat alcoholism and are being experimented with to break habits like smoking, drug use, and overeating. It is entirely possible that these methods can eventually be used to inhibit aggressive or other socially deviant impulses even in people with lifelong habits in the opposite direction.

In addition to manipulating emotion and body functions, classical conditioning has been combined with hypnosis to produce a dramatic sensory phenomenon called "conditioned hallucination." Originated by Osake Naruse, of the University of Kyoto, it works as follows: while a hypnotized subject watches a screen, the experimenter sounds a bell or flashes a light, then projects an instantaneous image on the screen at low illumination. He gives the subject a pad of paper, has him draw the image several times, then suggests amnesia for the whole experience and brings him out of hypnosis. Later he tells the awakened subject to watch the screen; he sounds the bell, projecting nothing, and asks the subject to draw what he "sees." People do, quite dependably. There are no practical applications of this phenomenon yet, but, as will be increasingly evident, the ease with which different techniques can be combined greatly expands the potential uses of all of them.

At first blush, there is nothing to wonder at in the fact that people can react emotionally to words or that their bodies respond to their perceptions, even when those perceptions do not correspond faithfully to what is going on in the physical environment. Both of these are familiar events of everyday life. The most elegant possible demonstration of classical conditioning of involuntary behavior, in fact, is toilet training, which is so common and so successful that people only wonder about it when it doesn't happen. By baring the principles involved in the creation of these reactions, classical conditioning initiates a technology for producing them at will, not as accidental and hence merely personal responses to the vagaries of individual circumstances but as deliberate products of social machinery which may be explicitly commissioned to manufacture them.

The Nazis did just that, in embryo form, with their propaganda machinery, especially through their youth groups. So did the Russian Communists, and so, in principle, did all the "true believers" described by Eric Hoffer, let alone the Wesleyan Methodists, Russian and Chinese brainwashers, and all the zealots of systematic religious and political conversion which have been described from ancient times down through William James and George Orwell to Aldous Huxley. The method of all these movements has been, first of all, to destroy the old loyalties and value systems that have guided their victims' lives, which means to destroy their personal meaning systems; this translates technically into "extinguishing old conditioned patterns." Once that is accomplished, they may try to replace them with new loyalties and new meaning systems or, having incapacitated their victims for further resistance, leave well enough alone. The early Nazi concentration-camp managers, as described in Bruno Bettelheim's *The Informed Heart,* and the subtler Chinese, in their Korean War prisoner camps, were often content merely to assault the prisoners' ability to resist their captors. Training youth to be loyal to the Nazi or Stalinist state, however, like inducing religious conversion or eliciting confessions of witchcraft, required that the breaking down of resistance be followed by a program of positive indoctrination. This has succeeded millions of times in religious conversions, especially in the Dionysian rites of primitive tribes and evangelical churches. But it has also succeeded many times in situations where the issues did not concern beliefs or attitudes but facts and events. Nobody knows how many innocent convicted witches or purged Bolshevik revisionists finally confessed to unspeakable and untrue crimes with absolute sincerity in their own guilt. Arthur Koestler gives a powerful fictional description of one such person in *Darkness at Noon;* and *Battle for the Mind,* by the British psychiatrist William Sargant, offers a detailed review of such phenomena and a plausible explanation of them in terms of Pavlovian psychophysiology, which is based on classical conditioning.

The techniques of breaking down established meanings, whether in propaganda campaigns or in eliciting confessions, are fundamentally the same as those described in the experiment where subjects became ill—the rapid alteration of individually meaningful signals makes it increasingly hard to respond meaningfully.

In propaganda, for example, the Nazis argued that the Jews were capitalists and Communists, democrats and tyrants, racist and mongrel, all at once, until the confusion of messages broke down the meanings of all these terms, leaving only one emotion-laden idea: Jews were bad. Orwell's Big Brother destroys denotative meanings totally with slogans like "war is peace" and "slavery is freedom." Where the intent is to break down more profound meanings, as is necessary to get sincere false confessions, rapid, meaningless stimulation is supplemented by anxiety and exhaustion, until the victim, ready to forgo life itself for surcease of fear and for rest or sleep, takes leave of the last semblances of will. If the method works, he has now become highly suggestible, and new ideas can be implanted.

At that point in "thought reform," as the Chinese call it, the devices of classical conditioning must be supplemented by the tools of instrumental conditioning to yield a more refined and systematic effect than either method could produce alone. The combined method still does not work very well; the "new" ideas are not accepted by most people, and are accepted only temporarily by most of the rest, as shown by studies of American prisoners during the Korean War. Even so, the resistance-breaking part of the process does tend to work and is evidently still a common tool of all the governments that became infamous for using it in the first place.

The combination of classical and instrumental conditioning methods is more effective on other behavior than on the manipulation of beliefs and attitudes because instrumental conditioning adds to the classical conditioning of meaning a technology for the teaching of habits and of skills.

Learning as an Instrument

If classical conditioning is the learning of codes whose signs have no intrinsic meaning in relation to each other, instrumental conditioning is the learning of connections where it is plain from the beginning that lawful relationships exist between events. Instrumental conditioning means the learning of behavior that serves a purpose, solves a problem, answers a question, or provides escape from pain or achievement of pleasure. In the instrumental learning situation, the stimulus is always a "problem" in the sense that it arouses the organism, who then tries to reduce the arousal by gratifying himself if the stimulus is pleasurable or by escaping if it is painful. He usually tries out several different responses; the one that turns out to be most useful in providing the needed relief or, to use the argot of the trade, which is most instrumental to the resolution of the problem, gets "habituated," or learned. Thus, when Thorndike incarcerated Harlem alley cats in Columbia Teachers College's Dodge Hall, in the original instrumental-learning experiments, they were aroused by the unaccustomed imprisonment, which stimulated them to violent efforts to break out of the cage. When a cat accidentally hit the latch which sprang the cage door, he rid himself of the irritation of imprisonment. Put back in the cage, he gradually learned to operate the latch deliberately and efficiently, resolving his problem. All habits are learned this way. As Thorndike used it, a habit always originates as a means of solving some problem and reducing whatever stimulated the animal to motion in the first place. In that sense, instrumental learning is always "solution learning."

Broadly speaking, instrumental conditioning is the essence of self-controlled behavior because it involves learning to control many different responses to a problem so that only the most useful one will finally be mastered. The greatest potential of instrumental conditioning for behavior control is to be found in the behavior-shaping, or operant-conditioning, techniques introduced under action therapies in Chapter 3. While these methods are still relatively primitive in some of their applications, they are the essence of scientific teaching and skill learning in general. Operating entirely with incentives given as the individual acts in ways which approach the controller's goals for him, virtually any skill of muscle or attitude of mind can be taught by this technique, if only it can be applied with sufficient ingenuity. B. F. Skinner, indeed, believes that its benevolent application can create a utopian society of productive, competent, and happy people. Some partisans of his view are now trying to establish a live "Walden II" community in the United States.*

As a practical matter, behavior shaping is increasingly used to train very complicated behavior patterns as well as simple skills in programs for the mentally retarded and in hospital wards for chronic psychotics. The former involve elaborations of teaching machines, based on the principles of operant conditioning. The latter is done by several methods, such as the manipulation of "pay schedules" in a "token economy."

A token economy is a control system in which an entire hospital ward is operated like a business and the patient uses poker chips as money. On admission to the ward, patients may be given a few tokens gratis. From then on, they must earn them as pay for chores or rewards for desirable activities. Earning tokens becomes a method of controlling behavior, partly because people tend to repeat acts which earn rewards, no matter how simple. More important, the value of tokens is enhanced by requiring that necessities as well as luxuries be paid for by them. On a token-economy ward, therefore, patients may have to pay to eat, to go to bed, to shower, to sleep, to use the toilet, and so forth. Training such habits of normal social intercourse may teach psychotic or retarded people invaluable skills for functioning outside an institutional setting.

The main difficulties in applying operant technology to any problem are the need of the behavioral engineer to have complete enough control of the environment so that he can reward the individual as he chooses, and his need to have suitable rewards to dispense once he has control. Sophisticated electronic equipment increasingly helps him gain complete control. Detailed information can be recorded electronically, fed into computers which translate it according to preprogramed schedules, and instantaneously activate machinery which distributes rewards.

* The Walden Two Society, Box 8971, Washington, D.C. 20003, publishes information about the communities developing and planned as outgrowths of Skinner's utopian novel.

It is not necessary to use fancy machinery or to have electronic technology available in order to make effective use of behavior-shaping methods. They have been critical for teaching all skills since time immemorial and do not depend on hardware. The treatments mentioned in Chapter 3 were generally accomplished with no auxiliary machinery at all. Some of the most effective applications of behavior shaping to date, moreover, are found in the group-therapy courses of Louisville University's Willard Mainord and the Palto Alto Veteran's Administration's George Fairweather. These groups provide thoroughgoing environmental control essentially by making rules which patients themselves largely administer, with no television cameras, computer consoles, or even candy dispensers at hand. It is the control of the environment, not of hardware, that gets behavior shaped.

The value of environmental control depends in turn on the extent to which one has rewards to give. David Premack, of the University of California at Santa Barbara, has demonstrated that an enormous number of events can be manipulated into becoming rewards and hence controls over an enormous number of activities. He has treated children who were problem eaters by first observing that they liked to manipulate things and then telling them they could not manipulate until after they ate. He has worked the same thing in reverse on children who liked to eat but not to manipulate. The method is no different in principle from one that Grandma might have elected, but is used more systematically.

Information Feedback

When classical and instrumental learning methods are combined, people's learning ability is sharply increased and refined, especially when information about their own behavior is fed back to them. One Russian experimenter, M. I. Lisina, found, for example, that she could not produce constriction and dilation of blood vessels to electric shocks until her experimental subjects were allowed to observe the recordings of their own vascular responses; then, knowing what the experimenter wanted, they were conditioned very quickly. Another Russian experiment, on bladder control, by E. S. Ayrapetyants, is even more interesting. He put liquid into people's bladders and recorded bladder distention and other functions related to the need to urinate, then showed his subjects the instrument readings. Some of the readings were faked, indicating little distention when there was really a lot; but subjects reported, in such cases, that they did not need to urinate, and their other physiological responses corresponded to the reports! And leaving stomach and blood vessels aside, Joe Kamiya at the University of California Medical Center in San Francisco, has been demonstrating for years that people can be taught to control some of their own brain-wave patterns by hearing a feedback buzzer whenever the desired pattern is occurring. Eventually, they learn to associate their subjective mental state with the buzzing so that, by reproducing that mental state, they can reproduce the brain-wave pattern whether or not the buzzer is on.

It is worth noting that all the experiments cited here involve body processes which we usually think of as involuntary. To whatever extent someone can manipulate a subject's involuntary processes, it seems, or can teach him to manipulate them himself, he is able to control them; the more precise this ability to manipulate, the more it represents a technology of control. The philosophical implication of these experiments for the meaning of volition is as important as their practical implications for the technology of control. Evidently, some body functions become voluntary in direct proportion to the amount of information feedback the subject gets from each past response of his body before his next response occurs; it is as if voluntary control will and knowledge were reducible to the same thing.

The Hardware of Information Control

Conditioning methods may not require auxiliary machinery in principle, but its use gives enormous boosts to these methods in practice. Classical conditioning has always used a lot of laboratory apparatus, especially to measure physiological effects. Operant-conditioning experts have long used relatively simple machinery like slot machines and bubble-gum dispensers to mete out rewards and a variety of clever and complex switches, relays, and automatic timers to program and administer them on exact schedules, untouched by human hands.

In the future, a great surge of additional boosts to conditioning technology will come from other fields, especially electronics. Television, computers, and telemetering devices have already made important initial contributions in this respect.

In California's Patton State Hospital, for example, the token-economy ward has twenty-one television cameras connected to a computer console, monitored by a nurse in another room. She records her television observations electronically by pushing different buttons on the console; the observations are fed to a central computer which arranges the dispensation of tokens for whatever acts she wants to reward, instantly dispenses them into a slot in the wall, and activates a voice which congratulates the patient.

Computers enable behavior-shaping methods to be used for programing very complicated kinds of teaching. At Washington State's Rainier School for the mentally retarded, for example, two teachers walk around the classroom punching a stenotype-like machine that records what the children are doing at their desks, feeds it to a computer which instantly assimilates the information, compares what each child is now doing with his previous behavior, and immediately reports what should be reinforced. This device permits teachers to deal with many activities of several children at once. Since most important life processes, especially interpersonal ones, tend to be complicated, a control process must allow for complexity to teach much about handling them. There is no obvious reason, of course, that the same method would not work equally well to individualize some of the teaching of normal children in school.

It is possible also to substitute telemetric for television observations and to use punishment as well as reward in such training programs. Telemetric equipment permits physiological measures to be transmitted by radio signals; computers can receive the information and act on it just as they would respond to buttons pushed by hand. Changes in blood pressure or heart rate resulting from emotional (autonomic) arousal can electrically signal a computer to activate machinery that rewards, punishes, or otherwise responds to the subject's internal state. With these devices, it is possible to do in vivo conditioning without wiring anybody up, tying him down, or restricting him to one place. Brain-stimulation controls use similar devices, but autonomic telemetering operates at a different physiological level and without irreversible invasion of the physical organism. Its effects are also less precise and dependable. As electronic communications and programing systems become more sophisticated, however, conditioning through such controls will become increasingly elaborate.

The Third Generation: Information Control with Electronic Tools

Many other developing electronic technologies contribute to control by information. Two important classes of them should at least be mentioned here. These are control by communication of information and control by elicitation of information. The former is represented by computer therapy, the latter by diagnostic machines, data banks, and electronic bugs.

The idea of a computer to do psychotherapy grows out of a practical problem, namely the terrible shortage of psychotherapists, especially in places like mental hospitals and jails, where they are most needed. It is made plausible, moreover, by the theoretical notion that there are only a finite number of verbal responses possible to any verbal stimulus, and only a much smaller number of statements or ideas that can be considered therapeutic. If it were possible for a machine to act *in loco therapeutis* by making those responses, a great economy of human resources would result, along with a net increase in therapeutic benefits. To whatever extent therapeutic results are a function of the ideas (which means the language) expressed by the therapist, a computer might be programed to do them as well as a human being does.

It is not a great leap in logic from talking about psychotherapy in mechanical terms, as many scholars have done, to building therapeutic machines, which is actually what reinforcing devices are. The great novelty and possible importance of computers, in this connection, is that they might be useful in insight therapy. Experiments to this effect are being done currently at several universities, both in computer centers and counseling centers. Computers have been programed to "make the same decision" as high school counselors, to approximate the behavior of interviewing psychiatrists, and in one case, to actually "advise" some forty ninth-grade children (it agreed with about 75 per cent of the statements of their human counselors). Kenneth Colby, a psychoanalyst now at Stanford University's computer center, has been working for several years on the development of a "therapeutic person computer conversation," basing his work on the still earlier efforts of MIT's Joseph Weizenbaum. It is less than a total success at present. He reports, for example, that the people who have interacted with it (by typewriter) have gotten frustrated, even though the computer uses personal pronouns to encourage a relationship with them, and consider the machine stupid, partly because it could not give therapeutic interpretations, but could only ask questions and make simple statements. Other factors, which need no elaboration here, might also make it hard for some people to really "warm up" to a computer, even a smart and loving one. Sooner or later, however, they probably will.

Computer therapy is still embryonic, but it is clearly only a matter of time before computers will be programed with very elaborate propositional (language) capacities. At that point, many people will forcibly—and too hastily—reiterate the laborer's classic expression of industrial shock: that it is immoral to let a machine do a man's work, especially here, where the work involves an intimate interpersonal encounter. In view of the purposes for which the therapeutic computer was originally devised, however, this criticism is not legitimate; the choice is between an "artificial" therapist or none at all rather than between two different kinds of therapists. On the other hand, if computer therapy proves useful in back wards of hospitals, where it is easily justified and desperately needed, then it is only a matter of time until it is tried in new situations. For such is the way of technological advance, as Muller says, that "invention is the mother of necessity." And when that happens, and viable therapeutic vending machines *are* available, the questions which will then arise will concern not only the technological unemployment of human psychotherapists but also the whole relevance of the interpersonal relationship to the conduct of insight therapy. The answer, at this juncture, is moot, but the question is altogether clear.

Electronic machines for diagnosis are more advanced than those for therapy, in part because the tasks set them are much simpler. They are also less threatening to the public, perhaps because we are rapidly becoming used to automated medical diagnostic aids. Even so, most people are unaware that machinery now exists which administers many of the tests clinical psychologists are still trained to give in person, like TAPAC (Totally Automated Psychological Assessment Console), which Allan Edwards invented in his laboratories at Los Angeles' Wadsworth Veterans Hospital, and which is being adopted throughout the federal hospital system. More important, even the scientists who use them do not usually observe that machines they design and refine solely to learn about behavior can be used as control devices whenever anyone starts to think of them in that way—the polygraphic apparatus which the experimental psychophysiologist uses to study skin resistance, heart rate, and temperature is the same lie detector which the police detective uses to interrogate suspected criminals. Not even the name has been changed. Despite the trite status of the adage that "knowledge is power," little thought is generally given to the behavior-controlling possibilities which come from having access to information about people until that access is gained by dramatic and frightening means. Modern electronics has now made that happen.

Constant progress in the development of electronic equipment for spying and eavesdropping, even in the dark, out of earshot, and at great physical distances from people, has brought the problem of the right to privacy increasingly to public attention in recent years. It can only become more serious as such bugging devices become steadily cheaper and more efficient. Elicitation of personal information about someone increases enormously the possibilities for controlling him. This seems most true if the information is obtained secretly or against his will. But it can be equally the case if the information is sought openly and voluntarily and, sometimes, even if it is quite impersonal or not actually collected.

The relationship of knowledge and power was an important unsolved problem in theology long before the United States Supreme Court became interested in evidence obtained by wire tapping or the American Congress devoted its attention to the ominous possibilities of a national "data bank." For clerics, the question concerned the relationship of divine omniscience to human freedom: could God somehow know in advance how everything would turn out without exactly making it happen that way?

As a practical matter, the problem did not begin with wire tapping any more than it did with private detectives, and it is, in any case, no longer merely a problem of the right to privacy; the issue is the right to anonymity. In a sense, this problem, more than any other, lies at the heart of the relation of the individual to any technical civilization. It begins with the very notion of public records of birth, marriage, death, and citizenship, and all the rest is an exponential extrapolation from that point. Most people find nothing objectionable in public record keeping and, in fact, most forms of welfare which governments provide would be impossible without it. Even so, public records are direct sources of control. If the state knows as little as the fact that you were born and are of a given sex and age, it can draft you, tax you, and make you go to school. If it knows your face, as from a driver's license, identification card, or even the official annual photo of your grade school class, let alone if it knows the subtler certainties of fingerprints or signature, it may seek you out. And if your address is recorded in a dozen places and by a dozen computers, as it is likely to be in this era of wide credit and fast accounting, it may find you with dispatch. In the Nazi massacre of Europe's Jews, the luckless Jews of

Holland fared far worse than those of France, despite greater efforts of the populace to hide and save them. The Dutch kept excellent public records, which the Nazis seized, while Gallic incompetence at record keeping saved many lives by making it possible for some people not to be identified as Jews or to go into hiding before they could be picked up for deportation.

So much has been written about the evils of social anonymity, especially in the modern megalopolis, that we all too easily forget the constraints imposed upon us by publicity. Village cultures do not suffer much from anomie, but rather from the pressures to conform to village norms. If everyone knows who you are and what your business is, you cannot deviate much from their expectations without risking your reputation, or worse. And most provincial people, afraid to take such risks, are therefore quietly condemned to the familiar.

The fear of exposure also makes electronic bugging a powerful means of negative control even when no information is gathered thereby. All that is needed is for the victim to know that his house, or telephone, is bugged—or that it might be—to induce him to refrain from any show of deviance. The watchful eye of Orwell's Big Brother can now be placed virtually anywhere to kidnap more information more efficiently than Orwell ever dreamed.

The fact that it functions mainly as a negative behavior control has important implications for resistance to control by bugging. Its controlling properties come only from people's fear of disclosing information that will compromise or harm them rather than from any positive contents it imposes on them. In other words, the power of bugging devices, once their presence is suspected, rests only in their crude coercive potential. No amount of electronic refinement will change that fact, so that ultimately people are capable of resisting such control, once they suspect it is being used, without having any more special training or equipment than has always been needed to combat such incursions on privacy. This does not make electronic bugging less objectionable, only less effective. Its plainly rude intention makes it less insidious in effect than in appearance.

Electronic bugs are of more concern here than are data banks only because they are designed to be used individually, on selected members of society rather than en masse. It would be a serious mistake to underestimate the potency of data banks on this account. Anybody who has been denied credit in a department store because of a computerized record of an altercation he had ten years earlier with a tailor on the other side of the continent, or because of a keypunching error in the credit-rating company's records, can testify to the effect of data banks on his life. Data banks are simply electronic extensions of public records, with the same positive values and the same dangers implicit in their uses—but at far greater speeds.

Overviewing Information Controls

Information controls have become increasingly sophisticated as increasingly effective means have developed for influencing internal behavior processes like language, thinking, imagination, and emotion. The chief means of individual control by information remains verbal, as it has always been, and the prototype for verbal control technology is psychotherapy, if not salesmanship. Insight therapy relies more on verbal exchange between controller and subject (therapist and patient) than does action therapy. The latter uses the special communication and influence made possible by hypnosis and conditioning to exploit a subject's imagination and emotions in order to teach new behavior patterns and to eliminate old ones.

In both classical conditioning and hypnosis, control occurs by capturing a state of mind or need, so to speak, and manipulating from it. The effectiveness of hypnotic manipulations, however, is limited by the uncertain roles which factors like a subject's susceptibility or a hypnotist's skill may play in producing effects, as well as the longevity of those effects. Conditioning effects are highly variable but are also too limited or short-lived for many important purposes. The next generation of control technology beyond these methods—that is, the next advance in control of internal processes—is the direct application of electrical and chemical stimulation to the brain centers that control specific behavior.

Operant technology, unlike classical conditioning, refrains from direct physical interventions in body processes. There is no tampering directly with mind or body. It depends on the inner drives of the individual to orient him in the right direction so that the manipulation of the surrounding environment will channel his behavior as per design. Operant methods eventuate in elegant teaching machines and elegantly controlled environments, not in radio signals and brain surgery. Comparatively, they are a less coercive method of control, though they can be considered, by their very reliance on an individual's voluntary quest for positive reinforcement, seductive. They are also slow to work but, among information controls, may be the most effective when they do. Like a diet without pills, they tend to take well or not at all.

All the information-control methods are making increasing use of communications hardware, but developments in this field generally supplement other methods rather than represent new or independent control technologies. The closest any of them come to the latter is found in computer therapy, information data banking, and electronic bugging. These topics illustrate the hardware of control by information best, perhaps, for people who understand technology best in terms of hardware. But they do not demonstrate any new principle of control by information, and the problems that arise from their proliferation are not new to modern society.

There is an interesting irony in the evolution of control technology that should be observed here for its own sake and as prelude to the technology of coercive controls. Insight therapy cherishes self-consciousness and abhors manipulation. But its very emphasis on motivations, and on the higher brain processes as the means to discover them, anticipates the methods of control that are most capable of destroying self-consciousness altogether: surgery, radio, and chemistry, which go directly to the brain to capture motives there. For it is in the brain that the final source of motivations is always to be found, though one must sometimes go the long way around, through a tortuous network of nerves and

glands, or ideas and feelings, to get there. And action psychotherapy, which begins its own polemic by vigorous disavowal of
the self, yields, at its most effective, operant technology, whose cardinal principle is that mind alone must be left free to exercise itself
as best its inner essence advocates, while all the stimuli around
must be enslaved.

With all their differences, the techniques of control by information share a common pose, namely, that their use does not coerce
the subject to comply and do the things directed but leaves some
choice to him of how to act. With several tools at hand, the choice
of any one reflects the risk a controller is willing to take of not
getting done what he wants. The less risk he is willing to take, the
more coercive his techniques become, and the less he relies on the
unbiased or reasoned transmission of information by itself to reach
his goal.

Even so, there is a clear limit to the coerciveness of any information method: it does not deliberately alter the physical structure
of the body in order to change behavior patterns. Knives, pills, and
injections are not fundamental to its effects, though they sometimes facilitate those effects. The use of such instruments represents another dimension of control technology. In information
control, the means of delivering stimulation are altered one way or
another in order to convey them more effectively to the organism.
In coercive control, the physical structure of the organism is
manipulated so that it will be more receptive to the stimulating
messages conveyed.

For most people, the alteration of structure is more frightening
than the manipulation of information because it seems more permanent and more destructive of what we often vaguely think of as
our essential selves. No matter how pervasive the intrusions of
sights and sounds upon our consciousness, or how complete the
death of privacy in our routine existence, we are still prone to see
ourselves somehow as entities inviolable. For simple information,
on the face of it, can be admitted or denied, seized or set aside, as
one might wish, and we remain ourselves.

We think our senses serve us, not we them, that our bodies

entertain and host our wills and that our ultimate allies, when all others go, are the limbs and parts we are accustomed to think of as servants which can be mobilized and controlled by the power of our thoughts and wills. Because of this conceit, the ultimate betrayal of the self does not come from the defeat of limbs or other parts whose loss is known by pain and mourned by our inner self. The inner self, itself, we think stays whole. It comes, rather, from the delicate perversion of the machinery of will, which transmutes at will—but someone else's will—hostility to acquiescence, resistance to docility, and all our feelings to their opposites. This is true coercion, where behavioral technology is pointed next, and this is where we next must look to see its promise and its threat.

5

Control by Coercion: Assault, Drugs, and Surgery

Considering how long it has been since people started using force to control each other, it is remarkable that they have found so few techniques for doing it. Throughout history, coercion has worked mainly through punishment, which depends chiefly upon pain and fear for its effects. The technology of coercion has been nothing but a catalogue of the many ways that pain can be inflicted and the fear of pain aroused; the laws and ethics of coercive behavior control have been discourses on the merits of punishment and the tactics of applying it. To this day, our views of the machinery and the morality of force still depend so much on our linking it to the instruments and rationales of punishment that many of us find it hard to think of control by force in any subtler terms. It is important to do so, however, because the coercive control methods which are now coming into their own, and which may be someday the dominant means of individual compulsion among civilized men, make conventional understandings of coercion obsolete. In the coercive technology of the future, pain and punishment will be used less and less in civilized society. The new technology will expose their inefficiency and their brutality, and its new devices will lend themselves alike to people's compassionate and practical motives, until traditional force is seen by everyone as stupid and unnecessary. Discussion of this development is the main business of this chapter.

The Natural History of Punishment

There are essentially two ways to punish someone: by frustration, in which he is deprived of something, and by pain, in which he is hurt. The variety of ways each can be applied amounts to an elaborate technology in its own right, engaging, throughout history, an enormous part of the administrative machinery of most societies. Even so, punishment, by itself, is a primitive and inefficient means of behavior control, chiefly because you cannot punish somebody until *after* he has transgressed. Ideally, control should operate to prevent transgressions in the first place. Thus, frustration punishments, such as jail or bondage, can do little more in the way of controlling people than prevent the repetition of misdeeds by the same person—and that unreliably. Pain can be used to elicit information or confessions from people but is good for little else.

Both kinds of punishment, however—frustration and pain—can be used to frighten people who have not done anything wrong, and it is this indirect control by the *fear* of punishment—that is, the fear of being deprived or hurt—which has classically been used to coerce people.

Fear is a more effective control method than punishment, because there are fewer obvious practical or moral restrictions on the extreme use of fear than on the use of pain. Fear is more flexible and looks less dangerous; there are more ways to frighten a person than to hurt him; there is less danger of arousing sympathy for the victim of fear than of pain; and fear can be made to last longer than pain. Even so, the potency of fear ultimately depends on people's experience and sensibility of pain, and the biology of pain is sufficiently peculiar, full of seeming irregularities, and little enough understood to make control through the agencies of pain undependable.

The ability to inflict pain is not entirely at the discretion of the punitive agent; it is possible to resist experiencing pain as well as to resist showing it, to overcome torture, to survive restraint, to find relief in unconsciousness, or, finally, to die without obeying physical tormentors. And while a given individual may not be able to withstand the brutal force of pain, it is still true, both in theory and in human experience, that some people can resist any degree of physical torment. Some choice rests with the victim of torture.

Fear does not offer the same options for resistance that pain does because it is invoked before anything painful has happened. Fear is aroused by threat, which works wholly upon the imagination, so the object of resistance is often more varied, diffuse, and harder to control than is the case with pain. The host of fearsome possibilities includes not only the threat of every kind of physical punishment but the excruciating mental pain of grief and shame as well, with their endless variants of embarrassment, loss of status, bereavement, and loneliness. Fear works on expectations of the future, and people's judgments of their prospects, for better and for worse, are cloudier and more intense than are their memories for what has passed. It is poignant uncertainty that makes us feel helpless in the face of threats.

With mental threats in particular, the victim's anguish is compounded by the fact that there is no prospect of surcease through death or loss of consciousness. Part of the horror facing the parents of a kidnaped child, for example, is that they will survive his murder, endlessly to repeat their present pain. The agony of a blackmail victim is not only that he may be exposed but also that the public humiliation he fears will be endless. Mental threats are most devastating because of their continuousness, their apparent promise of endless pain.

The potency of physical threats probably comes mainly from the sense of their permanence or irreversibility. Most people have experienced physical pain only as a very transitory condition and would probably have difficulty even imagining what continuous pain for a long time might be like. Most likely, the fear of physical pain becomes most extreme when it is translated in people's minds as the threat of death, which is frightening chiefly because it is permanent and irreversible, not because it is physically painful.

The contemplation of death is fearsome to many people because it promises to do away with their essential selves—that is, to end their existence, not temporarily, as in sleep, but for good and all. In the same way, the more any threat anticipates the permanent alteration of our selves, the more fearful is our experience of it. For this reason, unwanted structural changes in our bodies are more frightening to contemplate than many other far more painful things. It is said, for example, that criminals convicted of sexual offenses, when given the choice of penalties, will invariably prefer long imprisonment to sterilization, even though the latter is painless and has no effect on sexual behavior. And it is well known that many men who want no more children refuse voluntary sterilizations, preferring more inconvenient methods to the decisive contraception the physician has at hand. The very decisiveness of sterilization makes it objectionable to such men, just as many women are depressed that menopause ends their maternal capacities, even though they do not want children. For most of us, the selves we know are safest and most cherished, with all their faults, and are deeply entrenched in the environment we all know best, our own bodies. Whatever threatens to change the structure of those bodies, especially what we perceive to be important and familiar aspects of them, thereby threatens our very selves.

If the threat of structural body change is dreadful, the promise of desired structural change is excessive in the minds of many people. When such people undergo cosmetic surgery, they are often bitterly disappointed afterward to discover that improving the shape of their nose or changing the sag in their cheeks has not improved their ability to solve any problems or changed their relationships with people in any way. So much of their self-perception depends upon their perceptions of their body that they fall victim to the fantasy that corrective surgery of the one will heal the other too.

The Social History of Punishment

Social acceptance of pain and threat as proper means of coercion has always taken much of its ethical rationale from the widespread, maybe even universal, belief in the efficacy of pain as an agent of education and healing as well as of punishment. Religious, educational, and medical institutions in primitive and highly civilized societies alike have assimilated this belief, with some differences in their rationales for causing pain. Everybody seems to require a justification for hurting others that somehow makes the act impersonal and without pleasure for its perpetrator at the same time that it serves the "higher" purposes of God, society, or the victim himself. More primitive social codes advocate pain as a proper retribution for sin, justifying punitive social controls, sometimes along with a scrupulously legal God who runs a balanced and lawful world where infraction demands suffering.

The more sophisticated instructive character of pain is used to argue that punitive controls are instruments of training and reform, since the learning of avoidant behavior does result from painful experience. (The Stanford-Binet test of intelligence contains an item that goes: " 'You are to be hanged,' said the judge to the prisoner, 'and let it be a lesson to you.' " Seventy-five percent or more of American children ten years old are able to explain correctly what is foolish about the statement.) What is more, the ability to withstand pain has long been used as a measure of self-control, manliness, or individual worth, and people have long taken lessons in pain tolerance by techniques which are quite similar around the world, from the nail beds of India to the mutilation huts of Africa and the Pacific Isles to the lonely sites where the American Plains Indians tortured their bodies with starvation and exposure.

It is only a small step in logic from the punitive to the instructive view of pain, and both perspectives are neatly maintained by the belief that pain has a shriving function—that is, that scourging and suffering cleanse the individual of sin and leave him innocent again. The view presumed, of course, that he was innocent in the first place, that he has become contaminated by his experiences or actions, and that causing him pain expiates his guilt, sterilizes and disinfects his wounded character, and toughens his moral fiber. This detergent theory of pain is still popular in Western society, if not in all the world. It has provided the main rationale underlying much of medical and psychiatric treatment practically to this day and is still prevalent enough to sustain punitive methods of dealing with criminals and social deviants, despite their inefficiency for this purpose.

The belief that punishment shrives the individual is probably as old as the institution of sacrifice, which bore with it the idea that the gods could be appeased by depriving oneself of some precious thing, like the pick of the harvest, the hunt, or the womb. The belief is substantially the same in our time, with only the object of appeasement changed: we say that criminals who have served jail sentences have "paid their debt to society" and are entitled to resume their lives with no residue of guilt. The notion justifies our primitive desires for retribution, on the one hand, and, on the other, our image of ourselves as people who punish out of a kindly desire to restore errant individuals to society. The same belief applies, for most of us, to the protracted suffering of others, especially if their sufferings are troublesome to us, as is the case with Negroes, or if they arouse jealousy, as is often the case with Jews. Like Job's friends, we at once sympathize with these sufferers and wonder what hidden justice is being fulfilled in their tragic dramas.

The belief in expiative punishment was particularly congenial to the Platonic notion that body (soma) and self, or soul (psyche), were two distinct entities, united only until the mortal death of soma allowed psyche to pass on to judgment. Adopted in part by Hellenistic Judaism and taken whole by Christianity, this dualistic doctrine was most clearly and finally stated by Descartes and officially absorbed into Catholic theology. As a scientific theory, dualism justified shriving punishments both for the rehabilitation of criminals and the treatment of sickness. Instead of being implicitly connected with sin, the suffering body was seen simply as the contaminable vessel of the soul, which could be infected without damaging the soul and which could be scourged to purge the soul, much as fever purges the body of illness.

The Medical History of Punishment

Throughout history, all kinds of power seekers have been interested in pain and punishment, but it is finally from medicine, not politics or war, that modern coercive technology arises. Of all human enterprises in which some people manipulate others, sometimes violently, only medicine has always been nobly regarded, and only medicine has been officially, even heartily, approved by society to discover and use scientific products deliberately to change human beings. It makes no difference, in fact, if medical methods are punitive, because its motives are so palliative. Nor does it matter necessarily that its tools are dangerous; the doctor can, indeed must, be trusted to use them. Thus, dope is illegal, but prescriptions for it are not; knifing is illegal, but surgery is not. The motives of doctors are held above suspicion, for their manipulations are so clearly aimed at saving people's lives and well-being. Of all manipulators, physicians are the least accused of evil purposes in their altruistic acts.

Thus shriving was benevolently secularized in medicine into purgative treatments like bloodletting and some spectacular brutalities to the mentally ill. In general medicine, the theories seemed plausibly related to experience (some people did recover after bloodletting or vomiting) and they remained in effect into the last century. In psychiatry, where they have always been patent failures, they were transmuted into the scientific concepts of organic psychiatry, which continued to produce disastrous results for almost a century after its origins in 1845.

Physicians did not have to believe in mind-body dualism in order to practice purgative medicine, and psychiatrists probably never thought they would cure their patients merely by hurting them. Belief in Cartesian doctrine, on the other hand, if not in the dogmas of the Church, sustained the tendency to treat pain, like other mental processes, as a troublesome irrelevancy that doctors had to put up with. This has not entirely changed even now.

At all events, modern medicine, including psychiatry, developed in a social context where inflicting pain was always more the rule than the exception. Corporal punishment had barely disappeared from the British and American navies when chemical anesthetics were introduced to surgery; slavery in the United States and Russia was not yet abolished when the first textbooks in psychiatry were being written, nor yet when Freud was born; and it was barely established that a parent, slaveholder, or animal owner could not with impunity maim his child or kill his beast in the course of "instructing" him. Some of the most civilized elements of civilized society still viewed painful and humiliating punishments as part of a just social order and an intelligent educational system, although they had done away with stocks and pillories and public whipping posts and torture chambers generations earlier and had made legal provisions against them. Even today, thirty-seven of the United States still have laws providing for capital punishment of some crimes,* and all fifty states still use nonrehabilitative imprisonment as punishment for others.

In practice, the medical profession has never been ethically ahead of the social system of which it was a part, and psychiatry has often lagged behind the rest of medicine in experimenting with new ideas and materials in the sciences that underlie the healing arts. The enlightened modern view, which rejects corporal punishment and physical pain as instruments either of healing or of social control, is not a by-product of changes in medical doctrine but of changes in medical technology, especially through chemistry, which made it unnecessary any longer to rationalize the uses of painful treatments in surgery. The introduction of chemical anesthesia in 1846, one of the greatest achievements of clinical medi-

---

* Capital punishment is disappearing gradually from the United States, however; no execution took place in 1968, for the first time in the nation's history. And Ramsey Clark, then Attorney General, recommended in 1968 that all capital punishment be abolished.

cine in that century, was also the effective beginning of coercive behavior control through drugs, whose broader implications became evident only after 1952, when modern tranquilizers burst into public view. In the hundred years between, the fledgling discipline of psychiatry painfully established itself as a medical specialty, underwent several internal upheavals, and emerged as the dominant medical specialty of coercive control technology. The rude beginnings of that technology were already apparent in the highly punitive physical-assault techniques and drug therapies that dominated the first hundred years of psychiatric treatment. None of them worked awfully well, but some have worked well enough so that they are still in use and their merits still hotly debated.

Assault Treatments: The First Generation of Coercive Controls

Colloquially known as "shock" treatments, assault therapies are used mainly with patients whose disabilities are serious enough to require hospitalization, although electric-shock treatment ("electroconvulsive therapy" or ECT), the most widely used assault method, is occasionally given in offices as well. Chemical shocking agents were used even earlier than electricity to treat mental illness—perhaps as early as the eighteenth century. The first modern efforts at systematic treatment by this means were described by Von Meduna in 1935. He induced convulsions by intramuscular injections of camphor in oil, in his early work, and later used injections of Metrazol, a synthetic camphor preparation. Metrazol injections were superior to camphor, but terrifying to many patients, who experienced feelings of impending death and sudden annihilation during the interval between the injection and the convulsions. Sometimes no convulsion at all occurred after the injection, and the patient then felt anxiety, restlessness, nausea, and general discomfort for several hours.

Insulin coma therapy was another popular chemical shock treatment for mental illness. Before 1933 it was used in small doses for various symptoms, but pains were taken to avoid coma until

Manfred Sakel observed that some schizophrenics showed marked improvement after accidental insulin comas, which led him to induce them deliberately. The treatment soon became very popular and, at the International Congress of Psychiatry in 1950, was accepted as the best available treatment of early schizophrenia. It has also been used for other mental illnesses, such as involutional melancholia, but works best with schizophrenia.

The use of electricity for treatment has a fairly long history, dating almost from its discovery; since then, it has been applied to the cure of almost everything, and with little success. In 1938, it was found that the brain tissue of dogs was undamaged by electrically produced convulsions; when the same finding on human beings shortly thereafter was coupled with the observation that some people were relieved of psychiatric symptoms by the experience, ECT was in business. As currently practiced, the treatment consists of sending a small electric current through the front part of the patient's head, producing unconsciousness, convulsion, and on rare occasions, wrenched muscles or broken bones. At its best, the treatment is very distasteful, even terrifying, because, though it seems to be painless, patients awaken afterward with temporary loss of memory and frightening feelings of disorientation in time and space. At its worst, it can have dangerous side effects in damaged muscles, bones, or brain tissue.

Until 1950, ECT was the most common treatment for schizophrenia, but it is now clear that most schizophrenics are not helped by it. It is sometimes effective for treatment of depression, particularly severe or agitated depression, but even where ECT seems to work well, it is unclear why.

Since the advent of sophisticated drugs in the 1950s, all chemical and electric-shock treatments have been largely replaced. ECT has given way, for the most part, to antidepressant drugs, while insulin and Metrazol therapies have largely been abandoned in favor of strong tranquilizers. Most studies have found little difference in the effectiveness of insulin coma treatment and tranquilizers, but tranquilizers are cheaper and easier to administer than insulin, which requires close observation of the patient for a month or more. They have not, however, completely replaced insulin treatment; it is still used in some cases where tranquilizers prove ineffective.

Like insulin, ECT also seemed too traumatic, in comparison with antidepressants, its effects on memory too great, and the problems of administration too serious. Antidepressant drugs were not as successful as originally expected, however, and physicians were soon returning to ECT to treat depression. Reports still conflict about which is the better means of relieving severe depression.

In the long run, of course, changes in social mores make painful treatments seem cruel, while consistencies in the economics of public health make cumbersome treatments look wasteful. In face of these facts, it would make no difference even were the physical assault treatments as good as the pills and prescriptions that replaced them; they could never, under any circumstances, look as good. It was inevitable, therefore, that they rapidly give way to the tranquilizers, which soothe the spirits, and the energizers, which lift them, together initiating the generation of coercive technology through drugs.

Mood-Controlling Drugs: The Second Generation of Coercive Controls

As the mores of society retreat further and further from advocating pain and threat as means of manipulation, and as the machinery of technology makes it easier to coerce efficiently and painlessly, the basis of individual coercion increasingly will become the manipulation of physiological processes underlying the behaviors to be controlled. The medical arts will provide the practical outlets for the performance of these manipulations. As might be expected, therefore, the two most important methods for this purpose will be drugs and brain surgery. Drugs are, by far, the simpler and more flexible of the two.

The advent of control drugs can probably be dated from the introduction of tranquilizers into widespread psychiatric use in the early 1950s, though tranquilizing, energizing, and narcotic drugs of many kinds have existed for a much longer time. All such drugs are, of course, behavior-control devices. The rush to tranquilizers opened two vital doors to the future. Through one of them, a vast horde of behavior-controlling drugs would gain ever-increasing popularity, with ready-made markets eager for their appearance. Through the other, the domain of expertise in the use of behavior-controlling drugs would pass out of the hands of psychiatrists and, for the moment, once again to the medical profession at large.

Chlorpromazine, the first modern tranquilizing drug, entered the American market in 1952, producing an explosive change in organic psychiatry. Its full consequences have not yet been realized even in psychiatry, let alone in other aspects of modern life, but its immediate effects have been enormous. Not least has been the role of such drugs in reducing the use of all kinds of physical restraints in treatment and in eliminating most psychiatric surgery, with its permanent damage, and most shock therapies, with their terror. Unlike other drugs that had long been used as therapeutic adjuncts in psychiatry, tranquilizers gained almost immediate acceptance by the medical profession. It was estimated in 1960 that tranquilizers were then the third most common class of drug dispensed by general practitioners, appearing in more than 10 per cent of all prescriptions—more than 65 million a year. By 1965, 167 million prescriptions for mood-changing drugs were being filled annually, and it is estimated that by 1968 one in four American adults had used these drugs within the previous twelve months, with tranquilizers and sedatives far outselling stimulants.

By now, drugs are certainly the most common form of medical treatment for *all* psychological disabilities, and they are becoming more common all the time, as hard-working drug companies proliferate research which produces more and more of them and promotions which sell more and more of them. They have wrought a real revolution in the management of mental disorders, especially in hospitals, although in and of themselves they generally produce no cures of any kind. And variant drugs, with different powers over mood, perception, and activity, have spread their use beyond the confines of psychiatry, of medicine, of bourgeois propriety, and of the law.

There are several different technical categories of mood-controlling drugs in current use. Among so-called psychiatric drugs, the main ones are ataractics, or "strong" tranquilizers, most common of which is chlorpromazine; "minor" or "weak" tranquilizers, best represented by meprobamate (Equanil and Miltown are its commercial names); antidepressants, which tend to induce euphoria; and sedatives, such as phenobarbital, which have been in use since before World War I. In terms of what mood-changing drugs do to behavior, they can be classified as "tranquilizers," "energizers," and "hallucinogens." All of them work on the central nervous system, and their over-all effect is just what each name suggests: tranquilizers calm people down, energizers rouse them up, and hallucinogens alter their perceptions. Most knowledge about these drugs (including LSD) comes from medicine, especially psychiatry. Energizers and tranquilizers are obviously valuable for people whose symptoms include lethargy, on the one hand, or agitation on the other; they help to alleviate feelings of depression and, very often, of anxiety. Except for the old-fashioned sedatives like barbiturates, they tend to change mood more specifically and in more favorable directions than previous drugs did, without interfering, for the most part, in other aspects of consciousness, such as intellectual functions. And they do all this without any permanent effects—that is, they do not alter irreversibly any important body structure, even though they do effectively catalyze behavior.

Most prescriptions for psychological drugs are for the weaker tranquilizers, but there is really no substantial evidence for their effectiveness. They are *less* effective than barbiturates for reducing anxiety (they are also less dangerous), and most controlled studies suggest that meprobamate, the most commonly prescribed of the weaker tranquilizers, is no more effective than simple placebo. Also, adaptation to meprobamate occurs in a relatively short time, usually two or three weeks, so even its few benefits may be short-lived. The widespread use of the weak tranquilizers must be seriously challenged, therefore, especially their use outside the hospital on people who may not only fail to benefit from them, but who may be damaged financially by their exorbitant cost (the margin of profit on American drugs is so high that Congress has investigated the drug companies) and psychologically by foolishly relying on them to do what they cannot do—solve people's problems.

There is some evidence that strong tranquilizers are more useful than weak ones, but it is still quite mixed. Since they have been widely used, discharge rates from psychiatric hospitals have risen and the inpatient population has declined, despite a rise in admissions to psychiatric hospitals. While in the hospital, moreover, patients are more manageable, show fewer bizarre symptoms, and are less of a problem to the staff than formerly. Other innovations in psychiatric hospitals, such as increased staff and new psychotherapy techniques, may account for some of these data, but it still seems clear that schizophrenic patients, at least, have been relieved of many symptoms by the introduction of tranquilizers, especially chlorpromazine, into hospital treatment. Informed opinion also seems to conclude that tranquilizers delay rehospitalization, allowing a patient to stay outside the hospital longer than he could otherwise.

The revolution in hospital care that has resulted from the strong tranquilizers is less a product of their curative effect on patients than of the humanizing effect they have on hospital staffs. Even though it is the patient who takes the drug, its soothing effects on him permit the hospital staff to be more relaxed and congenial, to use less restrictive custodial methods, and to be more permissive and humane in their management of patients. Both in and out of hospitals, moreover, the equilibrating effect of the drugs may make patients more receptive to psychological treatments. Despite their limited value as direct treatments, therefore, the drugs have provided a major service in institutional psychiatric care.

The prototypes of "psychic energizers," also called "activators," "stimulants," or "antidepressants," are caffeine and nicotine, available at grocery and drug counters everywhere. More elegant energizing drugs in increasingly widespread use, however, are members of the amphetamine family; they are more widely sold as aids to reducing diets than as mood-changing compounds. The best-known and weakest member of this family is called Dexedrine. It is sold as a diet pill in a great variety of capsules, tablets, and spansules, varying in size, shape, and color; and occasionally it is laced with palliative side drugs, such as phenobarbital or chalk. Its major subjective effects are to depress appetite and to elevate mood, stimulating feelings of alertness, euphoria, and confidence in some people, and irritable excitement, nervousness, and restlessness in others. Taken in large doses and over long periods of time, it may also stimulate hallucinogenic effects. Unlike the effects of true hallucinogens, however, these are probably indirect, resulting from the fact that the drug keeps people awake and that anyone who stays awake long enough will inevitably suffer perceptual distortions. A stronger cousin of Dexedrine, called Benzedrine, stimulates similar effects with smaller doses; it has been accused of stimulating heart attacks as well. The most powerful of all these drugs, called Methedrine (colloquially "speed"), does the same things exponentially, causing hallucinogenic "highs" as well. A one-time favorite of San Francisco's Haight-Ashbury hippies, its effects are so serious that advertisements were soon being distributed throughout the district saying simply, "Speed Kills."

The dangers of most energizers, like their benefits, are easily overrated. In modest doses of short duration, they have proved useful to relieve depression and anxiety, let alone fatigue. Adaptation to them occurs fairly quickly, but they do tend to have positive short-term effects as appetite depressants; and while they do not improve intelligence or even test-taking ability, as some naïve users and researchers have suggested, they do produce useful boosts in alertness under some conditions.

Less is known about both tranquilizers and energizers than one might guess from the ease with which some doctors prescribe them or the high prices which the public pays for them. In some cases, they have no demonstrable effects at all; in others, the effects are just the opposite of those usually expected. A hyperactive child, for example, who is absolutely uncontrollable by means of tranquilizers or sedatives, may be calmed down by Benzedrine. The reason for this phenomenon is not known, and the selection of particular drugs for particular conditions is often done on a purely and rudely empirical basis.

Research on psychiatric drugs is often of poor quality also. Drug companies are not always eager to support studies over which they have no control, and the research which they do sponsor is sometimes inadequate in providing definitive information about the value of a given drug.

The profligate use of these drugs continues to increase for at least three reasons: doctors think they work, and lack both facilities and sophistication to examine their belief critically; pharmaceutical manufacturers are making money hand over fist from them, so they promote their use beyond reasonably cautious limits and without sufficient critical evidence of value or safety; and, most important, the public demands pills. People are more aware of their anxieties and tensions today than ever before, but are no more willing then they ever were to examine their lives critically or to change them radically as a result. Pills sound like an easy out, and physicians and patients alike are easily misled into thinking their results are valuable without asking whether another kind of treatment or no treatment at all might have done as well.

The very novelty of the psychiatric drugs is somewhat misleading. For many people who suffer the garden variety of personal difficulties, anxieties, and headaches, no drugs are of any special value, and aspirin may help as much as an expensive tranquilizer. The use of the mood drugs under medical supervision is usually not harmful, but it may not be very beneficial either. They may temporarily reduce some distressing symptoms of a psychological conflict or problem, but they are unlikely to have any effect at all on the problem.

Hallucinogenic or psychedelic drugs are the most widely discussed of modern mood changers because their chemical characteristics and behavioral effects are hopelessly confused by their promoters and prohibitors alike. As with energizers and tranquilizers, less is known about them than would seem to be the case from the public turmoil they engender, and less can be found out expeditiously, since their current illegal status makes it hard even for scientists to obtain them or to conduct needed research on them.

Natural hallucinogenic drugs like marijuana, hashish, and peyote have been known since prehistoric times and have been used in the religious rites of many peoples down to the present. Artificial hallucinogens like lysergic acid diethylamide (LSD-25) and THC (a kind of synthetic marijuana) have become well known only since the 1950s. All these drugs are illegal virtually everywhere because of their presumed harmful effects on users. Whether they do have typically harmful physiological effects is unknown, however. Unlike cocaine or opium derivatives, none is addicting; unlike barbiturates or alcohol, none of them clearly depresses brain functions. This does not mean that they are good for you either, only that they are poorly understood. What hallucinogenic drugs do share with sedatives and anesthetics, but in much greater strength, is the ability to alter subjective states of awareness in a way which, though difficult to describe, is most often seen as pleasurable and worth repeating. Users of the hallucinogens sometimes call them "mind-expanding" or "consciousness-expanding" drugs, but both the expansion supposedly involved and the benefits of experiencing it are vague. Hostile critics claim that the drugs cause temporary psychoses, delusional or hallucinatory withdrawals from reality which, unchecked, may lead to permanent damage. Their method of checking the effects, however, is to prohibit the drugs, though the occasionally very serious behavior aberrations that have been reliably associated with the drugs may also have occurred in otherwise unstable, disturbance-prone individuals. Nobody knows.

The facts of hallucinogenic drugs, such as they are, are that several million people, especially young adults, take them annually in America; that most of them experience dramatic but temporary changes in perceptions, sometimes of a bizarre sort; that a few undergo serious disorders, which may have resulted directly or indirectly from taking the drugs; and that public hysteria connected with them, often aided and abetted by the mental-health professions as well as law-enforcement agencies, contributes nothing either to restricting their improper use or finding out whether they have any desirable applications. Until they were widely touted and widely banned, there was some reason to think hallucinogens might be useful in psychiatric treatment, but clear evidence to this effect has not been found.

Judging from effects alone, the "second generation" of psychiatric treatments represented by mood-changing drugs may not suggest a particularly powerful, let alone obnoxious, kind of behavior control. At one extreme, some of them have little more power than aspirin, and those which are clearly powerful seem limited in capacity only to very general manipulations of mood. Effective energizers and tranquilizers are described all too precisely by the slang terms "uppers" and "downers" because they affect only the direction of mood, not the thoughts or acts that accompany it. An "upper" may support aggression, lust, giggling, or tearful Weltschmerz, and there is no telling from the drug alone which is most likely to result. Even the psychedelic drugs allow little more specific description than that they change "perception" to a "sort of dreamy state"; the contents of the dream are unpredictable from the drug, and "wow," "out of sight," and "way out" are among the most reliable descriptions to come from some users. Even so, the potential, if not the actual performance, of drugs to date implies their importance as behavior-control devices in the future.

From a social point of view, the first contribution of modern drug treatments to control technology was to lay the groundwork of popular acceptance for future drugs by their own almost instant public acceptance. Tranquilizers were popular almost as soon as they were known and before it was fully realized what they could do either for individuals or the mental hospital system. This did not result merely from the venality of drug companies or the naïveté of physicians. Nor did it come alone from the fact that the new drugs were cheap and powerful: many of the old ones had been, too.

The new drugs had the novel virtue of being administered orally, generally as pills. This made them easier to handle and less fearsome than previous treatments. Several people usually administer

ECT, and the experience may be dreadful. Powerful drugs like insulin, moreover, have to be injected—so even if they do not produce feelings of disorientation, they cause some pain—and at the hands of someone other than the patient himself. Pills are less frightening and painful than shocks or shots; they do not appear to insult the body, and nothing could be easier to administer. Many people have trouble finding their own veins, but everybody knows where his mouth is and can do his own pill taking. The patient feels more confident of controlling what is happening to him than when somebody sticks needles into him or attaches electrodes to his body. Finally, most people have positive mental associations with pills, a lingering remnant of the childhood myth that the things you eat are good for you. This "chicken soup theory" of the popularity of oral medicine suggests that the increasing use of drugs is, in part, a natural extension of health faddism, but in the hands of more respectable people. It is an elaboration of the heroic legend of nutrition, which purports, in the minds of the innocent, to guarantee long life, good health, beauty, and perhaps wisdom and happiness to people who will only eat the right things. And there is just enough truth in the claim; just enough research on the nutritional determinants of everything from heart disease to acne; just enough publicity on chlorophyll, cholesterol, hormones, and the preservation of smooth skin, profuse and glistening hair, bright and strong teeth, slender waists, and slick and well-flushed bowels, to sustain an optimistic zeal for every new orally incorporable promise to promote individual welfare. The same powders and potions may not go so well or quickly in France, where they are commonly administered by suppository.

Instant popularity does not always augur a long run, however, and the fact that mood-changing drugs are now doing better than ever means that the medical profession likes them more than ever. The reason is more technical than sociological. The transition from physical assault treatments to pills transferred the major instruments of psychiatry from mental specialists to general practitioners, few of whom would have dared administer insulin or ECT without special training but most of whom cheerfully assume that they are as able as the next fellow to prescribe a pill at the drop of a symptom. Since a large proportion of all medical cases involve psychological or behavior disorders, broadly speaking, the impetus for physicians to use the mood drugs is enormous. And the very grossness of their effects makes it easy to prescribe from the plethora of compounds at hand with little more information than the multicolored brochures and multiple samples left by the drug salesman.

As doctors use them more, the public wants the drugs more and, wanting them, expects to get them. Demand among "respectable" people for hallucinogenic drugs has already carried the transition in the mores of drug distribution a step further than that from psychiatry to general medicine, taking the control of mood-changing drugs outside the hands of doctors altogether and even outside the limits of the current laws. This has happened for what is finally the most important reason that behavior-controlling drugs will be more widely accepted and used in the future than was hinted by their early popularity: their proliferation, assured by a growing technical ability to produce them synthetically, and in turn giving them great promise as specifics.

The Search for "Specifics"

Every ambitious drug maker wants to produce "specifics," drugs which, to quote René Dubos of Rockefeller University, "act almost uniquely against a structure or an activity peculiar to the organism or function to be affected." Specifics, in other words, are drugs which do a single job; their effects are strictly known, and narrowly controlled. The ultimates in the technology of drug making are synthetic specifics, those invented in the laboratory rather than obtained from natural sources. The ability to manufacture them confers tremendous power over metabolic processes, once these are entirely understood and the engineering facilities for the operation are at hand. Both these problems are diminishing all the time, as the growing proliferation of drugs and biology journals testifies.

The search for specificity, according to Dubos, has been more responsible than any other single factor for the discovery of new drugs. The goal of deliberately synthesizing drugs, he claims, was first stated by Paul Ehrlich, who devoted much of his life to the search for a "magic bullet" that would cure syphilis.

A drug does not have to be synthetic to be specific. Penicillin, which is quite specific as medicines go, is a natural drug. The widespread use of a drug, however, probably does depend on somebody's being able to manufacture it in large quantities at reasonably low cost. Rauwolfia, a natural tranquilizer, was well known in India for over 2,000 years as an "insanity drug" but was not widely used in the United States until an Indian psychiatrist lectured on it in 1953, a year after chlorpromazine went on the market. Marijuana, peyote, and several other natural psychedelic drugs were well known and cheaply available for years before they were much used. It was the (accidental) discovery of LSD-25, a very cheap synthetic, that propelled the still rising tide of hallucinogenic drug use among middle-class Americans—including use of the natural hallucinogens, which have been outstripping LSD since its possible dangers have become well known.

Present skills at synthesizing drugs still exceed the ability to specify their action. "Powerful metabolic inhibitors have been synthesized . . . ," says Dubos, "but in general they lack selectivity." The endless output of new mood-changing drugs reflects this fact. Drug companies are creating new energizers and tranquilizers at such a great rate that as much effort is needed to invent new names (and claims) for them as to concoct new compounds, and their effects are about the same as with previous drugs. Discoveries in biochemistry, molecular biology, and other sciences, however, are continually broadening the scope of chemical syntheses and the knowledge of what drugs have what effects on what features of the body. Coming from both the theoretical and applied ends of biological research, the invention of new drugs will propel the discovery of new possibilities for increased control of behavior. And complete specificity is not needed for thorough drug control; behavior that cannot be controlled by the selective action of a single drug may still be susceptible to a combination of drugs from an armamentarium of relevant compounds. Aggression, for example, may be subject to drug controls, even if no one drug alone works well enough on it. There are several different hormone compounds now being studied which seem to have some promise for reducing hostile and aggressive impulses. So do some anticonvulsant agents, and so do some other drugs which have multiple and nonspecific effects as well. A drug whose primary function is to reduce hyperactivity may also be an effective inhibitor of aggression in one person, while a drug which primarily reduces anxiety may have the same effect on another. The aggregate of such drugs may provide an aggregate of control over aggression, even though a single pill, usable with a singular lack of selectivity for preventing aggression in anyone, cannot be envisioned. The concept of aggression includes too many different kinds of behavior, aroused by too many different kinds of stimuli and controlled by too complex a medley of too many brain and body parts, for its manipulation to be neatly subject to a single pill.

The simpler, the more specific, and the more accessible the physiology and anatomy which underlies a class of behavior, and the narrower and more concrete the stimulus conditions which arouse it and the avenues of expressing it, the more likely it is that specific drugs can eventually be produced to control it. This means, for example, that a specific drug will more likely be developed to improve memory than to curtail aggression. Work in that direction is well along.

Chemically Aided Memory

The physical basis of memory has eluded discovery for a long time, but much research continues to pursue the notion that memory depends on chemical changes in the brain which are chemically reproducible. James McConnell, a psychologist at the University of Michigan, has shown repeatedly that organisms as lowly on the phylogenetic scale as flatworms are capable of simple learning, and "cannibal" experiments, in which educated worms

were fed to ignorant cousins, seem to demonstrate chemical transfer of learning ability, though some attempts to replicate such
studies have been unsuccessful. For years, McConnell's research
group at Michigan has published *The Worm Runner's Digest,* a
delightful technical journal for keeping score on work in this area.
Some studies of chemical memory transfer have been made of
higher organisms as well. Allan Jacobson and his colleagues at the
University of California at Los Angeles have improved the memories of rats and hamsters with a brain-extract porridge from other
rats and hamsters who, to their regret, had previously learned
some simple response patterns by conventional training; and
George Ungar of Baylor University Medical School appears to
have successfully transferred fears in rats by similar means. There
is much equivocation in the scientific world about such results,
however, since many other scientists fail to reproduce them. Even
so, David Krech and his colleagues at the University of California
at Berkeley have shown definite changes in brain anatomy resulting from "environmental enrichment," the plausibility of a chemical basis for memory remains unassailable, and research continues
on various compounds that may facilitate or inhibit it.

The most popular current notion, in this connection, is that
memory is physically embodied in the brain's supply of RNA, one
of the nucleic acids which control the transmission of genetic information. Several experiments have attempted to improve memory by administrations of RNA, and at least one commercial
product, called Cylert, has been touted as a possible "memory
pill," based on its initial effects on rats; its initial results on human
beings have been mixed. The growing body of research on memory
drugs typically yields such ambiguous results. James McGaugh of
the University of California at Irvine has shown that some memory
drugs work only on the most stupid animals, not on beasts that are
smart to begin with. Even such a limited result would be very
valuable, however, if it could be applied to human beings.

At present, in any case, no true memory pill exists, and nobody
should bate his breath in momentary expectation of one, though
Krech expects to see it within a few years. Certain current drugs

do aid memory at times, but only by indirect means, as hypnosis does. A tranquilizer may make it easier for someone to concentrate, and thus to remember what he is reading, by removing the distracting effects of anxiety. An energizer may have a similarly beneficial effect on memory by arousing a person enough so he can pay attention. The direct memory pills of the 1960s, however, are no better than the garlic pills which grandmother used to make her smarter or the glutamic acid pills used for the same purpose in the 1940s (the same ingredients are available commercially as Accent in the United States)—and they will not even flavor or tenderize meat. But the basis for seeking a memory pill is sound, and as knowledge of the chemistry and physiology of memory grows over the next several years, as it surely will, the prospect of such an invention grows more real.

The Limits of Chemical Control

Complicated behavior like aggression may prove controllable without chemical specifics, and narrower kinds like memory may soon have specifics invented to control them, but the coercive power of drugs will always nonetheless be very limited. There are some things that even the most powerful drugs cannot make people do and other things, exemplified by placebo effects, which *people* can make even weak or inert drugs do.

General unfamiliarity with drugs, ominous publicity about them, and a subtle hangover from the halcyon days when we all believed in magic make many people feel that drugs can compel us to do all kinds of things over which they really have only peripheral effects, or none at all. The widespread belief in truth serums, and the true facts concerning the use of drugs for interrogation, is a case in point.

During World War II, Sodium Pentothal, an anesthetic drug, was widely used for its hypnotic (sleep-inducing, not mumbo jumbo) effects, which helped inhibited people to talk and repressed people to recover and communicate lost memories. Its success led many people to consider it a truth serum, a view that received respectively laudatory and ominous publicity in famous plays like *Home of the Brave* and novels like *The Manchurian Candidate*. In fact, Pentothal can no more compel people to disclose something they want to hide than can a stiff shot of whisky. Its usefulness lies in its ability to relax people so that they can recover experiences that anxiety *prevents* them from remembering, and it is not always effective even for that. The same is true of all other ostensible truth serums. Louis A. Gottschalk, when he was consultant to the Bureau of Social Science Research, reviewed research on this subject for the United States Air Force in a paper titled "The Use of Drugs in Information-Seeking Interviews." He concluded: ". . . drugs can operate as positive catalysts to productive interrogation . . . but, for many reasons, the use of drugs by an interrogator is not sure to produce valid results. . . . Even under the most favorable circumstances the information obtained could be contaminated by fantasy, distortion, and untruth. . . ." For all anyone knows, it may be impossible, even in theory, ever to develop a drug that forces anybody to tell the truth about anything, not because truly coercive drugs do not exist, but because, in a physiological sense, truth does not. Truth is what somebody perceives, and it is probably impossible for a person to perceive only one thing at a time, like the answer to a question without the question or a cherished secret without the cherished knowledge of its secrecy. This does not mean that secrets cannot be wheedled out of people or that drugs will not help to do it, perhaps by dulling their sensibilities to subtle or leading questions. It does mean, however, that ideas do not sit palpably in the brain, at least not in any form where they can be dissolved by some mental emetic and poured out the mouth reconstructed and whole. And as long as the effects of a drug must pass through the ideational centers of the brain in order to be expressed, the exact form of their expression will be uncertain. Even powerful excitatory drugs like epinephrine (adrenalin) do not dictate the precise behavior to result from their arousal of the autonomic nervous system or precisely which feelings will pervade consciousness from merely taking the drug. Stanley Schachter of Columbia University and Jerome E. Singer of New York State University at Stony Brook have amply demonstrated that the drug only excites the body, while the thoughts accompanying that arousal dictate whether the person will feel anger, fear, or overwhelming tenderness—and the drug does not dictate the contents of the thoughts. Even should a clever controller manipulate the situation so that his victim is first emotionally aroused by the drug and then given ideas that convert the arousal to anger, aim it at somebody, and provide the motive, opportunity, and equipment to kill him, there is no sure telling what will happen. The act of aggression is not the same as the impulse to aggress; it depends on the often complicated interactions of individual histories of aggressive experiences with the intricacies of motive and opportunity, and there is no such thing as a take-this-gun-and-shoot-Joe center in the human nervous system, though there are aggression centers in the brain. Pills for inhibiting certain kinds of behavior, like aggression, by suppressing appropriate brain centers, have better prospects than do pills for eliciting specific behavior because there are often many ways to do something but only one way not to.

Body Control Is a "Head Game"

What finally limits most of the coercive control of drugs over behavior, as suggested above, is the same thing that limits the coercive usefulness of pain: it must be processed through the central nervous system, including the brain, and its effects may be vitiated or nullified by what goes on in the cerebral cortex, the phylogenetically most advanced part of the brain, which controls critical and particularly human faculties like language.

In evolutionary terms, pain is probably a refined development of tissue irritability, which makes even the simplest animals move away from noxious stimuli in their environments—what Sir Charles Sherrington called the sensory adjunct of an imperative protective reflex. In human beings, this biological development has become so refined that to this day nobody is able to describe the anatomy or physiology of pain with certainty. What is clear about the nature of pain is that, far from being a simple, primitive somatic response, it is a complex behavior pattern that is interpreted, modified, and sometimes canceled by the central nervous system, so that the results of painful stimulation are anything but straightforward and obvious. Many experiences of pain, for instance, occur after the wires are cut; others, conversely, are not reported in situations where the pain nerve receptors have been intensely stimulated. Amputees often report excruciating pain in limbs they no longer have. Neurosurgery is sometimes used in the attempt to relieve this so-called phantom limb pain, but it often fails to work. An equally puzzling event is referred pain, in which damage to an internal organ, such as the kidney, is felt as a pain on the surface of the body, like the back, and may be triggered by mildly stroking normal skin. Conversely, men in battle may be wounded without noticing pain or may feel so little pain from their wounds that they refuse medical relief for them. In some experiments, finally, Pavlov trained dogs to interpret electric shocks, cuts, and burns as signals for food; eventually, they stopped showing any signs of pain in response to them.

As Ronald Melzack, of McGill University, and Patrick Wall, of the Massachusetts Institute of Technology, summarize it, pain is an extremely complex interaction "between stimulus patterns, the cells of different spinal cord systems, and brain activities," such that

it is possible for central nervous system activities subserving attention, emotion, and memories of prior experience to exert control over the sensory input . . . [and for] psychological factors [to] influence pain responses and perception. . . . The perceptual awareness that accompanies these events changes in quality and intensity during all this activity. This total complex sequence is hidden in the simple phrases "pain response" and "pain sensation." . . . Virtually the whole brain is the "pain center" . . . implicated in pain perception.

The complexity of pain makes the perception of it, at least in part, subject to control by the frontal cortex of the brain, where the critical and rational faculties of man reside; and this, in turn, makes pain a fickle agent of coercion.

Placebo effects, discussed briefly in Chapter 2, show that the power of the central nervous system over the body's response to drugs is as dramatic and mysterious as its control of pain. The genuineness of this phenomenon is established beyond question, but the fact is not always appreciated even within the medical profession. In an article called "Quantitative Effects of Drugs on the Mind," for instance, the distinguished anesthesiologist Henry Beecher reports: " . . . only after I had worked in this field for some years I realized that we usually had a high average degree of effectiveness of placebos in treating post-operative wound pain, and other conditions as well."

Upon this discovery, he began searching for other such observations and found many similar reports, in which placebos proved as effective as active pain-relieving drugs in from 21 percent to 41 percent of cases of postoperative wound pain, cancer pain, angina pain, and coughing. Even more important, he also observed that "the effectiveness of a placebo is much greater when stress is severe than when it is not [and] the average effectiveness of placebos in relieving pathological pain is 35 per cent, whereas the average effectiveness of placebos with experimentally contrived pain is only 3.2 per cent. In other words, the placebo is *ten times* more effective in relieving pain of pathological origin than it is in relieving pain of experimentally contrived origin."

The difference in treatment effects on pain produced in laboratory experiments and in live situations is not peculiar to placebos, however. The most powerful pain relievers, such as morphine, also have differing effects on laboratory and on real-life pains. Morphine may or may not relieve experimentally produced pain, but will always have some analgesic effects on pathological pain. Beecher's conclusion underscores the limitations that the central nervous system places on drug effects, which he considers "a new principle of drug action: some drugs are effective only in the presence of an appropriate mental state."

Placebo effects are not "mental" phenomena in the sense of being immaterial, incorporeal, or spiritual; they are physical events in the body, produced in connection with drugs which have no such effects most of the time. It is the statistical inefficiency of a drug that causes it to be used as a placebo in the first place, just as the statistical efficiency of morphine makes us regard it as a pain killer. The efficient result in question is the reaction of the body, not the chemical character of the drug. Placebos demonstrate the sometime independence of that reaction from drug control. A placebo effect, in other words, is an uncommon chemical reaction of the body to special commands of the central nervous system. How this reaction works is unknown, but the "chain of command" clearly originates in the most advanced parts of the cerebral cortex, where cognitive consciousness—that is, the understanding of language—occurs. It is misleading to say that placebo effects demonstrate the power of suggestion. If anything, they demonstrate the power of faith. The mere statement that a drug is powerful medicine has no effect until it is combined with a pill whose appearance makes it convincing. It is the resulting conviction which creates the placebo effect, not the suggestion! If the same conviction were instilled without a drug, perhaps by telling patients they had been given a drug in their sleep which would take effect shortly, or as may have already been done innumerable times by faith healers and hypnotists, then perhaps the same result would occur. At all events, unadorned suggestion does not produce placebo effects; the front part of the cerebral cortex is giving the orders that make them happen. It does the same thing sometimes to resist torture, to pursue what most people think are impossible goals, and to make the rest of the organism endure beyond ordinary measure until its purposes are fulfilled. Considered in that light, it is small wonder that it has some control over the effects of drugs.

The action of the cerebral cortex on the stuff of glands and nerves—that is, on body chemistry—shown so clearly in the peculiarities of pain and placebo effect, shows also that informational and coercive behavior controls are ultimately indistinguishable. Efficient control of human functioning does not depend on the means of input (the major difference between information and coercion), but on the ability to maintain the individual's sense of integrity while doing what the controller wants, so that one part of his self will not rebel against the urges of another. Despite their great potency and great potential, drugs cannot, in any absolute fashion, exert precise control over the parts of the brain that steer those urges. Such absolute control requires better access to the structures of the brain than pills or shots can give. This is possible today by a combination of surgery and electronics, which provides control over the control machinery of the brain.

Brain Implantation: The Third Generation of Coercive Controls

All the ancient dreams of mastery over man and all the tales of zombies, golems, and Frankensteins involved some magic formula, or ritual, or incantation that would magically yield the key to dominion. But no one could be sure, from the old Greeks down to Mrs. Shelley, either by speculation or vivisection, whether there was any door for which to find that key. There is, of course: the human brain, by now long known to hold the master mechanisms of control for almost every moving part of us, from breathing air to making love, and for all the parts that fantasize, compute, think, and know. All the complicated orchestration, the cacophony, and harmony of the body, and all the overtones from it which we call mind, are recorded, conducted, and broadcast by the brain. Because of its endless importance for so many aspects of life and well-being, the lucky accidents of evolution locked it behind a palisade of protecting bone, shielding it from harm and, incidentally, from investigation. Even after surgery made it possible to penetrate the skull, our knowledge of the living brain came only slowly and painfully to light; its tissues and its functions bore no labels, and its soft, squishy, and gelatinous depths presented a seemingly impenetrable barrier to easy discovery. This has been changing gradually, as knowledge of the brain has grown and been compounded since the nineteenth century, until today a whole technology exists for physically penetrating and controlling the brain's own mechanisms of control. It is sometimes called "brain implantation," which means placing electrical or chemical stimulating devices in strategic brain tissues, or ESB (electrical stimulation of the brain), referring to what is most commonly done to the brain once the gadgetry is in place. These methods have been used experimentally on myriad aspects of animal behavior, and clinically on a growing number of people with assorted miseries for assorted diagnostic and remedial purposes. It works with much reliability and is getting better all the time, and at an accelerating rate. The limits on what can be done with it in the future are not yet in sight. But what has been done with it already is more than enough to excite everyone and unnerve some.

The number of activities connected to specific places and processes in the brain and aroused, excited, augmented, inhibited, or suppressed at will by stimulation of the proper site is simply huge. Animals and men can be oriented toward each other with emotions ranging from stark terror or morbidity to passionate affection and sexual desire. Docility, fearful withdrawal, and panicked efforts at escape can be made to alternate with fury and ferocity of such degree that its subject can as readily destroy himself by exhaustion from his consuming rage as he can the object of it, whom he attacks, heedless of both danger and opportunity. Eating, drinking, sleeping, moving of bowels or limbs or organs of sensation, gracefully or in spastic comedy, can all be managed on electrical demand by puppeteers whose flawless strings are pulled from miles away by the unseen call of radio and whose puppets, made of flesh and blood, look "like electronic toys," so little self-direction do they seem to have. Memory can be aroused with an immediacy that, in ordinary life, it almost never has; speech can be speeded up from halting phrases to relative chatter; laughter and tears, anger and friendliness, and fatigue and curiosity—all these and more can be aroused, reduced, shifted, and maneuvered by stimulations of the brain. Developments in the isolation of distinct brain structures, in mapping the anatomy of the brain, in neurosurgical techniques and instruments, and in electronics, especially the miniaturization of equipment, make all these things realities right now. Improvements in all these areas can only increase ability to control behavior by intervention in the brain.

Clinical efforts at controlling psychiatric conditions by brain surgery are not new, but "psychosurgery," as it is called, was always more a matter of destroying brain tissue by lesions and ablations than of manipulating it by implantations. The most popular of these treatments has been "prefrontal lobotomy," in which the patient's frontal brain lobes are partially separated from the thalamus, a part of the midbrain involved in the experience of emotion. It was fairly widely practiced from the late thirties until the advent of tranquilizers in 1952. Its usual intent was to calm an uncontrollable patient, which, incidentally, made him more manageable in the hospital, but its occasional effect was to arouse a calm one. Lobotomies had other side effects as well, ranging from subtle behavior changes like the loss of intellectual abilities, especially the ability to do foresightful planning, to dramatic behavior changes like dying, which occurred in 1 to 4 per cent of these surgeries. Variations of the prefrontal lobotomy have been periodically introduced and promoted since, but the general opinion of psychiatrists is that their risks far outweigh their expected benefits, particularly since most damage inflicted by this surgery is not reversible.

In addition to its practical defects, ablative surgery is not as useful scientifically as one might hope because its often gross assault on a brain center tends to obliterate some brain suburbs as well, destroying more functions than was intended. Experimental conclusions drawn from brain lesion studies are therefore often misleading. "It is as if," says J. A. Deutsch, of the University of California at San Diego, "one were to amputate somebody's leg and draw the conclusion that he had thereby disinhibited a hopping reflex." Natural ablations may show the existence of specific brain control centers all too well, by dramatic changes in behavior patterns from traumatic head injuries, illnesses like meningitis, and chronic brain disorders like epilepsy, which leave a residue of brain impairment. Most information about human response to brain stimulation, in fact, has been a by-product of personal calamities in which neurosurgery was needed to repair brain damage or prevent further deterioration.

Even so, most knowledge about brain control mechanisms has come from experimental rather than from natural sources, and most of these have been ablation experiments on animals. Electrical stimulation research, from which implantation is derived, was opened up in 1898 by J. R. Ewald, a professor of physiology at Strassbourg. He developed a means of hooking an electric circuit to the waking brain of a dog and connecting the wires to a battery which he carried. Thirty years later, W. R. Hess, who later won a Nobel Prize for his work, used a related method to stimulate the brains of cats and discovered that they responded to the electric current as if they were about to be attacked by threatening dogs: their hair stood on end, their ears flattened, their eyes dilated, and they growled and struck out. In the absence of any ostensible dog to be threatened by, this reaction was labeled "sham" rage, and comparable responses to electrical stimulation were called "sham" hunger, and so forth, meaning that there was no apparent motive for the observed behavior. But the behavior expressed in such cases was hardly sham; it was forcefully real, and so was the motivation behind that. For rage and hunger and all the other animal passions do not reside in external objects or even in the stomach, glands, or gonads but ultimately in the brain, the master mechanism in which they are experienced and from which they are expressed. The key to control of the brain centers which guide motives and their expression is the key to absolute control over behavior.

Brain-implantation methods provide that key by making it possible to retain the structure of a brain center while an experimenter turns its functions on and off. Most brain-controlled behavior results from the activity of electric impulses, which either work directly on brain cells or stimulate chemical reactions which work on them, or both. Modern tools for managing that electrical activity had to wait on the solutions to some important engineering problems. Materials were needed that could be imbedded indefinitely in brain tissue without damaging it, fostering infection, or rotting; microscopically precise methods of introducing electrodes were needed; electronic equipment was required to transmit and receive electrical impulses according to exact schedules; and apparatus was needed that permitted experimental or clinical subjects, animals or men, to go about their business freely and not have to be strung by electric wires to cumbersome recording machines. Finally, a suitable means of making objective, long, and detailed observations of behavior was needed to assess what effects the stimulating devices were producing.

Interest, curiosity, need, and greed, the usual cluster of motives which combine with serendipity in an open market, to build better mousetraps and the like, were all conjoined by the early 1950s to solve most of these problems. Developments in synthetics provided the required materials, the needs of the communications and aerospace industries for precise and tiny tools and electronic packages enabled proper signaling and recording instruments to be built, and telemetry and time-lapse photography offered suitable means of using them.

Some of the most sophisticated techniques of surgery and implantation which evolved from these developments are represented in the work of José Delgado, of Yale University Medical School's Departments of Psychiatry and Physiology, and one of the world's leading students and most prolific expositors of this work. His method does little damage to brain tissue, permits his subject to move around unrestrained after surgery, with the stimulation devices working, and allows him to wear the apparatus comfortably for life, without functional deficits or even very obvious aesthetic ones (some women patients, he says, have "proved the adaptability of the feminine spirit to all situations by designing pretty hats to conceal their electrical headgear"). While the subject or patient is under anesthesia, the surgeon inserts fine steel or platinum electrodes in preselected brain sites using special maps to locate them and micromanipulator instruments to insert them. The wires themselves are coated with biologically inert insulation, such as nylon or Teflon, and are so fine that two dozen or more individual electrode tips may be extended to separate points of contact in the brain from a single external socket which passes current to all of them. Since brain tissue is insensitive, the electrodes are not felt; humans and animals alike can wear them indefinitely without discomfort. One animal did so for more than four years.

There are several different kinds of radio control devices. Radio stimulators are extremely small instruments for transmitting current to the brain by remote radio control. They can be strapped on the backs of monkeys or attached to people's belts. Activated by radio from yards away, they can operate on small portable batteries. Another variety, called a programed stimulator, is self-contained, delivering stimulation according to a prearranged schedule. Since it needs no remote radio control, the subject's mobility is unlimited by this device, which makes it therapeutically useful for human beings. A third kind of radio gadget provides prolonged continuous stimulation at low intensity. It has been used to pep up the posterior hypothalamus for weeks on end; the hypothalamus is part of the forebrain, controlling a number of autonomic, sexual, and involuntary functions. When used on the nerve which depresses the carotid sinus, moreover, the continuous stimulator has reduced high blood pressure both in dogs and men.

Administration of drugs into the brain by remote control may have even more important future applications than does direct electrical stimulation. Delgado and his collaborators have developed an instrument called a radio injector, which is implanted in the brain and, on radio command, releases chemicals directly into brain tissues. When a current passes through one chamber of this "micropump," its liquid contents, a volatile substance called hydrazine, is converted to expanding gas, pushing the liquid out of a neighboring chamber and into the brain at a constant rate, adjustable by means of the settings on the radio receiver. Chemicals have potential advantages over electricity as means of brain stimulation because of their flexibility and variety; their dosage can be controlled in fine degree, and there are a lot of different chemicals around that can be injected. One jolt of current, on the other hand, can differ from another in schedule and intensity alone.

At the present time, however, electrical stimulation remains paramount, and improves steadily, as its apparatus becomes tinier and tougher from year to year. In the fall of 1966, Delgado's laboratory was using a standard working transceiver (transmitter-receiver) slightly smaller than a pack of cigarettes, and was developing devices respectively about the area of a postage stamp and the thickness of a fingernail, and contemplating others of even smaller sizes, including a transceiver the size of a Sen-Sen. He indicated that it would be theoretically possible for someone to put a tiny computer in the brain in a few more years, and that such devices might ultimately be used for increasing intelligence electronically.

Animal Studies

Animals are more available than people for experiments, of course, which is why most implantation studies have been done on them. A phenomenal range and depth of animal activities can be manipulated by stimulating one part of the brain or another. Simple movements, voluntary or not, can be commanded from virtually any limb or muscled part. But attitudes, emotions, and drives can be directed just as well. Aggression, withdrawal, hunger, thirst, sex, and pleasure can be excited and inhibited so dependably and in such variety of expressions, that the very lives of the animals can be expended at the whim of the experimenter controlling the stimulation. Those whose stomachs are full can be made to eat themselves to death; the hungry or thirsty to refuse food; the serene become enraged and spend themselves in furious clawings at nothing; the sexually aroused copulate repeatedly until exhausted; and the placid quickly learn to inject electricity into a "pleasure center" in their own brains and continue injecting themselves, oblivious of anything else, until they are forcibly removed from the situation. Hess's early experiments on rage have been replicated innumerable times on innumerable species and his original findings refined and elaborated on dogs, cats, rats, bulls, and what have you.

Precisely what happens to what part of which animal under what stimulating circumstances is not simple, straightforward, or obvious, which is one important reason animal studies must generally precede experiments with human beings. Very brief stimulation in some areas of the brain, for example, may have lasting effects, as in studies where a cat, stimulated for five seconds in the amygdala, did not eat for three days thereafter, and normally voracious monkeys lost all appetite for bananas when the head of the caudate nucleus was electrically aroused. Other areas of the brain, like the motor cortex, quickly become fatigued, and may need a few minutes to recover from a few seconds of stimulation. Still others, like the hypothalamus, can be continuously excited with continuing effects, for weeks on end.

Depending on the particular brain site stimulated, and the nature of the stimulation, its effect on the animal's behavior may be either arousing or inhibiting. Stimulating the nucleous dorsalis of the thalamus, for example, enormously increases the amount of copulation in monkeys, but by stimulating the anterior part of the thalamus with the signal from a battery-operated transistor device in one hand, Delgado brought a "brave bull" to a dead stop in the middle of his charge.

In general, stimulation of a particular area in one species tends to produce the same effect as stimulation of the same or a parallel area in another. The larger the animal, the easier it is to locate a particular site in the brain—and the larger the species, more or less, the greater its intelligence. If size and site were the only considerations, it might be easier to control a man than a mouse. They are not, of course, because with our greater size goes a much greater complexity of functions, some of which are not subject to stimulation control at all.

Aggression and social behavior. Behavior patterns that involve the interactions of many brain centers rather than a single one also can be subjected to control by implantation. Aggression is one such pattern. It may be aroused by activity of the hypothalamus, the amygdaloid region, the thalamus, the temporal lobes, or still other places in the brain. Depending on where and how it is produced, moreover, it may be expressed as explosive rage, sullen hostility, irascible alertness, or violent attack. According to Kenneth E. Moyer, of Pittsburgh's Carnegie-Mellon University, there are at least seven, possibly eight, distinct kinds of aggression, each resulting from a presumably different interaction between some brain center and some external stimulus.

It is possible not only to elicit aggression, but also to get it in refined form, not just to turn it on and off, but also to turn it higher or lower at will by reducing the intensity of stimulation to a level which does not evoke overt rage. A usually affectionate and gregarious cat, for instance, put in the company of five other cats, while a low-intensity radio stimulation of the amygdala was applied continuously for two hours, turned sullen and irascible. He withdrew to a corner of the cage and sat motionless, uttering barely audible growls, and started spitting, hissing, and threatening if any other cat approached or if the experimenter tried to pet him. As soon as the stimulation stopped, he became his friendly self again.

Remote controls made it practical to study the effects of ESB on social activity; without them, animals would trip over each other's wires, short-circuit the recorders, and would perhaps from time to time hurt each other. Since we are finally more interested in human behavior than that of lower species, and since the human behavior of greatest significance is that which has social effects, it is important to learn what social behavior comes under the heading of physiological events or is subject to direct control of brain physiology.

One of Delgado's most important efforts has been the long-term observation of an entire colony of rhesus monkeys. This species is quite intelligent, as monkeys go, and, in addition, rhesus monkeys lead complicated social lives within their colonies, much like a Hollywood portrayal of life among the cavemen. Typically, one monkey emerges as "the boss"; he occupies large sumptuous living quarters, gets his pick of women and of food, and bullies his subordinates for recreation. There is not much fighting for position in monkey society, however, because its members ordinarily "know their places." Brain stimulation changes all that.

Radio stimulation of the boss's brain in one place inhibits his dictatorial posture, so that the other monkeys grow indifferent and ignore him; in another, the stimulation boosts his natural despotism, frightening them more than ever. To further confound things, if the radio stimulator that controls the boss is put inside the communal cage, then after a few days, even the most downtrodden victim of the boss's aggression learns to control the switch that turns him off.

Bryan Robinson of the Yerkes primate laboratory has reported an even more intriguing, and even romantic, find. In a three-monkey group with two dominant members, one male, one female, he made the subordinate male member aggressive by electrical stimulation. The female soon stopped attacking him, gradually shifted her affections to him, and eventually attacked her erstwhile friend. Those who remember Charles Atlas's 97-pound weakling could easily have predicted that she would do so.

Brain stimulation has also been effectively used to damage relations between a rhesus mother and her baby, whom she customarily attended and groomed almost constantly. When the mesencephalon of her brain was electrically stimulated, she began to ignore him completely. Only 10 seconds of stimulation created 10 minutes of maternal indifference, despite the baby's plaintive efforts to approach her. Once she did resume caring for him, moreover, a new dose of electricity again obliterated her attention.

In general, ESB has a more complicated and oblique effect on social behavior than on simpler activities. When a boss monkey is aggressively aroused, he does not strike out at random, but more often attacks a male whom he has long disliked and avoids attacking his favorite female lover. In such complex situations, electrical stimulation seems to work like drugs do: it increases the disposition to a certain kind of action, but does not dictate who will be the victim, object, or beneficiary of the act.

Human Brain Implants

Most implant studies have been done on animals, and despite similar results from one species to another, their relevance to human beings remains unsure. Easy denial of it is a fashionable dodge among people with philosophic or religious investments in claiming man's superior status among living creatures or in maintaining other special interests.

Even so, there is no certainty possible in arguments by analogy and no way, therefore, to know the relevance of ESB to human behavior without stimulating human brains electrically and watching what happens. A great deal has already been done, especially in clinical cases where electrical brain stimulations were needed in connection with surgery, sometimes requiring electrodes to remain implanted for months on end. Brain-implant controls have already been used successfully on people, experimentally or clinically, for changing speech patterns, relieving epileptic seizures, diagnosing and treating intractable pain, controlling some involuntary movements, and inducing and blocking hostile, aggressive impulses and an assortment of thought patterns, hullucinations, laughter, memories, sexual expressions, and pleasant shifts of moods—as well as physiological functions like heart rate, urination, muscle contraction, hearing, and blood pressure.

During the course of clinical operations, moreover, it has been possible for pioneering surgeons like McGill University's Wilder Penfield and like Robert Heath, of Tulane University, to use the surgical theater as a laboratory to study the effect of brain stimulation on other mental functions. Many but not all of these experiments have confirmed results obtained in animal studies. Since human beings are not available in large quantities for neurosurgical experiments, some comparisons between ourselves and lower species are limited to studies in which only one of us is represented. M. P. Bishop, S. T. Elder, and Robert Heath, for example, tried to discover on a human being the "pleasure center" which James Olds and P. Milner had found in rats at the University of Michigan ten years earlier, a finding replicated many times on rats and other species attending other universities. But since they had only a single person available for study, they were forced to conclude that their results, at best, were only suggestive. Similarly, J. M. Fuster found that stimulating the reticular activating system improved the visual perception of rhesus monkeys, but Gary Galbraith, of the University of Southern California, and Robert Heath were unable to parallel the finding on the one human being available for comparison.

More important than comparisons with other animals, however,

stimulation studies of human beings have elicited changes in thinking and emotion, in memory, in speech patterns, in motor functions, in sensations, and in perception. In some cases, patients
talked to a psychotherapist who tape-recorded the interviews while
different cerebral sites were stimulated. There were some remarkable results. One slow-speaking patient's rate of speech accelerated
from an average 8½ to 44 words per minute, amounting, for him,
to speaking in high gear. The friendly emotional content of his
remarks, moreover, sweetened ninefold. In other cases, thinking
has been blocked by ESB, so that people oriented in time and
space and able to follow the doctor's instructions in other ways
could not answer questions or pronounce a single word. "I could
not coordinate my thoughts," one explained. "My head felt as if I
had drunk a lot of beer." And another said, "I don't know why,
but I could not speak."

Hallucinations. The effects of brain stimulation on sensation
and memory are sometimes so powerful that patients' descriptions
of their electrically induced experiences sound hallucinatory.
Visual and auditory hallucinations have both occurred from stimulation of the temporal lobes. The stimulation, as described by
Lamar Roberts, of the University of Florida College of Medicine,
"can call back . . . past experience . . . as though a wire recorder, or a strip of cinematographic film with sound track, had
been set in motion within the brain." Past experiences go through
people's minds in vivid detail, and they are evidently aware of the
very things that captured their attention most strongly in the actual
event, while staying conscious throughout of what is happening in
the present. The whole thing stops when the current goes off and
starts again when it does.

The manipulation of human beings by electrical brain stimulation does not differ in principle from the same kind of manipulation in animals. What does differ, though, at times so dramatically
that it awes observers, is the fact that the effects of the stimulations
are expressed in ways peculiar to human beings. Animals too un-
doubtedly have memories and are capable of vivid recollections,
but they cannot convey them in a medley of words accompanying

their expressions of astonishment, anxiety, pleasure, love, or grief. Animals may feel pleasure akin to ours, but they cannot express amusement by giggling, laughter, or other such acts common to humanity and commonly observed under radio stimulation.

Electric sex. As might be expected, human sexual responses are also manipulable by radio stimulation. Several cases have been reported of shy and reserved women and at least one of a young boy being aroused sexually by stimulation of certain brain sites, flirting with their doctor as a result, and in two cases, including that of the boy, obliquely suggesting marriage to him! At least one projected case, moreover, involved a neurosurgeon's plan to treat a severe case of nymphomania by means of a permanent implant. Presumably, the same thing could be applied to sexual frigidity.

Control of aggression. There is probably no domain of radio stimulation more important for the near future than the control of individual acts of violence, a subject of increasing attention in this decade and of more concern in years to come. It has been an obvious subject of research since Hess's discovery of "sham" rage.

Dozens of studies to date have demonstrated the arousal of aggression by brain stimulation. Most report animal experiments, but increasing numbers of case reports indicate that the same phenomena occur in men. "Although the evidence is slim," says Dr. Moyer, "it appears clear that man, for all of his encephalization, is not free of those aggressive circuits. . . . Man is no exception. There are wild men as there are wild cats. . . . " Aggression is sometimes a result of brain pathology. Arson, rape, murder, and other acts of violence have often been associated with peculiarities in brain-wave patterns. Some of these conditions could in theory be controlled by implantations once the relevant brain sites are established and their operation understood.

A sizable body of studies on the control of aggression in human beings is accumulating. In Boston, an interdisciplinary team from Harvard Medical School, Massachusetts General Hospital, and Boston City Hospital operates a clinic for the study and control of violent people, directed by William Sweet and Vernon Mark, who are neurosurgeons, and Frank R. Ervin, a psychiatrist. Many of the patients referred to them have typically long histories of violent acts and significant numbers of psychological problems that are *not* a function of brain disorders in the usual sense. Some patients do have significant brain damage, however, ranging from epilepsy to tumors. ESB can be used effectively in some of these cases as a diagnostic tool. A twenty-year-old girl, for example, subject to episodic frenzies, was stimulated in several brain areas in turn in order to see which ones might be provoking her behavior. It was found that stimulation of the amygdala produced the frenzy, and termination of it ended her wildness. Moyer similarly reports how "a mild-mannered female patient became aggressive, verbally hostile, and threatened to strike the experimenter when she was electrically stimulated in the region of the amygdala. When the current was turned off, she again became mild-mannered and apologetic for her behavior. Her hostile . . . behavior could be turned on and off at the flick of a switch. . . ." Uncontrollable epileptic rage is also a well-known phenomenon. Vernon Mark cites a case in which a thirty-four-year-old engineer of some professional distinction was chronically violent over a ten-year period, during which he assaulted members of his family repeatedly and endangered many lives by his lunatic driving habits. He suffered from seizures originating in the amygdala. "Stimulation . . . of the left amygdala produced a feeling of 'going wild' and 'I'm losing control.' On the other hand, stimulation in the lateral amygdala, three millimeters away . . . produced a sensation of 'hyperre-laxation,' a feeling of 'detachment,' 'just the antithesis of my spells.' In his usual state, this patient was keenly aware of the slightest personal insult or threat, and his response was often sudden or violent. Under the effects of lateral amygdala stimulation, he showed bland acquiescence to the suggestion that the medial portion of his temporal lobe was to be destroyed." In this case, ablative surgery was necessary, and once accomplished, the rage reactions disappeared.

Brain surgery is fortunately not the only means of curbing aggression, but it is a valuable method to have in reserve when others fail. Even when violent dispositions are not the result of brain damage, implantation may still be used to cope with it and may be the kindest way of doing so. If the unusual distribution of male sex chromosomes called "XYY," for example, should turn out reliably to predict a genetic disposition to violence, as some scientists think it might, implantation might be more desirable than jail, if not than other treatments, since there is no evident way to remove a person's chromosomes and start him over. But since surgery is the least reversible of known coercive methods, the question will always remain as to whether it is justified simply because it is the most efficient.

At the present time, relatively few people combine the medical and scientific skills in their own persons to use brain implantation for many practical problems of human behavior, or to devise, execute, and test the research strategies or engineering tools and methods needed to expand knowledge in this field. There is no doubt, however, that the field will grow enormously as people become aware of its existence and importance. The combination of urgent need for it and of technological developments which promise to meet them guarantees that growth. Smaller and smaller instruments, better and better materials, more and more powerful batteries—all are in the works, and surely other things not yet envisioned here. No one needs to know what the limits of surgical control will be to know without a doubt, upon examining the work to date, that it will be possible someday to control very refined behavior by both chemical and electrical means.

Despite the fact that so many functions can be controlled by implantation, it is not clear that these methods, either in present forms or as projected for the future, are capable of producing human robots. Delgado does not believe "that a robot-like control of human beings is possible, because our personality depends on the functioning of millions of nerve cells with a multi-complex spatio-temporal integration of so many factors that its duplication by cerebral manipulation is not feasible." In particular, high-level thought processes, ideology, and other activities related to making rational decisions are not directly manipulable. The closer you get to intellectual processes, and to the top of the head, so to speak, the harder it is for radiosurgical controls to work. Perhaps commercial radios can be used ingeniously to direct higher thought processes, but implanted radios cannot.

We should not hastily conclude, however, that really important behavior is therefore safe from the effects of surgical control. What it demonstrates, if anything, is the large proportion of important activity which is not cognitive to begin with, but which rests instead in the middle, back, or sides of the head, and in the anxieties, hostilities, and lusts which mankind shares with lower animals. Even at their best and most independent, the cognitive processes may affect behavior less than writers, poets, educators, and romantics might like to think. The theoreticians of violence may talk endlessly, but there are no riots in the streets until someone's amygdala takes up their signal. Even the highest level of communion of cortexes, by itself, gets little action done.

In terms of what will come to pass, it matters little what the final limits are on this technology. Whether higher thought processes will someday be controllable by scientific means not known as yet, or whether men can be roboticized in frightening or beneficial ways, the course of this industry is clear for years to come. Sooner or later, someone will decide to put a small computer in the human brain to try and raise intelligence. Epileptic seizures will be overcome, some kinds of mental retardation will be conquered, and some psychoses will be subjugated too. But this technology, mindless and without morality, like all things not human, nor even living, will not direct itself. People will use it, just as people made it, and some of them will see that it has possibilities for more than merely medical control, helpful perhaps only to the controllers, not to those controlled. There is an intrinsic ambiguity about behavior control; whether its implications are more ominous or more promising to individuals and to society depends on how it will be understood, prescribed, exploited, and contained as it emerges in the future. Some of this can be foreseen.

PART III

The Meaning of Behavior
Control

6

The Prospects for Behavior Control

The increasing perfection of structural coercion techniques should make clear that it really is possible, or soon will be, for modern science to provide the means of profoundly controlling individual behavior. If there is doubt left by the brief description given here, the increasingly sophisticated application of these techniques in the next few years will make the point abundantly clear. The questions that will then arise will concern the prospects, dangers, and limitations of control technology, and the political, social, and ethical considerations that decent men must entertain in order to harness the power that will be available to the masters of this technology.

Predictions about the future effects of control technology often run to extremes. Ithiel de Sola Pool, of MIT, sees the early part of the next century as a golden age of interpersonal expression, largely derived from the behavior of modern hippies, and largely dependent on drugs. In a section of *The Year 2000* called "Other Twenty-first Century Nightmares," Herman Kahn and Anthony Wiener, of the Hudson Institute, foresee an equally probable era of repression and "dystopia," a term they apply to Huxley's and Orwell's awful visions of future political and social control. And both possibilities at once could come to pass, of course, with people enslaved in some respects and indulged in others.

155

It does not require any long-range image of behavior-control technology or much speculation about its future impact on society to see clearly what behavior-control developments are likely to be in the next several years and to draw some inferences about the effects they may have on the lives of individuals and eventually on society. In some respects, informational and coercive controls have different professional prospects and will have different effects on society. Both, however, will expand enormously as their applications and objectives move from the treatment of personal disorder to the reordering of human affairs at many levels, and the differences between them will become more and more blurred as all behavior technology becomes increasingly dependent on hard facts and hardware. In general, information controls, and some drugs, will have their main impact on individual mores and morals, fostering self-preoccupation, and their social consequences will come from the waves made in multitudes of individual lives. On the other hand, coercive controls, such as brain implants, will have their greatest impact from the top levels of society, stimulating political, ethical, and philosophical controversy as they emerge and undermining moral traditions by fostering skepticism about the assumptions on which those traditions are based.

Most important technologically inspired changes in society will, in any case, be products of general technology, whose effects on behavior, even when enormous, may be indirect and accidental. Contraceptive pills may have powerful consequences for sexual behavior, for example, but they have no *direct* effects at all on sexual motives, appetites, or opportunities. As behavior controls of all kinds grow beyond the narrow methods of healing to the broad techniques of mastering human behavior, their role in the general technology of our times continues to dictate the problems which it spawns. These are problems of success, not of failure, and it is the potential scope of their success that makes them grave.

The General Effects of Technology

Technology affects individual lives at three general levels: first, it confers life, sometimes wonderfully, sometimes tragically, on vast numbers of people who, for lack of technology, throughout history, died too young. Women survive childbirth today through the technology of antisepsis; healthy infants will live because of modern medicines; damaged neonates are doomed to imbecility or other handicaps because today's obstetrics spares their lives; numberless unknowing hosts escape pestilential death by the good grace of sanitary engineers. Second, it smooths our lives and eases them with comforting routines—flush toilets and tap water and electric lighting, instant communication, electronic recreation, and more. Finally, by the very pace of its development and use, it complicates our lives in unanticipated ways. Automobiles end the classic patterns of city construction in America, so quickly decentralizing urban centers that they cause a great displacement of people and of neighborhoods; the combination of labor-saving devices and improvements in income distribution inadvertently conspires to place young American upper-middle-class suburban housewives all at once among the most overworked and most pampered people in the world. There probably has to be some net gain, or benefit, to many people for any technological innovation to take hold, but the loss such innovations bring to some, as in technological unemployment, and the irritations and anxieties they bring to many more, who must adjust their lives to suit the new complexities, may be very troubling.

When technological change has some sharp and plain effect on how we live (which means on our behavior), it takes some getting used to. The appearance of trains and, later, of automobiles, for instance, strained the nerves of many a horse and rider for a while. But when it is phased in gradually, as part of a continuous stream of individually small changes, its effects are not so intensely felt. Invention of the jet transport plane has endless novel consequences, but a public already familiar with simpler air transport pays it no special mind. Most technical innovation is gradual; it does not spring forth full-blown from test tube or T-maze, from the furrow-browed thoughts of great scientists in white coats, nor even from most research orgies, in which huge programs drain buckets of easy money from the public trough. It evolves, most often, one step at a time, with each contributor, to paraphrase Sir Isaac

Newton, standing on the shoulders of the man who went before him to add small increments to the total structure of knowledge that results. In the past, this has allowed the pace of adjustment to most innovations to keep in lock step with the pace of development. But today the development of technology, for technical reasons, is accelerating constantly, and human beings are in danger of being suffused with more new things than they can handle. No one can say for sure what results this acceleration will have, but it must certainly cause some disruption to society. Behavior-control technology contributes to that disruption as part of general technology and, ironically, at the same time helps to alleviate it by doing what it is designed to do—controlling behavior. The way both roles are played differs somewhat for information and coercion.

The Prospects for Information Controls

Some of the future directions of information-control technology are clear, others not. The harder the wares involved, the clearer the future. It is very easy to see what will happen to the technology of behavior-shaping and instructional devices, fairly easy to say where action therapies are headed, and intriguingly hard to know what will become of insight therapies and all their spawn.

If there is one area where technological acceleration will help enable people to absorb the impact of technological acceleration, it is formal education. Three factors, all positive, are most responsible for this: first, our knowledge of the principles of human learning is forming and becoming sophisticated, so that we increasingly understand not only the rules of reinforcement on which most learning rests but also the facts of experience and development which make it possible to apply them intelligently to children of different backgrounds and tasks of different kinds. Second, the proliferation of equipment, from programed texts to videotape, makes it increasingly possible to present almost anything we want taught in effective packages which communicate subject matter in ways that make it most intelligible and memorable. Third, the use of computers as teaching machines creates almost limitless pos-

sibilities for individualizing the instruction of even the most complex topics and for even the most heterogeneous groups of students.
The technical future of education, by all means the most pervasive
behavior control in human history, is golden. What it will be used
for is another matter.

One thing that educational technology must be used for, of
course, is technological education. This is not a high moral purpose, by any means, nor is it the noblest social goal to which
teaching can be put. But it is needed to help the world's wheels
keep spinning, that is, to keep technology supplied with itself,
which we need, in turn, because we already have it. The irony may
be painful to some people, but none of the goals we examine will
escape this circularity.

Action therapies are becoming increasingly popular, in part
because they are polemical and in part because they are useful. On
either ground, these treatments will be more and more "in" for
some years to come; students will learn them, graduate faculties
will teach them, and the professional and general public will accept
and endorse them. This will be largely justified by their high rates
of success in treatment, but also by the good things they have to
say about approaching treatment. These are, first, their operational
assumption that behavior occurs lawfully, so any kind of human
problem can be viewed as part of a chain of cause-and-effect relationships. Second, their idea that since problems arise from a lawful source, their amelioration can be planned; therapy, therefore,
must have a planful character. Third, the actionist's emphasis on
learning as the basis for changing behavior is valuable not so much
because it is unique to them as because they make it palpable.
Finally, their demands for economy in treatment and for testing
therapeutic outcomes combine with the other things to give them
an aura of credibility that can only increase their appeal for years
to come.

Times change faster and faster, however, and once the polemics
cease, action therapists, with a few surly exceptions, will settle
back and do their work without finding new bêtes noires in Freud
and psychoanalysis, and will recognize that their contribution to

human welfare need not be limitless to be valid. By the same token, analysts and existentialists will also probably calm down about hypnosis, conditioning, and mood drugs, and reflect that there is indeed a lot of anguish in a lot of people for a lot of reasons. What helps, helps, and nothing else does; and whoever helps, exercises compassion in fact, even if his methods are unfamiliar, and his descriptions of them turgid, and his motives impure. The future of psychotherapy is unclear enough to discourage overzealous recommendations for what it ought to be or overconfident predictions of what it will be. There have been some wondrous benefits from psychoanalysis and wondrous failures from behavior therapies, and vice versa, and we can expect to see some more. Nobody should puff up his chest in righteous stupidity about what will work for whom now or in the next decade. As long as personal suffering has a future, so does the search for different means of coping with it.

Technology as much as maturity will justify some modesty in future claims for psychotherapy. For many problems, drugs and brain implants will some day replace psychotherapy as preferred treatments. Many problems of habit patterns for which action therapy is now used will be taken over by chemical and surgical procedures. Action therapy actually augurs such developments in its mechanistic assumptions, which presuppose that they are possible.

Insight therapies may have the dimmest professional future of all informational controls because of their poor success in treating symptoms. But at the same time, they may have the greatest impact on society because of their appeal as treatments for existential and personal identity problems. As our technological society advances economically, so that people have less and less to do and more and more time for doing it, the popularity of such problems will grow correspondingly. Kahn and Wiener point out that it has already reached noticeable proportions in "a concern for personality and relationships with others that is relatively new to American secular intellectual life of the last century." Terms like "commitment," "bearing witness," and "self-realization," they say, have an almost religious significance in New Left political circles, and "the need for companionship and a sense of belonging" gets increasing expression in social and political movements ranging from Black Muslims through hippies, free-love cults, and therapeutic communities like Synanon. They suggest that "new large movements of this general class in the postindustrial future" may recruit enormous numbers from small-town America, the lower middle class, and the children of successful parents who have, in adolescent eyes, sold out all decent values.

Insight therapies contribute to the existential orientation in three ways. First, their secularism and their scientific pretensions encourage people who are guilty, distrustful, or contemptuous of the value systems of most priests, doctors, and parents to talk to psychotherapists. Second, their methods for enhancing self-awareness and fostering self-preoccupation are readily transferred to relationships outside the consulting room and are as easily applied to groups as to individuals. Third, the self-preoccupation that happens in insight therapy can be translated into an ideology of self-realization or commitment which demands no loyalty to undeserving political, religious, or parental establishments. This shifts the burden of self-evaluation from external morality to personal integrity, a term for morals which reside within the self.

The extent to which this shift will be socially disruptive remains to be seen. It may not change things very much. In practical terms, the resulting "mentally hygienic morality" of self-interest may chiefly describe the boy who gives up medical school or teetotaling or the girl who forgoes being a teacher or a virgin because, in psychotherapy, they discovered that this behavior fulfilled a parent's wish, not their own. Or, contrarily, it may describe the businessman who forsakes making money to go back to school, the dissolute who reforms to seek respectability and whoever discovers by these means, designed to facilitate self-discovery, that he must "do his thing." Or tragically, it may describe whoever discovers through these same means that he has no "thing" to do. (Suicide is second only to automobile accidents as a killer of American college students.) There will never be a clear way to gauge this consequence, any more than there is a clear way to judge what the impact on the society would have been if psychotherapy had never been invented, or had long since been a perfect means of cure. St. Paul without fits, Luther without constipation, or a jolly Freud might all have left a very different legacy, maybe better, maybe worse. But good or bad, it is clear that information controls like psychotherapy tend to shake the moral tradition which directs aspirations and commitments outside the self and toward society.

The biggest future expansion of insight therapy will probably be in the direction of small-group encounters, including increasing numbers of the kinds of unconventional groups mentioned at the end of Chapter 3. These may be rationalized on both quasi-religious and quasi-medical grounds, to the effect that group meditation, nudity, body awareness, dancing, feeling and getting felt up, and so forth are at once spiritually valuable and mentally healthy. The same things have long since been said of group prayer, public confession, and Alcoholics Anonymous meetings. The important difference is not so much in the changed contents of the meetings as in the fact that personal morality and personal life styles will have shifted from broad social and religious conventions to the individual perspective of a psychotherapist or the narrow consensus of the immediate group, both of which will deny that anyone but the affected individual is responsible for his life and conduct. Hostile critics of insight therapy argue that its protagonists should admit to being what they usually pretend not to be—namely, expositors of moral doctrine, bearers of ideologies, and secular priests; but even were they to do so, it would probably have no great effect on the future course of the enterprise.

Another direction in which insight therapy will probably expand is, on the face of it, much more conventional; it is "sensitivity training," already by far the biggest commercial by-product of therapy. Sensitivity training is widely taught in adult extension courses and in the business schools of universities all over America and is widely used by business, industry, and government organizations to improve harmony among co-workers and to make people more aware of themselves and of the impressions they make on others (which, incidentally, might improve their ability to manipulate others). Its success at making people more sensitive is unknown, but its success at propagating itself has been astronomic.

Sensitivity groups are "person-centered," which means they have no problem to solve or purpose to promote but individual and mutual awareness. They actually work to control their members, however, by an indoctrination process which makes them emotionally dependent upon the group. The individual is first encouraged to admit something distressing about himself, which makes him anxious about the good will of the others. Sympathy from them then brings about his conversion and consolidation with the group; this leads to his participation in constraining "the next guy" to do the same. As one trainee put it, "It's funny how committed we each get after we're worked over by the group."

But getting people "committed" is exactly what insight therapy can do best, which is why it has an important, if diffuse, future. Committed to what? is another question, on the same order as, Educated for what? Jean-Paul Sartre would recommend politics; Abraham Maslow might suggest yoga; still others would opt for society, self-indulgence, God, revolution, or vegetarianism. What all champions of commitment share, and what insight therapy offers its effective, if cumbersome, technology to implement, is the belief that people must learn to feel that their commitments are drawn from within themselves, make their lives worth living, and are accountable to no one else. The widespread impact of this idea may shake to the core the glib belief that a free society of the future can rest on moral consensus, and the grim alternatives of anarchy and repression may be starkly evident results.

The impact of most information controls will be subtle, even at their most serious, for some time to come. Most of the problems they have faced thus far in the consulting rooms are individual ones, whose resolutions are not very far reaching. And those problems they have attacked in social settings, like hospitals and schools, are ones where the desirable resolutions are almost always clear. Nobody wants children to be illiterate, for example, or to be unable to interact amicably, and nobody wants schizophrenics helplessly lolling around in hospitals, in jails, or on the streets. In any case, information-control experts have not yet had very much real power over other people's behavior. They have accepted a manipulative role for themselves that has caused them sometimes to be accused of undue influence, but they have not yet heard accusations or, apparently, thought about the implications of un-equivocal influence. Those are more in the domain of coercive controllers.

The Prospects for Coercive Controls

Coercive behavior-control technology presents social problems for the same reasons that other new events do. Its effects are dramatic, and people have not been familiar enough with it for long enough to accept it, ignore it, or incorporate it into the routine fabric of their individual lives or common customs. How-ever, as it becomes commonplace to control epilepsy with brain implants, to help restore memory with drugs, and to treat psy-choses in "conditioning wards," much of the erstwhile public dismay over the dangers of coercive control will dissolve. It will not disappear altogether because the impact of coercive controls, far more than of informational ones, depends on the degree to which it is used for ambiguous illnesses or disorders. Everyone will accept the application of brain implants to conventional ailments like epilepsy or even mental retardation, because these conditions are unambiguously medical disorders. The same methods used to control homosexuality, marijuana smoking, or the aggressive im-pulses of anti-Establishment demonstrators, however, may not be so palatable. By the same token, using milder information controls like psychotherapy on the latter conditions may be easy to accept for the very reason that its methods are not powerful enough to force anyone to change; exactly the same reasons make those same methods seem banal nuisances when applied to epilepsy or retar-dation. Since inefficient control methods and unambiguous ail-ments have been around for a long time, they raise no new anxieties. Drugs and surgery do. But though they raise parallel anxieties in most people, their predictable impacts on society are not quite identical; drugs share some of the social characteristics of informational as well as coercive methods.

The Social Impact of Drug Controls

The medical importance of coercive controls makes it easy to overlook their nonmedical implications, which are, in essence, that their use need not be limited to curing people who are ill. As they become increasingly sophisticated, they will be increasingly useful to interfere in any behavior a controller wishes to manage, whether it involves physical impairment, social deviance, or whatever. Visible and palpable instruments, ranging from spectacles, peglegs, and wheelchairs, to trusses, diaphragms, and contraceptive loops, have long since laid the medical foundation for public acceptance of this fact. But the modern groundwork for such interference has been prepared by tranquilizing drugs, whose use for most psychological complaints, though justified, has notably different effects than does the use of drugs like antibiotics. Penicillin, for example, will attack pneumococci, syphilis spirochetes, and several other organisms without disturbing most other metabolic processes. This means that a patient who has pneumonia may be helped by it and that one who does not is likely to be unaffected. The drug may help, but probably won't hurt. A strong tranquilizer, on the other hand, tends equally to calm people down whether they are mentally disturbed or not. The domain of its action is clear enough, but the definition of the disorder which requires any action may not be.

The move from what are clearly physiological impairments to what are clearly not is a subtle one only because we are accustomed to the idea that what doctors treat, including head doctors, is illness, and illness implies, for most of us, physical malfunction rather than social malfeasance. The more the power to define disorder rests with people who are not the immediate victims of it, however, and the more the definitions rest on behavior rather than anatomy or physiology, the more tenuous they become. This is even more likely when the same people who define the illness also select and administer the cure. As the synthesis of specific drugs gradually yields pills to pacify aggressive impulses, expand or erase memory, and manipulate a variety of other intellectual and emotional functions which are now, for the most part, outside the direct control of anyone but the person in whom they occur, the ethical problem of who shall administer them to whom, and when, becomes more complicated. It is pretty complicated already, and general definitions of illness, social propriety, and the like seem increasingly irrelevant to understanding or resolving the issues.

It is a virtual certainty that the use of all kinds of behavior-controlling drugs will increase enormously as they become available. The two most immediate social problems that will arise are already portended by the limited variety of current behavior-changing drugs. The first problem concerns compounds which drug takers want to get and other people want to prohibit; the second concerns chemicals which potential takers want to reject and other people want them to accept. Neither problem is simple because existing medical, ethical, and legal norms and precedents conflict with each other and overlap with public whimsey and hysteria in these matters. Some hallucinogenic drugs, for example, appear to be less damaging and less habit-forming than alcohol, but custom has sanctioned the one and is only gradually relaxing its prohibitions on the other. In terms of their effects on behavior, they might be considered a special class of tranquilizer, less dangerous than alcohol or barbiturates and more appropriately used to treat ennui than anxiety. In America and Western Europe, ennui is probably as much the closing malaise of this century as hysteria was its opener and anxiety the malady of its middle age. Sleep-inducing drugs (also called "hypnotics" or "narcotics") and energizing drugs can be combined with them, and often are, to make a subjectively complete ring of controlled activity. To some people, this prospect has frightening implications for the abandonment of society in favor of a drug-controlled orgy of personal navel contemplations. This probably will not occur, at least not to any greater degree than it already has in the quiet misery of the millions of people whose conscious lives are now consumed in an alcoholic haze. Despite appearances, no new technology is involved, only smaller packages of dream stuff. And for what it may be worth as consolation, many of the college students of the 1960s who have sponsored such regimes will some day legalize them, and in some pathetic instances will fall victims to them; they are active rebels against the social order, not passive wrecks retiring from it.

The increased future use of "consciousness" drugs may not be entirely a matter of escaping ennui, however, any more than the widespread use of alcohol can be explained away entirely as a form of escapism. Both share some appealing characteristics as socializing agents (for example, Ogden Nash's "Reflections on Ice-Breaking": "Candy/Is dandy/But liquor/Is quicker."), and both provide novel mental experiences, many of which feel good. Among college students and hippies, most of whom, significantly, come from high socioeconomic backgrounds, many drugs have important advantages over alcohol: they are more powerful, less sloppy to handle (both to take and to hide), sometimes easier to acquire (either by being cheaper or simply by not requiring a license or proof of age), foreign and frightening to adult authorities, and often, among peers, less associated than liquor is with debauchery and more with religious experience. The quest for certainty in a complex world, and for ecstasy in a painful one, is probably as important today as it has ever been in human history, and as much the business of religion to satisfy. But educated young people are probably less able today than ever before to find these things in creeds and institutions they regard as obsolete, or sometimes as obscene. Drugs seem to provide many of them with the ecstatic experiences of religion. Drugs (and alcohol) have long since done just that in primitive societies, but they can be nicely rationalized in contemporary terms as well: they can be made in laboratories, and they permit the illusion of transcendance to be conjured up precisely, to be self-controlled, and to be freed of cant.

In the long run, a great deal more social upheaval is likely to come from the indirect behavioral effects of drugs whose primary

functions are aimed in other directions. The effectiveness of antibiotics in the treatment of venereal disease, for example, seems to
have produced some increase in the incidence of it. Birth-control
pills have promoted an ever more rapid liberalization of sexual
mores which may, in turn, eventuate in radical changes in the
structure of families and the nature of marital relationships. David
Krech believes that the forthcoming development of IQ pills and
memory facilitators will create new labor crises because the
Nouveau Smart will refuse to be "the hewers of wood and the
drawers of water. . . ."

Such indirect consequences of drug developments are more
reasonably viewed as new problems in the impact of technology on
cultural stability than as a new order of social problem. This suggests that for them, as for most problems in the ordering of individual behavior and the general welfare, there is no single domain
of moral excellence, scientific expertise, or professional skill that
can alone resolve them.

The second immediate problem of drug controls concerns their
use in the face of the victim's objections. This can sometimes be
resolved in practice by mood-changing drugs, once they can be
administered at all, because insofar as mood is the emotional basis
of will, manipulating the one tends to coerce the other. This
creates its own moral conundrum. The problem thus far concerns
the character of doctors, not of their medicines, which is why the
medical profession is a prime target for worry in the use of behavior-control technology: it is the most important craft in which
individuals go to behavior-control engineers who have technical
power, ostensible skill, the protection of privacy while at work,
legal sanction for what they do, and patients who have little choice
but to trust. Coercion to take drugs depends on the people involved, not on the drugs.

The practical virtues of drugs rest to begin with, however, in
their transitory effects and ease of self-administration. These tend
to make any kind of drug usage voluntary. It is no easier to force
somebody to swallow a pill than it is to make him submit to
electric shock. The coercive power of drugs only begins after they

are taken; whether they are taken has nothing to do with their chemical properties. In that sense, virtually *all* control drugs are devices for increasing self-control! Short of shoving them down someone's throat or sneaking them into his cocoa, the use of drugs to control behavior is as much in the "victim's" hands as is his attending psychotherapy sessions. The only difference between them comes after that decision is made, for the predictable effects of drugs are far more precise and potent.

The combination of voluntarism, precision, and transiency gives control drugs many of the same long-term prospects and problems that result from information methods like insight therapy, but magnified many times over: they tend to shift the basis of personal morality from external to internal standards. But where psychotherapy does this almost inadvertently, by a tentativeness and imprecision which cannot help inviting self-doubt, drugs do it almost boldly, by supporting a kind of self-control that stimulates self-confidence and providing a feeling of certainty about results that fosters skepticism toward moral traditions. Combined with the routinizing impact of general technology, these traits augur enormous shifts in individual morals as a by-product of future behavior control.

Technology and Personal Morality

Morality means the choice or evaluation of what is good or bad. Most of us are disposed by temperament or training to order our lives so that we do not have to treat all life's problems as moral dilemmas, and are able to routinize our lives enough to reduce most of our moral conundrums to fleeting breaths of conscience— at cheating the telephone company or the internal revenue service, at telling small lies of convenience, at lifting someone's old idea or joke, at consummating a seduction by protestations of love, and so forth. The issues are sometimes bigger, though, involving risk of life and limb or honor, going to war or refusing to, risking everything for loved ones or for strangers, committing oneself irrevocably to some movement or principle or deity. For such unroutinized things, a sense of morality is important, because it gives guidelines for conduct at what most of us consider the highest level of our individual self-consciousness, that of judging our ultimate value as human beings. Morality is the supreme court of self-esteem.

By fostering routines which smooth living, general technology tends to undermine the exercise of moral sensibilities; it reduces the number of conscious and deliberate choices needing to be made, which tends to lull us into accepting whatever we are used to, good or bad. Vegetarianism might be more popular in our humane and antiseptic society, for instance, if meat did not grow in Saran-wrapped supermarket cases, and if we had to kill our own animals and perhaps wave flies off stinking carcasses in the open air. The routinizing process also changes the basis on which people previously made choices about how to act which, in turn, changes the basis on which they subsequently evaluate their acts. Since the Social Security laws have been passed, for example, people need not worry about how or whether to support their aging parents, so the relevant moral tradition is weakened by disuse. Behavior-control technology augments the threat to remove moral tradition as the main basis of contemporary personal morality in two ways: first, by orienting the individual toward himself, while much of our moral tradition orients him toward society and social institutions, and second, by its increasingly precise effects, which tend to demonstrate that many of our moral traditions and moral impera-tives depend for their social support on uncertainties, if not on falsehoods. Changes already occurring in the status of social institutions like the family and of mores like sexual practices show that this process is well along.

Traditional sexual mores in our society, which have long been bound to premarital abstinence and absolute monogamy for women, avoiding sex education for children, censoring pornog-raphy, and condemning homosexuality, have been largely obliter-ated in barely three generations by a chain of increasingly precise technological inventions which undercut the traditional means of enforcement—namely, penalizing women. Primitive mechanical contraceptives began to undermine conventional sexual practices, the automobile furthered the process, and modern chemical and mechanical contraceptives (pills, intrauterine devices) completed it. They did so empirically, however, not by argument. Condoms and diaphragms both existed since ancient times, but only the vulcanization of rubber and mass production made them feasible for general use. The condom is relatively limited in value, however, because its use is controlled by the male. The diaphragm is controlled by the female, but requires experience to be used efficiently. And neither device is certain to work. The automobile provided a major parallel step in liberalizing sexual practices by its powerful influence on the attitudes which make people willing to engage in sexual acts—it fulfilled the indispensable prerequisite for maintaining middle-class dignity during sex—namely, *privacy*. To-day's contraceptive devices complete the process by providing almost absolute control over pregnancy and placing it entirely in female hands.

Drastic changes in American sexual practices are already evident as a result of all this. Premarital sexual relations are more widespread and widely approved than ever before; sex acts once considered "deviant," if not more widespread, are more often widely admitted and legally sanctioned; extramarital sex is increasingly accepted with nervous sympathy and amusement; movies like *Guide to the Married Man* and *The Secret Life of an American Wife* and books such as *Married Men Make the Best Lovers* attract wide audiences; sex clubs and wife swapping are more and more public and publicized; sex education of children is increasingly explicit and widespread; pornography of all kinds is published more prolifically, and more safely, than ever before.

All this is largely a result of the increasing certainty of effects of control devices and their having been vested in the hands of the people most victimized by not having them—women. They have practically obliterated the concept of sexual morality based entirely on reproduction. The over-all effect of this process on society is unclear, but it may also have obliterated the sexual motive for marriage in our society and left only two rational motives for it:

the desire to have children together and the promise of affectionate companionship. These may be more wholesome bases for marriage than have ever existed, but that is not yet clear, and it is beside the point. What is clear is that one of their consequences is to further weaken the already weak role of the family in society.

The family's role as the arbiter of propriety has been declining steadily for a long time as technological change has reduced the economic interdependence of family members and increased their physical mobility. Behavior-control technology further constricts this role by making the family less than ever a sufficient repository of experience to guide the behavior of young people. Peers become more important than they ever were, though they are neither more experienced nor wiser, because they share the interests of the present and the risks of the future, and formal education becomes more important because it holds the keys to scientific knowledge. Robert Morison feels that the declining prestige and power of the family resulting from these factors will eventually require that the individual's identification with family be replaced by identification with society. Skinner's familial perspective in *Walden II* adds up to the same idea.

The changes that occur in the contemporary morals of sex and family life are not explicit results of a narrow behavioral technology but inevitable by-products of technological changes which include behavioral technology. These changes result from controls which are fundamentally in the hands of the people to be controlled. As such, they have no direct effect on the political or legal structure of society, no matter how massive their impact. Those effects are likely to occur when exorbitant control becomes possible, as in brain-implantation methods.

The Prospects for Structural Controls

The availability of very reliable techniques like brain implantation puts some social problems into sharp focus because their finality is so much clearer than that of other control techniques. Anyone can "pop" his own pill, but somebody else must operate on your brain, even if you want it done. The effects of a pill, moreover, will wear themselves out, but an implantation will not. And the drug, after all, may not work, or may work differently at different times or on different people, but implantation has an aura of standardization about it that suggests a ghastly appendectomy of the mind.

The limitations of such control are unknown. At the present time, there is no theoretical "limiting velocity" in molecular biology or genetics or psychology of the kind that is still widely accepted in physics. Good theoretical reasons are given by Roger Williams, at the University of Texas, and Jerry Hirsch, of Illinois, to believe that every human being is unique in his genetic composition, so that the ultimate ability of biologists to create or manipulate protoplasm would not even begin to give them the power to create human automata from scratch. The point is moot, but even were it clearly impossible ever to manufacture the androids of science fiction, this would not much reduce the practical ability to control most socially significant individual behavior with the machinery which is now rapidly coming to hand.

The most important practical constraints on the widespread use of coercive behavior controls are economic, not ethical or scientific ones. For most political purposes, which is where pervasive behavior control appears most threatening at first blush, it is probably not needed in any refined form. The harsh reality of political manipulation and its bloody corollary, military force, is that man is already the fanciest conceivable machinery, widely available in huge lots at pathetically low cost and docile (educable) enough for most purposes, that with relatively little maintenance cost, he can be gotten voluntarily to do just about anything. Under the circumstances, no one is likely to go about scrambling people's brains just because he has the means for doing so. It is not hard to imagine some situations where massive controls might be used, probably through drugs, and probably to inhibit rather than elicit an activity such as aggression. A subjugated population might be kept docile by dosing its drinking water with a tranquilizing chemical. But such a method is very risky unless one really wishes its victims to be "hewers of wood and drawers of water." Any chemical given to thousands of people through a public water supply would have to be so potent that were it to squelch aggressive impulses in everyone, it would probably do the same for any other kind of active impulse. People might then be as incapable of productive obedience as of rebellion. On the other hand, there are certainly some societies where the ruling powers would be glad to have large portions of their population subjugated in just such a way.

The political issue of behavior control arises only in the face of actual or potential political opposition. In such situations, Delgado feels that there is no great danger of massive use of structural controls, despite their availability, because

this technique requires specialized knowledge, refined skills, and a detailed and complex exploration in each individual, because of the existence of anatomical and physiological variability. The feasibility of mass control of behavior by brain stimulation is therefore very unlikely, and application of intra-cerebral electrodes in man will probably remain highly individualized and restricted to medical practice.

It is almost certainly true that brain implantation will not be used on large masses of people. By its nature, the technique permits great refinement of control, which is hardly necessary to apply en masse. The argument that it is difficult to do, on the other hand, may turn out to be specious; the development of better and better means of brain mapping, easier methods for individual identification of critical brain centers, and easier, more efficient techniques of surgery in which, for example, laser beams may supplement or replace knives may make the whole business cheap and easy enough for every man to have his own brain implant.

Efficient coercive controls do not have to be available at bargain basement prices or to be useful on large masses in order for them to have very serious political and social effects. "Politics," as T. H. White says so cogently, "is an exercise in leadership." The political potential of brain implantation is more than fulfilled when it is used on political leaders, not on masses. And only a few people ever lead in any political or social organization.

Even in totalitarian states, coercive controls are not likely to be viewed as a punishment for political opposition, but rather as a politico-medical treatment, a restorative for social deviance of one kind or another. In democratic countries, they may be applied in exactly the same way to other kinds of social deviants, especially to criminals and the mentally ill, although Kahn and Wiener note that not only has "the Soviet Union already sent some of its important literary men to mental institutions," but "the United States sent Ezra Pound to one, and did so as an act of kindness." In all cases, the same question arises: would not political deviants be better off docile than dead? Is not assassination a less humane method of control than implantation, or, for that matter, imprisonment? But by the same token, why should people be incarcerated in prisons or mental hospitals if, by safe and certain means, they can be provided with treatments which will make any kind of external restraint unnecessary? One can retort that they would really only be substituting one restraint for another, replacing the jail around their bodies with one inside their heads. But for some people at least, this can be dismissed as academic sophistry—all people carry some jails inside their heads if they live in a modicum of harmony with other people, and the restraints provided by drugs or brain implants operate at the very level of motivation, so their "victim" does not want to do what is forbidden; rather than feel unable, he prefers not to do it.

Most people do not even realize, at the present time, the extent to which coercive controls have already advanced, so their implications for public policy may seem far-fetched. The 1967 *Task Force Report: Science and Technology* to the President's Commission on Law Enforcement and Administration of Justice does not mention specific individual coercive controls in its discussions of crime corrections and preventions, though the report's authors are obviously sensitive to the existence of such devices and concerned about them: "Their availability raises grave questions about their social value, and there is doubt whether any of them would be acceptable in a free society. As with many technological devices that raise such value questions, decisions whether or not to use them, even experimentally, must be carefully weighed."

The fact is, however, that such devices are already being used in clinical medicine, and many of them are experimental only in the sense that they are not yet used by very many people on very many things. If decisions about their use in medicine have been "carefully weighed," as the task force recommends for their use in controlling crime, then the balance has swung in their favor and will swing even further as people become aware of their tremendous boon to victims of so many clearly medical maladies.

The problem which must then be faced is that the uses of the future will come, at first, from the uses of the past, which will have been entirely and justifiably medical. But the problem will put us back at the same old cigar store, however modernized: applying brain implantations to uncontrollable seizures—or uncontrollable sex impulses, for that matter—raises no issues as long as the desires of the patient and the doctor coincide. But control of seizures is not so far removed from control of rage; and control of sex acts, from control of appetite. And when the condition to be corrected is a form of behavior rather than the action of a microbe or a wild gene or even the squiggle on an electroencephalogram reflecting some damage to the brain, then the line between the social deviation called illness and that called crime is a very narrow one. And the distinction between correction and punishment may be just as difficult. Nothing better illustrates the failure of our society to cope with this problem so far than the ambivalence of legislators and psychiatrists alike toward the whole class of crimes without (external) victims, like prostitution, sexual deviation between consenting adults, or the use of narcotics.

In most respects, the problems to be posed by coercive controls in the future differ from those of the past chiefly by being more sharply put. It is no mere academic exercise to offer the alternatives of therapy or jail to a homosexual when it is absolutely certain that the therapy will rid him of his sexual proclivity. A legal precedent already exists in one case where a woman on the public welfare rolls who bore several children out of wedlock was given the choice of sterilization or jail. However repugnant such a judgment may sound to Americans at this time, it can easily be softened by experience as custom soothes conscience to sleep and more and more ex-deviants report satisfaction with their new status. When enough such reports have accumulated, moreover, so that almost nobody chooses to go to jail, a confluence of economic pressures can then tear down the prisons, which, however desirable, also does away with choosing and leaves the cure as the *only* answer to the crime. The factual extent of control over individuals does not change, except perhaps to be enlarged, even if all punishment changes to treatment, all public malice to social benevolence, and all vengeful motives to rehabilitative ones. "As antisocial behavior becomes less tolerable as a result of the increasing complexity . . . of society," ask Kahn and Wiener, "are we not likely to treat what we cannot tolerate?"

Coercive technology may be most startling or threatening because of its precision, but the most important problem it finally presents may concern the nature of its assault on behavior rather than its potency. Both drugs and surgical controls are effective primarily in the manipulation, not of overt behavior, but of the underlying moods and motivations which produce it. In changing motivations they effectively change the meaning of coercion from its historically psychological connotation to a new concept, which is physiological. Coercion traditionally implied the *violation* of will in compelling some behavior; in the new technology, coercion is the *subversion* of will in compelling some body process. But virtually all of our concepts of individual liberty and of social responsibility, its antagonist and counterweight, have been based on the assumption that human beings retain inviolate some faculty which ultimately enables them to judge their intercourse with others and, by judging, ultimately to oppose them. The main subjective means of measuring just how coercive something is, therefore, has always been its source of motivation and its strength. If I think the motive for doing something comes from within me, I consider it voluntary; if the motive comes from someone else, I feel it is forced upon me as long as it is something I do not want to do. If the motive is weak, then source alone goes into the definition. If the motive is strong enough, it makes no difference where it comes from—most people will see themselves as victims, whether of external coercion or internal compulsion, which lawyers translate as "irresistible impulse."

The ironic thing about chemical and surgical coercions, from this definition, is that their main function can be said to be that of internalizing motives so that people will themselves desire what we want them to. This makes it necessary to resolve the practical issue of coercion before the pill is swallowed; afterward, the corpus delicti will testify only for the defense.

The new technology thus creates a great conundrum: it makes possible the nullification of all those human rights which are predicated on individual consent. Once consent can be flawlessly engineered, then doctrines like the Nuremberg code, which begin with "The voluntary consent of the human subject is absolutely essential" to do medical research on him, become meaningless. And if the treatment of an individual's body is not subject to his own jurisdiction in any meaningful way, then nothing else can very well be—for nothing else is so surely or inviolably himself and his rightful possession, if anything is, as is his own body.

Even here, government and the common welfare have already made serious inroads and established prerogatives which make the individual's body processes objects of social scrutiny and control. As Delgado points out:

In civilized life, the intervention of governments in our private biology has become so deeply rooted that in general we are not aware of it. Many countries, including the United States, do not allow a bride and groom to marry until blood has been drawn . . . to prove the absence of syphilis. To cross international borders, it is necessary to certify that a scarification has been made on the skin and inoculated with smallpox. In many cities, the drinking water contains fluoride to strength our teeth and table salt is fortified with iodine to prevent thyroid misfunction. These intrusions into our private blood, teeth and glands are accepted, practiced and enforced. [They] generally benefit society and individuals, but they have established a precedent of official manipulation of our personal biology. . . .

Relatively few people see vaccinations and blood tests as objectionable, especially since they do not sacrifice an individual's bodily health to any alleged common good. Coercive controls, however, represent a new degree of intrusion, which may undermine the very basis for disputing what is proper and what is not.

Certainly, in any case, control technologies will not prescribe their own moral proprieties. Self-awareness frees the bonds that tie people to contemporary norms. Skepticism frees the bonds that tie them to traditional ones. Behavior specialists who are deliberately working toward control technology—that is, toward a planful effort to change human activity—are willy-nilly working toward the defeat of obsolete moralities in people's lives. But while this might relieve some individual pains (and create some), it cannot possibly serve a common social purpose, and as the impetus of technology speeds the world along, the common risk to mankind from a lack of common purpose is growing. As behavior technology becomes more and more capable of success, the issues it engenders become clearer and more urgent. They are the same ones that people who are responsible for the common welfare have always faced, but they are writ large by the tremendous power which technology confers. The moral imperative which confronts today's behavior controllers, from physicians to politicians, is the recognition of the power which tomorrow will bestow. Some of them cannot accept this thought and, threatened by the rapid changes they observe, nurse the idea that their familiar world can be preserved by judicious restrictions of the power of technologists. Perhaps, indeed, intelligent restraints can protect society somewhat from being overwhelmed by precipitous change. One reasonable bill to that effect has been introduced in Congress, proposing to create a Technological Assessment Board, which would study new developments and warn the public of any dangers it foresaw in them. Most of its concerns, however, and the technological dangers it anticipates, would focus mostly on industrial problems because they are easier to assess. And when it did treat behavioral problems, it would have to be more concerned with the physical dangers of structural controls than with the threat to morals posed by drugs or psychotherapy, for the same reason. There is probably no sound alternative—for, in fact, it does no good to pine for the family if it is going out, or to whistle after the sex pill in fear of licentiousness, or to outlaw the drugs, panicked by autistic ecstasies, or to thump the Bible, conjuring hellfire for a cool generation. Even were it possible to delay such changes, they could be totally prevented only by brute repression, for which a free society would finally have to pay a higher moral price than could ever come from trusting its free and equal citizens to make no poorer use of the biochemical powers in their hands than they do of the political ones. The course of personal morality, and of voluntary controls, in a democracy, must probably be left to run its course, subject to preaching, but not repression.

Structural controls offer no such easy options. They are becoming steadily more important tools of behavior controllers, who, having already inadvertently usurped the roles of parents and of priests in their capacity to influence the young of our society, will soon find that they have become instigators and accomplices in an enterprise that moves to fill the roles of tyrants and of God. For when the genetic code is cracked, as it will be, and it becomes possible to intervene with razor delicacy in the temperaments of progeny to be born ten generations hence, to free our feelings of despair by talking to computers, to contain aggression by pacifier pills and lust by radio, today's aspiring controllers cannot then decently retire from their manipulative roles by nervously explaining that they never intended to control so very much. Nor can they withdraw from these considerations now, by arguing that powers of control are already too excessive for more development to be decently permitted; the practical effect of trying to ban it would only be to guarantee that these controls became the properties of the worst possible people, who would use them for the worst possible purposes. Such a ban would be morally indefensible as well because there are many cases where we would use such controls right now, if they were at hand, and where in their absence, now use harsher and more painful means. The new control devices, by making that which is mandatory seem desirable, are generally kinder to their victims, if more frightening to their observers.

The fundamental moral issues in behavior control do not

change, of course, no matter what technology develops around them. They are now, as ever, only these: Who shall be controlled? By whom? How?

By what right may one man curtail another? And within what limits? And who is to decide? Who executes the judgment? And who takes the mantle, or fasces, or scepter, or holy oil, or oath, and from whose hand, to transmit or change the massed experience of endless human struggle with these same imponderables? The new technologies sharpen the questions and lend them urgency by making them more answerable in fact with each new radio device or chemical. But *de facto* answers to questions of power are not enough for decent men, so we must study how to force these powers into decent harmony with our individual and common lives.

7

The Machine Model of Man

Political philosophers, theologians, and social theorists take their points of departure on moral questions from assorted beliefs about the facts of human nature. Scientists, engineers, and technologists try to find those facts and only rarely to help construct philosophies, theologies, and political theories from them. Perhaps they should help, especially now, as the facts proliferate and understanding them becomes more urgent and complex.

The facts of behavior-control technology, and some of its potential problems, are now becoming evident. The next question that arises from them asks what they imply about human nature; that is the subject of this chapter.

Europe and North America are by now several hundred years deep into technology, so almost no one in these places is choked with nostalgia by the thought that mechanized production reduces the variety of goods that would exist if everyone spun his own cloth and stitched his own suit from it. If anyone thinks about it at all, he may decide that, for most people, the gains from mass production offset the losses many times over.

The mechanization of society, on the other hand, is not taken so lightly, at least not by many people who have a say in it. In politics, in economics, and in every social arena where a few people must direct the behavior of many others, there is an endless ideological teeter-totter between pressures to vest the control of public conduct in law or principle and counterpressures to leave the same behavior to the discretion of individuals. Even so, people more and more accept the fact that social controls grow with the growth of technology, and formal opposition to government regulation of things becomes increasingly the prerogative of people who do not have to govern. Among those who do, planning is recognized as the essence of responsible conduct; and planning is nothing but automating, regulating, systematizing, mechanizing, routinizing, or regimenting—that is, controlling the events with which one is concerned.

Many people find it hard to think beyond goods and government, however, to face the prospect that individuals can be mechanized much as industrial production has been. Some of the same people who can speak glibly and optimistically about "planned economies" or "social planning" or "social action programs," would be fearful and reticent to talk about "programed persons." For some of them, this idea implies fearsome limits to human freedom that undermine political freedom or religious morality. Others, including many people who welcome the benevolent uses of behavior control, do not think its philosophical underpinnings or implications about human nature need to be thought about at all, as long as it can be practically applied. On the face of it, they have a good case.

The standardization of human behavior is, after all, precisely what drill sergeants and educators, as well as traffic cops, dental hygienists, and gym teachers, try deliberately and conscientiously to achieve. Behavior control, in this sense, is easily rationalized by one or another practical necessity, not the least of which may be its value to the regimented person. In many respects, the new technology of behavior control will be similarly rationalized. Practical necessity always tells its own story, makes its own rules, pleads its own defense, and, often as not, gets away with its own crimes. Theories and philosophies are made of weaker stuff, either harder to come by or harder to defend.

The trouble with arguments from practical necessity, however, is that one man's vital need may be another's deadly bane: viable social systems require at least tacit agreement among their members on a number of rules about how people ought to live and conduct their lives in relation to each other. A society could not last long if half the members believed that everyone should give away his best possessions in order to gain social status and the other half believed that everyone should hoard possessions for the same purpose, or if half the population believed in turning the other cheek to insults and the other half believed in vendettas. Some common set of beliefs or principles must be shared by the members of society for the orderly conduct of affairs and the negotiation of differences to be possible. Such sets of beliefs inform moral and legal codes.

If the technology of behavior control is to be used wisely in democratic societies (tyrannies and savageries can only use it tyrannically and savagely), some ethical notions must be applicable to it. But ethics themselves depend on theories about the nature of man, at least of the men who make up the in-groups and out-groups of any real society. The ethical applications of behavior control will incorporate the views of human nature implied by it. Those views are borrowed from the scientific beliefs that made the experiments that found the results that built the technology in the first place. So the underpinnings of the ethical system are fastened to a scientific model of man.

That Man Is a Machine

The most important idea about human nature attaching to behavior control technology is the notion that man is a machine. This does not mean that he ages, rusts, falls into disrepair, must be fueled, is difficult to maintain, hums, whirs, or goes chug-chug-chug, though many of these things are the case. Nor does it mean that he is merely a soft, warm computer, a lucky blend of inexpensive chemicals. Both the promise and the dangers of behavior-control technology are implicit products of the meaning of this concept. And both have equal portent whether or not the idea is literally true.

What it really means when we say that man is a machine is that his behavior is lawful and limited. This is true of everything else in the world as well, and its implications for understanding man are not new or special; but they are not always appreciated.

The idea that human behavior is lawful implies that its guiding general principles should apply to individuals as well, without requiring that one focus on idiosyncrasies every time he confronts a human problem. This does not mean that people are exactly alike, but only that they are enough alike so that experience with a small sample can teach a rule for dealing with the whole population of similar human events. A young surgeon does not have to relearn how to do an appendectomy every time he must do one, even though no two are exactly alike; most are alike enough so that mastering the principles and observing the details of the operation, then practicing on some cases, trains him adequately for the task.

Another way of describing the generality of lawful behavior is to say it is predictable, which means that by understanding the principles involved, one can anticipate the outcome of events without actually going through them. Events cannot be controlled just because they can be predicted, as is sometimes mistakenly thought. Astronomers do very well at predicting movements of heavenly bodies, but they are unable to direct the traffic. Even so, prediction is an important first step toward control, which is generally unachievable without it.

The idea of human limitations is another convenience for understanding behavior offered by the portrayal of man as a machine. Machines have a finite number of parts, and there are strict limits on what they can do. Viewing man similarly is useful for studying him because it suggests that one needn't know everything in order to know anything about him. In other words, one can learn useful, even indispensable things about his individual parts and their functions, without always having to learn much about the total organism.

The value of this "molecular" (also called "reductionist") approach to the study of behavior is disputed by some scientists, particularly by psychologists and biologists. The "molar" view (also called "organismic," "holistic," or "morphological") which says that one must examine the total organization of a system in order to understand it rather than study isolated individual parts is, for many reasons, more popular among psychotherapists, and has been almost sanctified in clinical medicine by the adjuration to "treat the whole patient." Each approach has been useful, sometimes indispensable, for attacking scientific problems to which the other method was poorly suited. But the molar view lends itself to more complicated descriptions of events, and hostile critics of mechanism, therefore, have sometimes erroneously looked to it for congenial arguments.

Operational Models and Truth

The idea that behavior is lawful is, of course, the most elementary axiom in the scientist's creed and, in a general way, is also common to much of the theology of Judaism and Christianity. The notion that human behavior has limitations is also widely accepted when stated in very general terms. And as long as any practical derivatives of these ideas are beneficial or harmless, no one takes exception to them. The theoretical trouble with calling man a machine begins when it is clear that someone believes the statement is true, and not merely a figure of speech; the practical trouble begins when anyone can act as if it were true, whether he believes it or not.

Outside of philosophy and religion, it has not been necessary to ponder much the relative natures of man or machinery, not even among scientists and engineers, the people who are now acting on the comparison. They are more seriously concerned with operational problems like that of establishing practical definitions and standards for evaluating facts, than with the ultimate nature of things. Thus, it has always been proper for anatomists and physiologists, whose business requires that they study the body as a piece of elegant machinery, to treat the "human machine" as an operational model, one they could make practical use of without believing it gave a true or complete picture of human nature.

The distinction between the "practical" and the "true" is only meaningful, however, as long as there are situations to which "mere practicality" does not apply. It is all right, in other words, to say that we will look at man *as if* he were a machine for merely practical purposes, provided that there are some respects in which the analogy does not hold and he can be seen some other way. In the sciences, it is hard to see what they might be, and it is getting harder all the time.

With diffidence put aside, it is plain that most scientists do not really think that the machine model is an analogy at all. In *The Organism as an Adaptive Control System,* John M. Riener describes living creatures as "Environmentally Modifiable Physico-chemical Regulatory Devices," and man is certainly an organism, whether or not you want to call him a "device." And if you speak of man as "an information-processing and information-gathering system," as Harvard psychologist George Miller does, where is even the pretense of analogy involved? Norbert Wiener defines "machine" in virtually the same way Miller speaks of man—"a device for converting incoming messages into outgoing messages," and he is making no analogies at all. So too, when John von Neumann writes a *Theory of Self-Reproducing Automata,* he means "self," he means "reproducing," and he means "automata" quite literally. When a computer "calculates," is that a mere analogy to thinking? How about to doing arithmetic? Or to calculating? Is it casual anthropomorphic error which makes us use the word "calculate," or vain anthropocentric illusion which surrounds it with quotation marks?

If thinking is defined by an activity, rather than by an actor, there are machines that think—perhaps not cleverly, but very quickly. If learning is described as a certain kind of process, with no discussion of who does the processing, then by any reasonable standard, some machines can learn. Any definitive discussion of manufacturing or of production or of reproduction, which does not demand, Mad Hatter fashion, that the manufacturer's pedigree be certified before the discourse starts, must recognize that machines can make things which, finally, include copies of themselves. And without a doubt, they can be themselves so made that they will operate and maintain themselves, decide on their own needs, and reproduce themselves accordingly.

If metabolic processes and reproductive ability were enough to define life; and if mobility alone, added to them, defined an animal; and if the ability to think sufficed, when cumulated with the rest, to depict a human being; then we would have to say that structures of silicon and steel and copper wire could be living human animals, for these are properties which today's machines, or tomorrow morning's at latest, will possess. This does not really mean that you must let your sister marry one. All men may be machines, but no other existing machines are men, at least, not yet.

What, then, *is* a man, and what connection with his parts and mechanisms counts toward his humanity? Most parts do not account for very much that is human. Prosthetic skills make artificial parts for natural people; transplant techniques put natural parts in natural people. Automata function as artificial people, and can, in fact, be hooked to natural parts. Should androids some day exist, they will be seen as artificial or natural people, depending on political, not scientific views of them.

Gross parts like limbs and organs do not define a man, either by the composition of their molecules or by their functions. And today's behavioral technology invades the brain as well as lesser parts, with chemicals and steel and plastic parts that can usurp its highest functions, so that the orchestration of all a man's acts comes to depend on artificial things which are no natural part of him. When the discovery of chemical anesthetics started this progression more than a century ago, no one realized how comprehensive the extent of imposed control could be. No one does yet.

But when tomorrow's technology goes a step beyond today's, raising man's IQ, improving his artistic skill, and his athletic prowess, will the affected person then be more, or less a man? As the merely operational virtues of the machine model impose more and more on the "truth" and come more comprehensively to account for everything that happens to the body, the question eventually occurs of why we continue to distinguish them. Perhaps we do so only to protect our sentimental attachment to old creeds which we have neither faith to believe in nor courage to abandon. In relation to behavior, it is the doctrine of free will that is ultimately most threatened by the machine model of man, and which ultimately must be invoked to oppose it.

The important questions that arise from the machine model are, finally, practical, not just intellectual ones. They probe the legal as well as scientific, moral, and spiritual status of people and of people parts. If he were to lose some parts or lose the functions that make them meaningful, at what point would a man cease to be himself? The extreme problems caused by learning to produce man or variations of him in the laboratory will not be realized in this century, say Kahn and Wiener, but the basic question need not wait for androids to appear to leave the realm of theory. It has already been asked in euthanasia trials and autopsy cases; and the answer traditionally given is that all the parts of man are sacred. But that tradition, perhaps once valid, will no longer serve mankind; technology has made it into a *de facto* falsehood by the same process it has used to make man into a *de facto* machine, whatever his original essence was.

It makes less practical difference to the scientist than to many others whether or not the machine model of man is literally correct. He can use no other broad theory to design or interpret experiments, and does not use theory of any kind as a catechism to keep faith. Science is a way of working, not a religion; its models of human nature are intellectual conveniences, not personal credos. There are all kinds of machines that provide useful scientific models of man in one or another situation; some of them liken him to a computer; others, to a hydraulic system; and still others, perhaps, to a cuckoo clock. What they share is lawful functioning, no more, and scientists officially assume no more than that about them. They believe, with Albert Einstein, that "the good Lord is not a crapshooter." Scientific mechanism implies a belief that the universe operates lawfully, for molecules and men, but the belief is an intellectual convenience for the scientist, not a dogma over him. It is more than a mere inconvenience to people for whom human nature is a moral problem, however, and it is from them that the main opposition to the machine model arises.

Humanism Versus Mechanism

The view that man is *not* a machine, here called "humanism," is rarely stated very bluntly by scholars because, put strongly enough and in detail, it is obviously untrue. Any intelligent observer can see that a good deal of human software works by the same mechanical principles as does the hardware of other machines. Bones provide leverage for muscles by Archimedes' rules for all levers; blood is pumped through the circulatory system by an honest-to-goodness pump; perspiration on the skin evaporates in the same way as does sweat on a glass of beer. The more sophisticated statement of humanist belief is that man is not merely a machine, or that he is more than his apparent machinery. In the past, when all machinery was crude and primitive, man had to be carefully elevated above all other animals, almost up to the angels, in order to sustain this belief. At present, with animals little better than they have ever been, but machines improving all the time, it means defending the superiority of his faculties against computers. Many advocates rush to take the case.

Psychologists, biologists, theologians, artists, and philosophers have all contributed to this endeavor, usually in the technical jargon and from the special perspectives of their own fields, and sometimes in dazzling displays of intellectual virtuosity. The diversity of background and approach from which human mechanism has recently been discussed, and frequently rejected, ranges from the fundamentals of molecular biology through neurology, psycholinguistics, and philosophy, and from the dignified proceedings of a 1964 Vatican Conference on the physical basis of consciousness through scathing literary attacks on behavioristic psychology.

Regardless of the exact subject matter or professional background, the humanist position typically favors the molar approach to behavior, arguing from one speciality that even the lowest levels of cellular organization involve functional products which are more than the sum of their chemical and molecular parts, and emphasizing from another that the self is a whole and unique entity which identifies a human being and sets him permanently apart from all machinery, however elegant. It is easy to see how, in psychology, this idea gained currency from the clinical experience of psychotherapists, many of whom object strongly to the machine model of man: psychological problems are only presented by whole people, whose selves are not seen but are, presumably, as unique as the therapist feels his own self is. The humanist argument, however, is not limited usually to such simple expositions. It is often stated in such complex form, spiced with neurophysiological speculations, larded with psycholinguistic "transgenerations," or torturous analogues or rejections of analogues from computer simulations, that one sometimes cannot tell, at first blush, that the approach is either molar or antimechanist. For example, Arthur Koestler's complex, often brilliant attack on behavioristic psychology talks about "hierarchical organizations" and other technical ideas from Gestalt psychological theory, showing its antimechanist intent most dramatically only in the title: *The Ghost in the Machine*.

The arguments cited above have all appeared in books published since 1966, but despite appearances, the philosophical basis of modern humanism has not changed much since Descartes, whose argument reduced to the position that man is more than his machinery. Descartes indicated clearly that man was a machine distinguished from other biological machinery by having a soul, derived from no material power, but reflected in propositional speech, an ability which he thought would never be replicated by any machines that man himself could build. Modern partisans of this view who wish to avoid the theological problems of the soul, or of its secular (and mortal) counterpart, the mind, substitute the term "self."

While the humanist polemic ostensibly concerns freedom as a scientific, not a metaphysical issue, its underlying aim has always been to establish personal responsibility as the basis of morality. Cartesian dualism required the separation of mind and body in order to give man's incorporeal, immortal, and free will space in which to operate. It is will, in that view, which identifies man, and it is freedom which confers the capacity for moral choice upon him and makes responsibility possible. This ancient perspective is beautifully and tragically expressed in the naïve version of the Faustian epic, in which man bargains the long future of his soul against a transitory but enormous increase in the pleasures of the flesh. The Devil makes the deal because there is no way he can get access to the soul without Faust's acquiescence, and the contract is signed in blood to signify, per Biblical dictum, that the essence of man has been committed. In modern form, the argument stays much the same; secular disciples of Descartes may forego incorporeality and immortality, but they cling hungrily to the idea that will is free within its mortal host. Regardless of the semantics used to get there, the humanist perspective conclusively insists on man's unique freedom to make choices. The molar scientific proposition it relies on says, more modestly, that the most significant human behavior tends to occur at such a complex level of organization that its individual determinants are either trivial or unmeasurable. Even if this is true, however, predictability implies restriction— and the humanist position demanding, above all things, human freedom, cannot be fully satisfied by it.

Thus humanism is rooted inextricably in a moral system which is threatened by the machine model of man, and which would demand political or religious opposition to that model even if it were "true" and even if it were evident that the humanist argument is mounted on errors of observation, which assume that the appearance of uniqueness is uniqueness, or on errors of logic, which neglect the possibility that hard-machines may feel like people but don't say so. The argument eventuates as special pleading for man's exalted place in nature, offering responsible stewardship in exchange. While it may be inept as a tool for engineers to work by, it can be gravely studied to judge its rules for men to live by.

The Dangers of the Machine Model

Treated strictly as a scientific matter, the humanist doctrine cannot oppose the machine model very well. The molar-molecular controversy is really a question of the best tactics of investigation, and both are strictly mechanist positions. The concepts of self and of individual uniqueness fit the mechanist scheme without violence to it. The humanist position is a poor logical and empirical antagonist of the machine model. Its early Renaissance dogma that "man is the measure of all things" cannot be extrapolated into the dogma that he is the physical measure of things. The humanist argument for freedom is sensible only as a moral prescription; as a scientific description of human behavior, it addresses the facts incorrectly. Were it stated precisely about behavior-control technology, for instance, it would either deny that one is possible or insist that its limitations will be severe. The first claim is demonstrably untrue; the second, unverified and unlikely.

The humanist's only valid basis of resistance to the machine model is psychological; it challenges the moral uses to which this concept can be put. There are two important reasons for fearing the easy application of mechanistic theory to morality: it may encourage an impersonal approach to human beings, and it may discourage personal responsibility for one's conduct.

It is dangerous enough to use the products of science thoughtlessly, as Philip Wylie accuses religious men in *Opus 21:* "to flush one's toilet and kill one's enemies." It may be even more dangerous to make the rules of scientific operation a basis in some minds for reducing the image of man to an elegant pile of junk. For the notion that the difference between man and the machines he invents is nothing more than the physical difference between hardware and software (which is little more than the distances apart of each one's molecules and the speeds at which they cavort) may offer dangerous leverage and comfort to all those persons and forces in modern society who are, to begin with, no respecters of persons. And however absurd, pathetic, or in error it may seem to be, the sentimentality which ordains the frantic assertion, "I'm a person, not a thing"; the irritability engendered by discovering that one's salary, income tax, and gasoline bill are the victims of an insane digital computer; and even the political conservatism which makes a few of us pine hopelessly for a return to Jeffersonian democracy are guardian attitudes against the depersonalization which both technology and totalitarianism promote.

The other psychological danger in the mechanistic view is, as Norbert Wiener puts it, that of encouraging "the gadget worshipper" in his desire to avoid personal responsibility and place it elsewhere.

. . . on chance, on human superiors and their policies which one cannot question, or on a mechanical device . . . It is this that leads shipwrecked castaways to draw lots to determine which of them shall first be eaten. It is this to which the late Mr. Eichmann entrusted his able defense. It is this that leads to the issue of some blank cartridges among the ball cartridges furnished to a firing squad. This will unquestionably be the manner in which the official who pushes the button in the next (and last) atomic war, whatever side he represents, will salve his conscience.

The common contemporary problems of personal identity and personal morality have been restated often and well, though not always with cogent proposals for their solutions. Maintaining individual identity in a complex society is not easy, and, on the face of it, the machine model does seem to support what James Bugental calls "the dangerously pathogenic trend toward the mechanization of man," in which we treat ourselves and others as "interchangeable units," and identity and individuality "get washed out in the process." And coming from an ethical tradition in which morality depends upon free will, it is not clear how the idea of personal responsibility in our society will survive the demise of its intellectual underpinnings.

But the image of individual facelessness in a technological nightmare cannot, in any case, be fought effectively by the force of outworn intellectual habits which constrain most of us, however educated and secularized, to nurse an anthropocentrism in which we do not really believe. Maybe the only reason the idea of human mechanism threatens personal identity is that it offends anew the conventional human vanity which says we differ nobly from all other creatures God has made and, accordingly, should differ even more from products of our own invention. If so, it is no more dangerous than Galileo's once shocking discovery that the earth was not the fulcrum of the universe, or Darwin's that man was not uniquely discontinuous with life on earth, or Freud's that he was not controlled by his highest faculties alone. All these ideas offended human vanity in the same way at one time, but we have revised our images to incorporate the new models of reality they imposed without wrecking mankind in the process. Perhaps there is no more to fear from mechanism in this regard. This is not to say that the modern problem of identity is unreal, only that its source is poorly understood. Clearly, overpopulation and slavery threaten individuality because they really do cause men to be misused like interchangeable parts, but the machine model, perhaps, implies no such concrete danger. It is important to challenge our habitual thinking in this respect, for no attack on the problem of personal identity can hope to be successful if it is any less intelligent than the forces that misuse man.

There is no gainsaying the value of a morality of personal responsibility, but its value has nothing to do with its origins, only with its effects. Habit alone leads us to assume that there is no other basis for personal responsibility except the doctrine of free will. That is true when the sole basis for morality is coercive; then responsibility must be linked to freedom in order to have a rationale for penalties. But saying there are no other grounds for responsibility is tantamount to saying that fear and avoidance are the only motives for moral conduct, which is untrue. There are also incentive motives and sympathy motives, and they may be more powerful than any others. They are motives a machine can have and act upon, even though it cannot be held responsible by being threatened in advance and punished afterward for lapses.

If there is anything we know about man as a machine, it is, first, that part of his machinery is animal in that it can suffer pain, feel tenderness, and experience all the sentiments which together are compassion; and second, that he is a thinking machine, or calculator, programed for conceptual thought of many kinds. One kind, by which he defines himself, is reflexive thought; that is, thought about himself, awareness of himself as an object. By cogitation about what he is, he learns to define his self apart from all its parts—to know that his leg, which he can feel, is not him, that his will, which he perceives and always feels is free, is not him and not free. Only man knows that his humanity is in the interaction of his parts, and that it is altogether real and totally impalpable. Only the child of man asks where all the music goes when the tape recorder is shut off; and only man can understand that it goes nowhere, that it was never there as an entity, but only as an energy transformation, just like his self.

Man is not merely the animal machine with propositional speech, or only a compassionate computer. He is the machine that can make propositions *about himself* and can tell the difference between his parts, which are his property but not his self, and their processes of interaction which enable him to reflect, and which are his soul.

This ability to objectify his thoughts and separate intelligence from feeling, while losing neither one, gives him two great moral capabilities; it enables him to compare his sentiments emotionally with those of other creatures, that is, to feel compassionately. And it enables him to make intelligent judgments of the world, that is, to think dispassionately, disregarding all feelings briefly while he calculates what effects his acts will have, and then anticipates how much of them his feelings will accept. The only moral question man need ask is how to act. He can do this even with a material soul, even if there is no moral force in all the universe but himself, even if God is dead or never called on man to play some special role, and even knowing that freedom is, finally, the illusion of itself.

And might not the anthropocentric fallacy of the old morality in fact promote an unnecessary, even cruel and dangerous creed? The ancient religious quest for supernatural purpose in human history tried to give man superior status among natural things, not just to soothe his fears for survival or well-being in a dangerous world, but also to justify his callous disregard for the kinship of sentience, of pain, and of life's struggle, which simple intelligence shows him that he shares with other creatures. The secular quest for freedom and uniqueness in our species may do the same thing, making it all right, for instance, for a man wantonly to kill his poor relatives on the phylogenetic scale or other men, as if he knew that "the anguish of all creatures" clearly differed for man and beast, Jew and Gentile, white and Negro. And if the day comes when first-rate androids exist, so Man and Machine can be added to the list, it would require no novel thinking to arrange for their mistreatment. Most of man's lugubrious enslavement of his fellow creatures has been eased along by just this kind of morality.

At all events, man does not need the backing of a moral code in order to assert superiority over all the other creatures on this planet. He could be brutal or compassionate, whatever moral claims he made, and he would have the same options on how to act whether he called himself an animal, machine, or god. All that is required to act is power, and man has power to rule the world.

The machine model of man is not important as a credo underlying the developing technology of behavior control. Its challenge arises from the fact that however limited its concrete moral or material uses, it is to all intents and purposes correct. If so, then it makes no difference how dangerous it may be, except in a Platonic state, where discussion of it might be suppressed; there is no alternative to recognizing its potency and confronting its consequences.

If it is understood that there is no self-abnegation inherent in the machine model of man, and that there is still nothing to scorn in him if all his stuff is molecules, then the problem becomes the manageable one of how to find the basis for a compassionate mechanism to guide the technology he elaborates, not how to combat it with worn and threadbare myths. No ideology inheres in scientific work, and man must always borrow wisdom from some moral creeds to guide its use—but not from false ones. Sooner or later, people will abandon an ethic which depends on what they know is false. Technology is not an accidental force but one whose products and effects may be foreseen. The machine model does not intrinsically demand, nor does it justify, the brutal mechanization of society, but without absorbing what it means, that may be impossible to avoid. And its absorption likewise can be no accident, though it is fearsome for most of us, schooled in the old myths, to contemplate that man's *deus ex machina* is finally man himself. But there is no choice. Only by dehumanizing man conceptually can we learn where his humanity lies, and only with that knowledge can it be preserved.

8

The Ethics of Behavior Control

Control means power. Behavior control means power over people. In times past, it meant power over life and death and some visible activities in between. Now, it is coming to mean power over all the details of people's lives—of attitudes, actions, thoughts, and feelings, of public postures and the secrets of the heart. Many sciences feed technologies that harness them to human needs and, at the same time, fashion and refine ever-sharper and profounder tools for exercising power over men. The nature of these tools, their prospects, and the view of human nature they inform, has occupied most of our discussion to this point. Now, we must consider the greatest moral problem of their management: how to keep the delicate balance of personal liberty and public interest so painfully achieved in free societies from being tipped or overthrown by naïveté or malice in handling these instruments. Technologies do not create or answer moral problems; only men do that. The final issues of their moral intercourse, accordingly, do not depend on how men are able to use their tools, but on how they are willing to use each other.

The moral problem of behavior control is the problem of how to use power justly. This is no new question, but critical questions in human experience rarely are. The proper use of power is seldom obvious to thoughtful men, especially if they lack religious revelations or "natural" ethics for deciding what is just. But if the basic questions never change, the answers sometimes do; they sometimes must in order to serve man's nobler purposes, however tentatively, or to avoid catastrophe, however narrowly. The right use of power over man's behavior is no plainer now than it was in eras when the tools of power were few and gross. Now, they multiply and grow more potent at such a frantic pace that customary social instruments of control like law are inadequate to manage them, and it grows harder all the time to know how they can be managed wisely, and by whom, and for what ends. We need new ingenuity to see how they should be exploited or contained. Where discussion of behavior technology has begun, people have agreed that its expansion is inevitable, that its misuse may be disastrous (for its individual victims, to be sure, but for the rest of us as well), and that some extreme misuses already have occurred, especially, and ironically, in health research. But few discussions have been held as yet, perhaps because the field is still too new, or still too inchoate, even for many of its explorers to have noticed that they have a tiger by the tail. Thus it was no surprise, in 1966, when the United States Public Health Service ordered all the scientists it sponsors to obtain the voluntary consent of experimental subjects in advance and to guarantee no harm would come to them, that many research workers felt a needless leash was being put on them. In the first place, they said, most subjects in most experiments volunteer; in the second place, details of some studies (like placebo research) cannot be told to subjects in advance; in the third place, nobody *intends* to harm his subjects; in the fourth, almost nobody does; and in the fifth, the benefit intended to humanity, and usually served, makes occasional accidents bearable. So the arguments run, most often correctly.

Even so, most of us would agree, there probably should be some restrictions on research, and certainly there must be much discussion of them, as long as it is true that experimenters have power over subjects or that their ability to use it declines or grows with the decision to tell or hide what they are doing or intend. All good people who have power over others, even just a little power and even for just a little while, need access to an ethic that can guide their use of it.

The Meaning of Justice

In man's long struggle for control over his destiny, perhaps his greatest triumph has been the invention of justice, the idea that power over men must be controlled. But the idea of justice is a mere fiction until it is expressed in law, its ostensible instrument of control, and until the law itself is reinforced by powers as strong as those it seeks to curb. Without power at their disposal, the legal formulas prescribing the just use of power or redressing its abuse are meaningless. In this sense, power is real and justice is not.

The natural history of justice is such that restraining laws usually evolve as aftermath to wild outbursts of destructive power and are conceived to check its further excesses. The Nuremberg trials thus take place after genocide has happened, not before, and codes to prevent such crimes against humanity in the future only follow on the heels of their disastrous past. So, too, the United States Supreme Court does not acknowledge the existence of a law until a case occurs in which someone has broken it, thus connecting the words of statutes to the facts of human experience. Law is a device for channeling power over people, nothing more. And it cannot work well until it is clear where the unchanneled flow of power will work its ravages.

The problem of how to plan the general control of power over people applies to the control of behavioral technology as well. Until its dangers are apparent, there is no just way to legislate its use; as the dangers grow visible, tentative strategies for controlling them can be conceived and executed when the need is clear—but not before. It would pervert justice to suppress in her name evils that are only hypothetical.

Absolute and Relative Ethics

People who are frightened and repulsed by the prospects of behavior control may find it frightening and repugnant to hear that the ethics of managing behavior-control technology to be just cannot be absolute. An absolute ethic is sure to be useless or disastrous because it will anticipate either too much or too little harm from a technology whose details cannot yet be forecast and whose impact cannot yet be known. A fearful ethic, which restricts its use too much, binds progress at no profit to anyone; most people who understand the value of placebo studies, for instance, would probably agree to being subjects in them if it were safe to be. A cavalier ethic of permissiveness that allows, say, doctors to secretly inject cancerous matter into old people, ambiguously calling it a "cell suspension" (this happened in New York in 1963), may help to bury the victims of cavalierly good intentions. It may also lend science to new depths of mischievous misuse.

The rigidity of absolute ethics guarantees not only that they will be unjustly harsh or lax, but that they will soon be obsolete as well, especially as the progress of technology accelerates. The ethical questions of technology must largely follow the machinery, as justice must largely follow power. As new machinery brings new impact on people's lives and new need to probe the ethical formulations which preceded it, it will be clear that some old rules have become patently impractical guides for conduct. New ethics, in turn, may seem absolutely valuable in their time, until new realities once again require that newer rules be formed to cope with them. Practical ethics are thus expedients for defining good and bad behavior, conveniences serving limited purposes for limited periods; and they evolve, instead of springing forth full blown, at a pace set by changing circumstances more than by reflection or decree.

Absolute behavior-control ethics cannot be meaningful at all, but neither will tentative and cautious ones be meaningful solely by virtue of their modesty. Even a limited ethical code must try not just to follow but to anticipate the dangers to avert and hopes to reinforce by its prescriptions. This means it must abstract some moral principles from past experience and make some general rules to guide specific acts. The intellectual pitfalls in this process are the same for the ethical congressman trying to decide the proper legal status of marijuana users and the moral theologian seeking immutable rules for the status of living creatures we may some day find on other worlds. They are the dangers of fuzzy logic and sloppy language habits which rob concepts of their meaning or pervert them to connote things they do not mean, which can have deadly effects applied to human attitudes and affairs. Viewing concrete things like human beings abstractly, for instance, lends itself to treating them indifferently, while the converse process of treating abstract ideas like "society" or "government" concretely disposes us to take nonentities too much to heart, as if they had some palpable existence of their own. Such practices put words at such a distance from their referents that meaning perishes along the way, giving rise to vagaries and euphemisms which mask reality and mislead the innocent. It would matter little if only harmless vanities were served as a result, like titling everyone from chairman of the board down to the lowliest office boy, as some firms do, or calling garbage men "scavenger contractors," as the city of Chicago once did. But the same usage has also served well to disguise unconscionable horrors, soothing the squeamishness of people who might be unnerved by confrontations with ugliness which they approve in abstract form, like Nazis titling their mass murder plans "the final solution of the Jewish problem."

In ethics, abstractions become dangerous and euphemisms poisonous whenever they mask the basic unit of concern, the individual human being, or when they describe things in ways too far removed from the palpable, sensory experience of the listener to be meaningful. In politics, where demagoguery is more common and works better than in some other crafts, the manipulative possibilities of airy double-talk are even more plain. The Left has a richer vocabulary of such nonsense than the Right in Communist countries; the opposite is true among fascists; and the democracies are probably middling muddled. The thickness of prosody goes with the amount of oratory.

Decent moral ideas are hard to formulate and dangerous to use, at best, and despite the dangers, just and practicable codes of ethics cannot be freed entirely of generalities, cannot be based firmly on sensory experience rather than ideology—and cannot be done without. What we can do to construct a meaningful ethic for behavioral technology is study critically our common ethical vocabularies, ideologies, and myths in order to explore how well they can address the new problems and new prospects of our times.

It does not take very elegant analyses to see that some of the ethical abstractions in common use can retain their ideological sanctity only if people do not think much about subtleties which make their meanings doubtful. Everyone presumes to know what freedom is or what will means, for instance, as long as they refer to common things in everyone's experience, which can be understood in simple terms and acted on accordingly. The subtleties of analysis tend to subvert traditional ethical ideas by showing that their traditional meanings are too simple to be accurate. Technology contributes to the subversive process by inventions which complicate or simplify life in ways that make old ethical doctrines appear irrelevant—like medical techniques which keep a man's vegetative functions alive long after his animal passions and intellectual processes have died, so that euthanasia laws start to lose their meaning, or welfare laws which seem to make a gratuitous virtue of personal charity to widows, orphans, and the aged. Either way, technological invention can suck the breath of life from common referents, render their former meanings meaningless, and undo the ethical doctrines that had once served the *status quo*. The ideological cornerstones of modern man are constantly ground down by the innocent creations of his engineers.

Freedom and Control

The most important ethical problems of behavior control concern its relationship to freedom because freedom is the antithesis of control. And the most vital questions are those of political freedom in particular because politics is the most important kind of behavior manipulation. Political freedom is the right to do whatever one wants. The moral question is: to what extent can individuals demand or be denied this right? To what extent can they be compelled to discharge responsibilities to other men? In what respects should men be free to engage other people cooperatively, antagonistically, or not at all? It is all one question and has probably been much the same since neolithic times, when the elaborate division of labor in human societies began to make people interdependent and, in doing so, began to compromise individual liberty.

The contemporary version of this ancient problem differs from early ones in some important details which sharpen its focus but do not change its fundamental character. First, as society becomes progressively more technical and complex, it may also be more delicate and vulnerable to bottlenecks and breakdowns, so that anyone who removes himself from it or rebels against it may endanger the welfare or survival of everyone else more than at any time in the past. Second, more powerful means exist today than ever before for coercing social responsibility. Third, and most important here, behavior-control technology makes it possible not only to rationalize coercion in terms of the common good but also to engineer individual consent in ways that make it possible to be responsible and happy all at once. The intellectual tradition of the West has not prepared us for this phenomenon because the engineering of consent has always been inordinately difficult.

For most of history, the struggle for freedom has been concerned with restricting the power of rulers over their subjects. This was almost always achieved by force and maintained by the machinery of government, but in the Anglo-Saxon world, at least, it has moved toward freeing individuals more and more from the control of others, whether peers or patrons. All the great legal codes from the Magna Charta through the Bill of Rights enlarge the measure of free speech and action to which we are entitled. The Nuremberg code, the most recent milestone in the discourse on freedom, guarantees freedom of the will as well, by forbidding the coercion of consent. By making possible the engineering of consent instead of its coercion, however, behavior-control technology shifts the problem of individual freedom a step further than legal codes have yet thought to cope with.

Political man, the hypothetical creature on whom Western

democracy is based, is traditionally responsible for his own behavior, which means able to act upon the choices of his individual consciousness; it, in turn, is supposedly under his own control and no other. Talmudic law went so far as to assert that "man is eternally liable" for doing damage, even while sleeping, because his capacity for consciousness enables him to foresee the outcome of his acts. The capacity for consciousness, and hence for responsibility, is the ideological foundation, in our society, of individual liberty.

But the nature of consciousness, its control, and their relationship to responsibility are not always obvious. Small children cannot take responsibility for property or for government or, in most respects, even for deciding what is needed most in their own education (though B. F. Skinner, in his utopian *Walden II,* says they should). Nor can the insane be prosecuted for criminal acts because presumably they lack control of their behavior. And just what having control means is also problematic. The legal basis for criminal insanity in most of the United States, called the M'Naghton rule, says that someone is criminally insane only if he does not know right from wrong or cannot distinguish between them at the time of his crime. An extenuating principle, called "irresistible impulse," says that people may sometimes know an act is wrong but feel helplessly compelled to do it anyway. Most psychiatrists, and many lawyers, feel that neither idea corresponds much to the realities of human behavior.

Whether responsibility is seated in a consciousness identical with intellect, as the M'Naghton rule implies, or in some steering unit of the brain that couples passion and intellect and that harmonizes them, as the notion of irresistible impulse would indicate, it is always directed toward a hypothetical group of individuals who, taken together, are society.

There has always been a dynamic tension between the concepts of freedom and responsibility; they are antagonistic modes of conduct. If a person acts as he pleases, he may be set on a collision course with others, who call themselves society and tag him antisocial or psychopathic. But if he acts responsibly toward others, he may not be free to satisfy himself. Individuality always courts social deviance, and social responsibility never promotes it. Their blending in permanent harmony has always been the fantasy of utopias, societies which do not exist. We have always assumed that social deviance and social responsibility were the chosen behavior styles of individuals in control of themselves, and in control at the deepest level of awareness—that of their own desires. It is at that level that behavior technology challenges the utility of these concepts by making it possible to populate utopia with automata, who are free at every level of behavior *except* desire. Behavior technology can cope with social deviance in the happiest possible way—by eliminating personal license and still leaving the individual with the feeling that he is free to satisfy his needs. But the very power to guarantee that people will act responsibly and feel free completely unhinges the conventional political morality on which modern democracy is based.

In a complex society, where many kinds of individual regulation are unavoidable, and where social responsibility of some kind must be advocated as a positive value, it is easy even for lovers of freedom to forget that the idea of responsible freedom is a contradiction in terms and that the ultimate doctrine of social responsibility is "statism," a form of slavery, politically expressed in government by tyranny. To free men, the state is not an entity around which men's lives should be organized and to which they should be devoted, but a fiction, convenient and dangerous, for regulating their many cross-purposes. The theoretical danger inherent in abstract concepts like "the state" or "social responsibility" is that they can be used so easily to hide the machinations of power, which are always concrete and specific, beneath a dunghill of verbiage, which is neither. The practical danger, which increases all the time as its machinery improves, is that behavior technology will be used to assist such operations.

Information control already has been, of course. In the "total states," it is used extensively in the primitive form of "big" lies (like Nazi propaganda) and in slightly more advanced form (like the propaganda of Russia and the Arab countries) by using words, as Gore Vidal says, "for transient emotive effects, never meaning," for example, calling liberal Czech reforms "reactionary" or the Israelis "Nazi." In future autocracies, such as the one George Orwell projects, words are so freed from their referents that it is not necessary to resort to abstractions for emotionally stimulating gibberish; even concrete, simple language has its meaning destroyed by using it for doublethink, like "War Is Peace" or "Slavery Is Freedom." The final extension of political abstraction, however, is seen in Kafka's works, where words no longer refer to anything at all, not even to contradictory words. When the protagonist in Kafka's *The Trial* is accused of "crime," he is not charged with any act or even with an epithet that implies an act, like "revisionism" or "counterrevolutionary tendencies." To be accused by the state is to be guilty. This is the apogee of statism.

The danger to a free society from behavior technology, however, is not that a few tyrannical rogues will first propagandize us into giving them power and then scramble our brains or our television sets to keep it. The danger is that even its most benevolent use runs the risk of eroding freedom when it takes place *by the decision of anyone other than the person on whom it is used.* And in a free but complex society, that decision must sometimes be made by other people, and even against the subject's wishes. The ethical challenge emphasized by behavior technology is that of how to preserve or enhance individual liberty under circumstances where its suppression will frequently be justified not only by the common welfare but for the individual's happiness.

General technology contributes even more to the complexity of society than does behavior technology, of course, but it has a more ambiguous impact on individual liberty. Emmanuel G. Mesthene, of Harvard University's program on science and technology, argues that technology has created a society of such richness and diversity that people are more individualized and more aware of their worth and rights as individuals than ever before in human history. Certainly, technological improvements in economic efficiency, such as automation, reduce society's dependency on individual participation in production. That may make it possible for people to withdraw from economic production without damaging society, but it does not free them necessarily from other social involvements, like going to school or serving in the army, and it does not necessarily let them go publicly against the grain of social convention without risking condemnation or retaliation. Any increase in personal liberty which comes from the technology of production can be used up easily by a repressive social organization that finds "useful" things to occupy people's time. And behavior-control technology can probably make the people like it. Thus the problem of individual liberty is specific to it. Liberty, in the age of behavioral technology, must have an ethic to defend it and must not depend on the illusion that any "natural" benefits of general technology will work in its behalf.

The Ideals and Myths of Ethics

Every code of ethics involves a "mythology" and an "ideology." Ideology informs the code's goal and is always explicit; mythology informs its origin and may be implicit or explicit.* Ethical ideology is more important than mythology because it can be acted on and mythology cannot. We use our myths to reinforce our purposes, not to shape them. Even so, mythology has some importance of its own; it reassures people that their goals are worth pursuing, which is probably why they universally concoct elaborate histories to justify their goals. Virtually all tribal, ethnic, and national legends have a moral to the story.

The transmission of ethical tradition to children through myths, as part of their cultural heritage rather than as an articulate ideology, helps it to be maintained unconsciously. Most people want to be good by their own lights, but not to have to study for the purpose. Observing ethical tradition makes it possible, in general, to be good without having to be smart, at an intuitive level. Intuition is closer to sensory experience than is intellect, so

---

* A myth is literally a story handed down by word of mouth, i.e., a traditional tale, in Latin, a legend. It may or may not be true. The widespread myth that the term applies only to fictional history is untrue.

the precepts and examples of mythology seem sympathetic and easy to appreciate, while the abstract convolutions of ideology may seem cold-blooded and irrelevant. Abstractions lack pity and malice alike. Even so, ethics require ideologies more than mythologies. For one thing, the incidents of myth and midrash may have no useful lessons for distant times and unforeseen events. For another, just principles are distillations of experience, not recitations of it; and the ancient tales of any people teach eventually as much of cruelty, corruption, ignorance, and hatred as they do of virtue. Ideology may itself originate in the myths of group tradition (religious ethics sometimes have), and new myths may constantly be written to suit contemporary ideology (like official Russian history), but in any case, myth serves ideology, not the reverse. The essence of ethics is its ideology, from which come both law and revolution.

The current ideology of freedom in the West is served by the myths of English history, the American and French Revolutions, and romantic anecdotes of the Periclean Greeks and ancient Jews. It is also sustained, however, by the scientific myth of will which, like the dualistic idea of mind, implies some topography of liberty inside a man.

Since there has been no shortage of governmental tyrannies available through most of history, the ideology of freedom has usefully focused on overcoming them. But it has never been easy to find a neat ideological basis for individual freedom within a democratic society because it has generally been so clear that the common welfare required the individual to accept some restrictions on his spontaneity and fulfill some duties of citizenship. The only domain in which it has been almost universally accepted that people have no social bonds is in the articulation of purposes, goals, or ideologies. By cherishing the belief that ideology moves behavior, on the one hand, and that it is freely willed and manipulated by the individual who believes it, on the other, we have had a basis for the pretense of absolute freedom. No matter what limits society must place on the expression of animal passions or the fulfillment of personal desires, we have said, individual freedom always exists in the one domain where nobody can be hurt by its expression and nobody can question its inviolability—the human mind. Ideology, which is not physiological or even material, but which can contain or unleash the fiercest energies of men, is free; it is the expression of man's ultimately free will.

But behavior technology can empirically deny just this belief and treat both ideology and will as merely organismic apparatus, and neither one as free. The idea that ideology expresses any absolute quality of freedom independent of anatomy is simply a new phrasing of mind-body dualism, this time expressed as a political-ethical secularism instead of the usual religious pietude. The message of behavioral technology, sent more forcefully by drugs and psychotherapy and conditioning and brain implants than it could ever be by proposition, is that will is ultimately not free, nor is ideology, nor man. Freedom is as much a scientific fiction as it is a political reality, and its political support cannot come from that pillar of intellectual respectability.

It is the threat presented to their pet mythologies of human nature that most frightens some people about behavior technology, rather than its challenge to personal liberty or traditional morality. With the power of science increasingly in evidence, they are fearful if their choice beliefs such as free will are not sanctified by science, which ordains the priestly blessings of our age. But science is not an entity or institution which can harm people whose ideas are unscientific, and nothing concrete hangs upon the myth of will to justify their fears. The ethical problem of behavior control is real, indeed, and needs specific guidelines for its resolution. Myths, after all, will be adapted to the purposes they serve.

The Ethics of Awareness

Behavior technology represents refinements of power which have never existed before. Even the most powerful tyrants of the past have been unable to enslave people so thoroughly, let alone to get them to like it. There can be no greater power over men than to make them want to do what one wants them to do. Advocates of an ethic of happiness might find such use of power justified, even compassionate; making people want what they cannot help getting protects them against the pain of feeling suppressed and seeing their wills defied. As Skinner suggests, freedom is an important idea only to people who feel oppressed; and happiness, only to those who are miserable. An ethic of individual liberty finds such exorbitant control generally unacceptable, however, not only because of its effect on its victims but also because it gratifies the lust for power in its perpetrator, which is the greatest vice conceivable to this ethic.

Even in the freest society, of course, some people must sometime bear the responsibility and burden of wielding power over others to supervise the allocation and distribution of resources, to organize protection and aid for the weak, the ignorant, and the infirm, and to maintain the physical machinery of civilization. Some candidates for power will want it because they see its value as an instrument for serving human needs. Others will be intoxicated by it, will delude themselves that having power makes their lives more worthwhile than other people's, and goaded by their invidious need, will lust after power for its own sake.

Those who find power inherently attractive will be most disposed to violate the freedom of others when it serves their quest for power. But even among those who seek power only instrumentally, there is no sure way to know whose wish to use it for serving others is self-delusion or an outright lie, or whose pure motives will later be corrupted by having power, or who would put it to foolish uses in the first place. Even the best men who seek power tend to want it, and even the best motives are no assurances of wisdom, honesty, or incorruptibility. Hitler, Zapata, and Huey Long may all have started their careers from different premises, ideals, and motivations, but once they had power, the victims of their repressions could not have known the difference.

Whether or not people want to be governed, in the ethics of liberty, does not count. Even if people choose their slavery, as many Germans did under Hitler, no one has the right to enslave them, any more than I may murder someone just because he asks

The Ethics of Behavior Control 213

me to. As long as it was true historically that there was no sure way to enslave people except "against their will," individual consent or will was a reasonable criterion for liberty. Once will itself can be readily manipulated, though, it stops being a useful measure of the limits for exerting power; it becomes a meaningless epithet about the human condition which only obscures the lust for power by focusing attention on the victim instead of on the violator. Behavior-control technology brings no conceptual novelty to the process; it just makes it easier to maintain power over others once someone wishes to do so.

Behavior control means that some people have power over others; freedom means that they do not. The ethical problems of freedom and control reduce to the conflict between these simple meanings, no matter how elegant the technical apparatus of power becomes. And these are finally practical, not philosophic problems, for the commitment of human beings to human freedom does not rest finally on their dialectical abilities, still less on freedom or determinism in the universe at large or in the soul. Ideology is not self-contained discourse but an articulate guide to action, whose purpose is to validate pledges long since given or to exact them against an uncertain future. Men who are pledged at once to freedom and to civilization, who can no more forsake the public interest than they can permit repression of its members, need an ethical ideology against the repressive power of behavior technology. They will not find it in foolish dithyrambics on the scientific reality of will, nor do they need to seek it there. It can be found, if anywhere, only in the realities of power.

There is no antidote to power but power, nor has there ever been. But there are ethical uses of power. In order to exercise justice against lawlessness, it is necessary to array lawful power. In order to unseat tyrants, it is necessary to mobilize revolutionary power. In order to defend individual freedom, it is necessary to enhance the power of individuals. If behavior technology endangers freedom by giving refined power to controllers, then the antidote which promotes freedom is to give more refined power over their own behavior to those who are endangered. Since everyone is endangered, this means facilitating self-control in everyone. And self-control does not mean simply the ability to inhibit impulses, but the general mastery of one's own behavior. The key to mastery of self is not will, which reduces, even subjectively, to nothing more than our perception of ourselves as struggling, demanding, or insisting. It is "awareness," a set of higher processes in the brain with which we recognize ourselves as having self and from which we derive the special human powers of control which animal passions could not supply.

Awareness is the conscious processing of information, which includes selecting it, storing it, and acting upon it. And the processing of information is the essence of behavior control. What we have called "information controls" meant simply the manipulation of stimuli presented to the individual, and what we have called "coercive controls" meant the manipulation of body processes in order to manage their responses to different stimuli. "Stimulus" is a technical term for any information to which the individual responds, which means any information he processes. The difference between self-control and control by others rests only in who is manipulating what stimuli. *All* behavior control is stimulus control, and awareness is the key to self-control because it enables the individual to maneuver his own sources of stimulation.

Will does not offer many options for self-control, only for mindless heroics. It is possible, for instance, to study mathematics in a room where a radio is blaring or where other people are carrying on an interesting conversation. But it is easier, and more effective, to turn off the radio or to leave the room—that is, to change one's relationship to the disturbing stimuli, either by manipulating the noise (information control) or changing the body's ability to respond to it (coercive control).

Such humble examples of stimulus control may hardly make it seem like the basis of all self-control, still less link it with elegant terms like awareness. But the idea becomes more plausible when we consider how, time out of mind, some humble ancestor observed that he could bring the warmth of fire home instead of seeking out a natural blaze, that his arm grew longer in the hunt if he held a stick, and that his fist grew harder with a rock in it. It is not such an unconscionable distance for the mind to travel from observing, remembering, and acting on the simplest tools man used to control events around him and from which his conquest of the world began to the endless complexity it has reached today, or to the still unforeseen events where the same processes of mind will take it next.

Awareness is the instrument of control par excellence, replacing, in the advanced state it has achieved in human evolution, much of the biological armor that lower organisms use to battle for survival. The armamentarium of human invention, including modern technology, is an expression of the power placed in man's hands because of his great capacity for awareness. Until now, his awareness has been directed at the things around him. Behavior-control technology has itself arisen from man's awareness of the relationship between his surroundings, his body parts, and his experiences of mood and thought, which he has labeled "mind." The solution to the problems of behavior control requires more focusing of human awareness on the subjective self, not to the exclusion of its surroundings, but for the expansion of its own contents. And there are no other solutions possible because there is no alternative to man's continuing to acquire knowledge, to build tools from it, and to use them. The only answer to man's increased general awareness is to increase his personal awareness. The only defense against the intrusions of science and technology, the cohorts of massed knowledge, is to expand and fortify his consciousness of self, the armor of individual knowledge. The only deterrent or reply to behavior control is to increase his technical mastery of his own behavior. Man's shield and buckler and, finally, his most potent weapon, is his individual power of awareness. It has always been.

All this brings the Biblical story of man's history full circle. The problem and its cure are born alike of Eve's temptation, and pain and pleasure both are sired by intelligence. So it finally comes to pass that knowledge is the only guardian against itself.

With this the case, we then must ask what ethical prescriptions follow from this ideology. If ideology does not mean just ideas, but ideas to be acted on, what actions do the ethics of awareness demand? There are at least four. Of technology, it demands that individual development be maximized and people provided with the instruments of self-control; men must know their tools. Of politics, it demands that men be free and the machinery of government forever vulnerable to individual action against it; men must have their rights. Of free men, it demands that they be conscious of the need to share the world with other men and exercise restraint on their own willfulness; men must know some limits. Of society, it demands that it renounce coercion as its chief instrument of control and substitute persuasive means which individuals may finally take or leave, even at some peril to us all; men must take some risks.

As it expands, the technology of behavior control clearly holds as much promise for serving freedom by developing tools that enhance awareness as it seems to threaten freedom by compromising will. Drugs to increase memory or improve intelligence or expand consciousness, electronic tools (inside the brain and out) to restrict dysfunctions and to heighten skills, educational instruments and techniques (from programed textbooks through hypnosis and conditioning) for speeding learning and for self-control of brain processes and body functions, and ways of thinking and meditating which simply turn consciousness upon itself are all parts of this technology. They are all developing apace, and they are all contributing to individual awareness, and hence to increasing internal behavior control. Without knowing what the social effects of such developments will be, the technical processes involved are clear, and the ethical imperative is clear as well: all the devices of self-control must be made available to all the members of society who can use them. If technological upsets result, such as might happen when erstwhile unskilled laborers get trained, or smart, and then decide not to do menial work, we will have to cleverly invent automata to do the work which people have outgrown. Man is thus ethically committed to a technical contest with himself whose future limit is not evident: he must keep making new things to correct the indecencies which are sometimes by-products of the new things he has made.

The politics of democracy have long since exploited the ethical imperatives of awareness whenever they have linked responsibility to consciousness, despite the useless further link so often made of consciousness to will. Political freedom is thus more ethically advanced and practically protected currently than are any other aspects of individual self-control, though in the nature of political activity, it must always be guarded. In the democracies, moreover, there are external stimulus controls on the misuse of governmental power which protect people from stupidity and corruption as well as malice by distributing power among many offices and individuals, by limiting the time anyone can hold power, by making him subject to recall while in office, and by spreading initial access to power among a wide electorate. But all these situational controls finally depend for their effectiveness on the mutual awareness shared by free men and their rulers of the nature of political power and its dangers, which makes it possible to concentrate power in the hands of a few without destroying the liberties of the many. If politicians did not know that the people expect them someday to relinquish power, they might try to subvert the democratic process; if the people did not expect the same thing, they might let them. What gives free men power over their rulers is awareness of their own power. What maintains individual freedom in any civilization, however elegant its technology for manipulating individual motives, is the power of individual awareness.

The politics of freedom are not only matters of resisting government, however, but of maintaining oneself against infringement from any outside source. Here too, knowledge has always been one of the best guardians against exploitation, just as it has always been one of the best tools for manipulating others. People who know their rights are not easily deprived of them, and people who study the weaknesses of others are not easily prevented from using them. To this day, the slave markets of Arabia specialize in ignorant and innocent victims who literally do not know that there are laws against their being kidnaped and enslaved or that there are people from their native lands who want to find and free them. And the bank accounts of confidence men are full of funds seduced from foolish people whose vanity prevented them from taking counsel in their ignorance and whose greed made them victims of their own main chance illusions.

The only ethic of freedom which is ultimately defensible in modern society is one which limits freedom as well as advocates it. If people demand that they be free in everything they do, they will finally be free in nothing. If individuals refuse to observe some restraints on themselves and to fulfill some public obligations, free society cannot survive. The question is where social controls should come from. Edmund Burke said, "Society cannot exist unless a controlling power upon the will and appetite be placed somewhere, and the less of it there is within, the more there must be without." The ideology of awareness demands that social controls must ultimately be seated within the individual himself. The apotheosis of awareness is the exercise of freedom within channels of restraint, ideally chosen and navigated by the individual himself. Ideal control is self-control.

This "modern" ethic of individual liberty and limitation has been stated simply in two ancient principles, a positive one of action and a negative one of restraint: (1) People are entitled to do what they want up to the limit that (2) they may not hurt other people. What hurting others means is not always clear. Hurting someone's sensibilities, for instance, may be more or less damaging than hurting his body. And neither the positive nor the negative version of the golden rule is comprehensively workable—doing to others what one wants done to oneself, or not doing to them what one does not want done to oneself. But the same fundamental assumption always operates in this ideology; it is that life is precious, that it is only evident once for each individual, and that there is no such thing as a group life. An acceptable ideology for such an ethic must be one that promotes the life of the individual and that protects the lives of those around him as well. Only the awareness of himself in relation to others makes that possible.

If awareness is to be the chief instrument of social control, society must eventually operate through the medium of education rather than coercion, of persuasion rather than law. The chief burden of social conformity must fall upon the individual rather than upon enforcement agencies. And insofar as the latter retain responsibility for the control and rehabilitation of individuals, their work should be directed increasingly at seating the means of control within the individual himself rather than on making him a ward of society.

The shift from coercive to educational means of social enforcement seems to be taking place rapidly in advanced social climates like that of modern Sweden. It is worth noting, in this connection, that Sweden has a very high suicide rate; this may be the price of internalizing control. The more the responsibility for a man's behavior rests with himself alone, the more likely he will act as his own judge and executioner when he feels that his needs cannot be met or his guilt not expiated. At all events, from the ethical point of view espoused here, the phenomenon does not demean Sweden's social order; aggression against the self is better than aggression against others, and Sweden also has a very low crime rate.

Self-control means choice, not inhibition. A social system predicated on individual awareness and control must ultimately be reconciled therefore, to the right of the self-controlled self to act in ways which depart from the conventional and which are currently forbidden only because they offend the tastes of others, without damaging them more palpably. The self-controlled self has the right to terminate, just as it has the right to take drugs, masturbate, and think its own thoughts. So too do pairs of individuals have rights to make contracts repugnant to others, provided they do not infringe on them. Infringement is hard to define, of course, and has long been a practical issue at law, but the principle involved is clear nevertheless: there can be no such things as crimes without victims in this ideology, for it is only the existence of victims which makes possible the definition of crimes. The ethics of awareness can permit no other argument because to say otherwise would allow that there are crimes against society. But society is not an entity, the state is no real thing, and government is not an organism which lives and breathes and hurts. Abstractions cannot be victims.

In a society which foregoes coercion, some individual expressions are clearly worse than others, that is, they clearly infringe more upon other people. A practical ethic therefore emerges. It says, for example, that if aggression cannot be controlled, murder should still be avoided. It suggests a whole hierarchy of undesirable conditions:

If someone is to be killed, suicide is better than homicide.

If another person is to be harmed, verbal aggression is better than battery.

If society is intolerable, withdrawal is better than wanton destruction.

If withdrawal is necessary, temporary means like alcohol or hallucinogenic drugs are better than enduring ones like psychoses.

If psychosis is needed, introversive ones like depression are better than projective ones like paranoia or extravagant madnesses like mania.

The ethics of awareness must eventually require a noncoercive society, but it is not clear what life in such a society would be like. There is little doubt that the nature of some social institutions in contemporary society will change as new machinery makes old mores obsolete, and it is possible, under the circumstances, that we will enter a long term moral crisis as people find themselves freed of the chains of tradition and adrift, desperate for something to which to bind themselves. The ethics of awareness will be especially frightening to desperate people because the argument that social limitations should be vested in the individual may seem to them to offer no moral certainties. Society does run some risk from this ideology, as it always has from human freedom. But there are no alternatives to freedom except tyranny.

The guiding principles of this code, at all events, are clear: life is always precious, and it is only individual; awareness is the choicest instrument for the control of behavior; control should be vested internally and not in other people's hands. Informational and coercive methods are both useful for expanding awareness and, to that extent, should both be used. Society is a convenient fiction for the interdependencies of many individuals. It should subserve the needs of individuals, therefore, whose main responsibilities toward it are negative: to refrain from hurting others. And its main instruments should be the good opinions of oneself and other individuals, not the threat of force. Thus the ethic of awareness, the ideological instrument of liberty in a scientific world.

The Mythology of Human Nature

The myth of will cannot sustain the ethics of the future, so other myths must take its place. Man is a tale-spinning animal, whose massive curiosity about the world and about himself makes him fashion histories and explanations endlessly. He cannot do without myths, and whether they place him high or low in the scheme of things does not matter in the end. Merely giving him a place satisfies his deepest need: to know. The factual truth of mankind's myths is also unimportant; today's common knowledge is tomorrow's superstition in many things which still may serve today's needs well enough. Tomorrow's myth of human nature probably must be that of "the aware machine" because it is more acceptable in a scientific age where will can be controlled than is the dualistic notion of an inviolable core of self in man. Factually, it is also more true, but this is less important; like any ethical mythology, its chief use is to reinforce ideology, not to fashion it. In this respect, all myths are ultimately meaningless.

But the ethical systems they support are meaningful indeed to the individuals affected by them, and a mythology that replaces will must not only be easier to reconcile with facts but also must be no less suited to serve human freedom. The more clear it is that will is, in absolute terms, a fiction, the more important it is to protect the individual whose rights have hitherto been borne upon that myth. For he is the same creature, with the same endowments, sentiments, and intellect, whether he is guided by soft machinery or an immortal soul. Only fools and villains need to devalue what they understand, and only they will withdraw compassion from human sufferings or manifest indifference to human strivings on finding them defined and limited by mechanisms and mortality.

The value of perceiving man as machinery is that it does not demean his functions or potentials at the same time that it suggests they may all be understandable. No matter how much he is ruled by law, which is the essence of all machinery, man still remains the choicest artifact of God's invention on this planet, and such a one as reconstructs himself, extends his energy in all directions, and rules the earth. Seen this way, man as machinery is surely nobler and more dignified than the natural man of Romantic philosophy, whom we know to be a savage. And seen this way, he is immensely more than the cousin of the other animals he has been linked too tightly with since Darwin was misread.

In fact, the mechanistic myth of man frees us somewhat from obsession with his animal origins to meditate more than we have upon his human purposes. A great deal of energy has been spent on the sterile issue of whether man rose from baser origins and to what extent he has escaped from them. As Sir Arthur Keith (quoted by Robert Ardrey) wrote: "I feel confident that, if evolution had succeeded in tracing man from a fallen angel and not from a risen ape, . . . antagonism to evolution would have gone by the board."

The immanence of control technology depending, as it does, on our attributes as machinery, makes it irrelevant any longer to debate the ethical or political implications of where we came from, a matter which, in any case, is useful only to racists and their like, who call on history to justify the evils of the present. Control technology makes it possible to substitute concern with human purpose for concern with origins, to ask what are the decent uses of human beings, at what costs and for what rewards, rather than to consider pedigrees as claims. Regardless of where we have come from, this technology insists, humanity is going wherever it goes together.

An animal, but unlike any other animal; a machine, but softer than most machines; a sentient computer with passions, whims, and locomotor skills—man is the animal that makes machines. So far, his products are what Eric Hoffer calls mere "half machines lacking the gears and filaments of thought and will . . . that turned the machine age into a nightmare. Human beings had to be used as a stopgap for inventiveness. Men, women, and children were coupled with iron and steam . . . the machines were consuming human beings as fast as coal."

For human beings not to be the stopgap for his inventiveness, man must not turn back upon himself, deny his genius with machinery, or fail to make himself the object of its inquiry. What he must do is recognize the precious character of each one of his kind and seek to maintain these kindred mechanisms in ways that serve them individually well, nurturing them, repairing them, and giving them the freedom to fulfill whatever purposes their inner gears and filaments ordain. The world must be controlled so that the maintenance of each precious life in it can be ensured.

Mankind's greatest skill is the ability to *maintain* what he has created. It is the expression of his powers of control.

In his essay, "Strategy for the War with Nature," Hoffer describes the maintenance of *things* as one of the most glorious and precarious accomplishments of civilization. He is puzzled by it too: "Even a lethargic or debilitated society can be galvanized for a while to achieve something impressive, but the energy required to maintain things is of a different order." The proper maintenance of people is even less understood than is the maintenance of things, but it is more important finally; behavior technology is one important craft to serve that end.

No one knows right now if man will ever travel to the stars or find other life—higher or lower than his own—on other planets. But however distant or farfetched that adventure, it seems more likely that he will find life in other places than that he will find a second life for human beings on earth, either buried in their bodies in the form of lasting self or in a soul resurrectible beyond the grave. If anything seems sure in knowledge by this time, it is that human beings live just once on earth, in a unique configuration of parts and events unrepeated in this place. One life—one chance to live, and love, and leave behind a world worth living in. Maintenance provides the culmination of technology; it is the conscious sequel to invention, which sustains the profits human genius has accrued. It is the civilization of tenderness, the gentlest character of our animal heritage. Maintenance is the act of awareness that contemplates death without despair, but with the tender resolution to leave behind ourselves a useful world for those we love. This is the final triumph of this soft machine which thus, knowingly, defeats death, conquers nature, and controls the future of a world it will not see.

Additional Readings of Interest

The first two chapters of this book introduce a field that has been little explored until now in an integrated fashion. The individual disciplines involved and the specific implications of behavior control are discussed in detail from Chapter 3 on. The suggested readings accordingly begin with the third chapter.

Chapter 3: Control by Information (1): Psychotherapy

Bandura, A. "Behavioral Psychotherapy." *Scientific American,* March 1967, pp. 78–89. Nontechnical discussion of contemporary work on "behavior modification," a common term for action therapy. It covers role modeling, desensitization, and operant conditioning in some detail.

————. *Principles of Behavior Modification.* New York: Holt, Rinehart & Winston, Inc., 1969. This is likely to be the most important scholarly work on psychotherapy for some years.

Ford, Donald H., and Urban, Hugh B. *Systems of Psychotherapy: A Comparative Study.* New York: John Wiley & Sons, Inc., 1963. Analyzes the theories and practices of most of the important psychotherapy systems, including all the insight methods, existential therapy, and Wolpe's methods. It does not include other action therapies, such as behavior shaping, which was then only on the verge of its great popularity.

London, Perry. *The Modes and Morals of Psychotherapy.* New York: Holt, Rinehart & Winston, Inc., 1964. A comparative analysis of the technical characteristics of insight and action therapies and the moral implications and conundrums of each. It views psychotherapy as an incipient "secular priesthood."

Wolpe, Joseph, and Lazarus, Arnold. *Behaviour Therapy Techniques: A Guide to the Treatment of Neuroses.* New York: Pergamon Press, Inc., 1966. This is a "cookbook" of action therapy methods, which clarifies, better than any theoretical exposition possibly could, the experimental and pragmatic character of these methods.

Chapter 4: Control by Information (2): Hypnosis, Conditioning, and Electronic Tools

HYPNOSIS

Chertok, L., ed. *Proceedings of the 1967 International Symposium on Psychophysiological Mechanisms of Hypnosis.* Berlin: Springer, 1969. The papers presented at this conference, sponsored by the International Brain Research Organization, are all quite technical but provide the most current summary of work in this area.

Gordon, Jesse E., ed. *Handbook of Clinical and Experimental Hypnosis.* New York: The Macmillan Company, 1967. A comprehensive collection of papers by assorted specialists. It summarizes much of the theoretical, experimental, and clinical status of hypnosis in America.

Lassner, J., ed. *Hypnosis and Psychosomatic Medicine: Proceedings of the International Congress for Hypnosis and Psychosomatic Medicine, Paris, 1965.* Berlin: Springer, 1967. A broad sample of work from many lands and in many languages. It concentrates more narrowly on medical hypnosis than do other works.

London, P.; Hart, J. T.; and Leibovitz, M. "EEG Alpha Rhythms and Susceptibility to Hypnosis." *Nature* 219 (1968): 71–72. This article reports the first discovery of a relationship between electrical brain wave patterns and hypnotic susceptibility.

Moss, C. Scott. *Hypnosis in Perspective.* New York: The Macmillan Company, 1965. This is a shorter work (also available in paperback), which summarizes current knowledge in a brief but clear text and samples some representative experimental and theoretical articles from the technical literature.

Naruse, G. "Hypnosis as a State of Meditative Concentration and Its Relationship to the Perceptual Process. In *The Nature of Hypnosis,* edited by M. V. Kline. New York: Institute for Research in Hypnosis, 1962. The originator of the study of hypnotically conditioned hallucinations describes his ideas. Most research on the subject since then has still not appeared in print but does tend to support Naruse's early work.

Conditioning

Brown, J. A. C. *Techniques of Persuasion: From Propaganda to Brainwashing.* Baltimore: Penguin Books, Inc., 1963. This is an excellent summary and critique of actual methods and the literature analyzing them.

Condon, R. *The Manchurian Candidate.* New York: McGraw-Hill Book Company, Inc., 1959. A fantastic fictionalization of Chinese brainwashing methods and the effects of hypnosis on American soldiers in the Korean War, this novel makes heavy and often accurate reference to the technical literature on classical conditioning and hypnosis.

Griffith, Samuel B., II. "Communist China's Capacity to Make War." *Foreign Affairs* 43 (1965): 217–36. This is a cogent description of the use of persuasion methods within the Communist Chinese Army.

Honig, W. K. *Operant Behavior: Areas of Research and Application.* New York: Appleton-Century-Crofts, 1966. This is a collection of technical papers giving a comprehensive summary of applications of operant conditioning, its interactions with classical methods, and the use of hardware in conjunction with conditioning.

Rice, Berkeley. *The New York Times Magazine,* 17 March 1968. "Skinner agrees he is the most important influence in psychology." The article gives an excellent description of Skinner, parts of his theory, and many of its implications for behavior control and scientific views of human nature.

Sargant, William. *Battle for the Mind: The Mechanics of Indoctrination, Brainwashing, and Thought Control.* Baltimore: Penguin Books, Inc., 1961.

Skinner, B. F. *Science and Human Behavior.* New York: The Macmillan Company, 1953. A splendid and detailed discussion by the originator of operant conditioning. It is written for the interested layman and describes the implications of behavioral science for human affairs, heavily emphasizing behavior control.

Computer Therapy and Electronic Tools

Abelson, Philip H. "Privacy." *Science* 158 (1967): 323. A review of A. F. Westin, *Privacy and Freedom,* New York: Atheneum Publishers, 1967. It describes Westin's theory that the human need for privacy is biologically based, reviews the accelerating development of electronic devices for spying, and warns of the uses to which these are increasingly being put.

Bellman, R.; Friend, Merril B.; and Kurland, L. "Simulation of the Initial Psychiatric Interview." *Behavioral Science* 11 (1966): 389–399.

Bennet, Chester C. "What Price Privacy?" *American Psychologist* 22:5 (1967): 371–76. This article takes the opposite view to the position Abelson represents, asking what title people have to privacy which serves antisocial interests.

Colby, K. M., and Gilbert, J. P. "Programming a Computer Model of Neurosis." *Journal of Mathematical Psychology* 1 (1964): 405–417.

Colby, K. M.; Watt, J. B.; and Gilbert, J. P. "A Computer Method of Psychotherapy: Preliminary Communication." *The Journal of Nervous and Mental Disease* 142 (1966): 148–152.

Glueck, B. S. "The Use of Computers in Patient Care." *Mental Hospitals* 16 (1965): 117–120.

Kamp, M., and Starkweather, J. A. "The Electronic Computer as an Interviewer." *California Mental Health Research Digest* 3 (1965): 103–104.

Loughary, J. W.; Friesen, D.; and Hurst, R. "Autocon: A Computer-based, Automated Counseling Simulation System." *The Personnel and Guidance Journal* 45 (1966): 6–15.

Starkweather, J. A. "Computest: A Computer Language for Individual Testing, Instruction, and Interviewing." *Psychological Reports* 17 (1965): 227–237.

Chapter 5: Control by Coercion: Assault, Drugs, and Surgery

DRUGS

Abelson, Philip H. "LSD and Marihuana." *Science* 159 (1968): 1189.

Baker, Rodney R. "The Effects of Psychotropic Drugs on Psychological Testing." *Psychological Bulletin* 69 (1968): 377–387. This is a comprehensive review of research which concludes that mood drugs do significantly affect psychological test performance.

Beecher, H. K. "Quantitative Effects of Drugs on the Mind." In *Drugs in Our Society,* edited by P. Talalay. Baltimore: The Johns Hopkins Press, 1964, pp. 77–89. It discusses placebo research.

DeBold, Richard C., and Leaf, Russell, eds. "LSD, Man and Society." Middletown, Conn.: Wesleyan University Press, 1967.

Dubos, René. "On the Present Limitations of Drug Research." In *Drugs in Our Society,* edited by P. Talalay. Baltimore: The Johns Hopkins Press, 1964. This is an authoritative discussion of synthesis and specificity in drugs.

Gottschalk, Louis A. "The Use of Drugs in Interrogation." In *The Manipulation of Human Behavior*, edited by A. D. Biderman and H. Zimmer. New York: John Wiley & Sons, Inc., 1961.

——. "The Use of Drugs in Information-seeking Interviews." In *Operant Behavior: Areas of Research and Application*, by W. K. Honig, Chapter 42. New York: Appleton-Century-Crofts, 1966.

Jarvik, Murray E. "The Psychopharmacological Revolution." *Psychology Today*, May 1967, pp. 51–59. This article is an excellent nontechnical history of psychopharmacology.

Katz, Martin M.; Waskow, Irene E.; and Olssen, James. "Effects of LSD." *Journal of Abnormal Psychology* 73 (1968): 11–14.

Noyes, A. P., and Kolb, L. C. "Pharmacological Therapy." In *Modern Clinical Psychiatry*, Chapter 33. Philadelphia: W. B. Saunders Co., 1958. Textbook prescription for the use of mood-changing drugs.

President's Commission on Law Enforcement and Administration of Justice. *Narcotics and Drug Abuse*. Task Force Report on Narcotics and Drug Abuse for the President's Commission on Law Enforcement and Administration of Justice, Washington, 1967.

Snyder, Solomon H.; Faillace, Louis; and Hollister, Leo. "STP: A New Hallucinogenic Drug." *Science* 158 (1967): 669–670.

Uhr, Leonard, and Miller, J. G. *Drugs and Behavior*. New York: John Wiley & Sons, Inc., 1960. Collected papers by specialists, primarily research and theory. It is a major comprehensive work on the subject.

Uhr, Leonard, and Uhr, Elizabeth. "The Quiet Revolution." *Psychology Today*, July 1967, pp. 40–43. The article discusses what should be done about hallucinogenic drugs.

MEMORY

Three excellent articles on the physiology of memory and search for a chemical memory booster.

Deutsch, J. Anthony. "Neural Basis of Memory." *Psychology Today*, May 1968, pp. 56–61.

Halstead, Ward C., and Rucker, William B. "Memory: A Molecular Maze." *Psychology Today*, June 1968, pp. 38–41, 66–67.

Perlman, David. "The Search for the Memory Molecule." *The New York Times Magazine*, 7 July 1968, p. 8ff.

PAIN AND PUNISHMENT

Melzack, Ronald, and Wall, Patrick D. "Pain Mechanisms: A New Theory." *Science* 150 (1965): 971–79. A discussion of the most important theory of pain in this century. The authors attempt to account for the different psychological phenomena reported in connection with pain.

Solomon, Richard L. "Punishment." *American Psychologist* 19 (1964):

239–53. An authoritative discussion of punishment as a means of behavior control, this article concludes that, in general, it is un-effective or has capricious effects, but there are important areas of potential use which should be studied.

Szasz, Thomas S. *Pain and Pleasure: A Study of Bodily Feelings.* New York: Basic Books, Inc., Publishers, 1957. This is a psychoanalytic study of the physiology, psychology, and sociology of pain, the uses to which it has been put, and response to it.

ELECTRICAL BRAIN STIMULATION

Delgado, J. M. R. "Chronic Radio-stimulation of the Brain in Monkey Colonies." In *Excerpta Medica International Congress Series* no. 87. Tokyo: Proceedings of the 23rd International Congress of Physiological Sciences, 1965. This article describes the behavior of rhesus monkeys in response to ESB.

———. "Free Behavior and Brain Stimulation." In *International Review of Neurobiology.* Vol. 6. Edited by Carl C. Pfeiffer and John R. Smythies. New York: Academic Press, Inc., 1964. Delgado reviews his own and other research on ESB, particularly with cats and monkeys. It includes an excellent summary chart.

———. *Evolution of Physical Control of the Brain.* New York: The American Museum of Natural History, 1965. Surveys historical foundations of contemporary brain stimulation research on man and animals. This extremely well-written and interesting review touches on all the major problems of philosophy, experimentation, and instruments in the field.

Heath, Robert G. "Electrical Self-stimulation of the Brain in Man." In *Control of Human Behavior,* edited by R. Ulrich, T. Stachnick, and J. Mabry. Illinois: Scott, Foresman & Company, 1966. This describes use two psychotic patients made of self-stimulation units worn at the belt and operated at will.

Moyer, Kenneth Evan. "Kinds of Aggression and Their Physiological Basis." *Communications in Behavioral Biology,* abstract no. 08680058 part A, 2 (1968): 65–87.

Rosenfeld, Albert. "The Psycho-biology of Violence." *Life,* 21 June 1968, pp. 67–70. This is informative popular description of current uses of ESB and drugs in the diagnosis and treatment of uncontrollable violence.

Sheer, Daniel E. *Electrical Stimulation of the Brain: An Interdisciplinary Survey of Neurobehavioral Integrative Systems.* Austin: University of Texas Press for the Hogg Foundation for Mental Health, 1961. Comprehensive collection of papers by outstanding authorities on virtually every aspect of ESB. Many of the papers are quite technical, but it is still one of the most important references to consult for detailed background in this field.

Chapter 6: The Prospects for Behavior Control

Dobzhansky, Theodosius. "Changing Man." *Science* 155 (1967): 409–14. This is a comprehensive and optimistic discussion of man's biological future based on favorable cultural and technological changes favoring positive evolutionary changes.

Elkinton, J. Russell, ed. "The Changing Mores of Biomedical Research: A Colloquium on Ethical Dilemmas from Medical Advances." *Annals of Internal Medicine,* supplement 7, 67 (September 1967). This is an interdisciplinary discussion of the dangers to be foreseen from advances in the life sciences, including dangers of behavior-control technology.

Kahn, Herman, and Wiener, Anthony J. *The Year 2000: A Framework for Speculation on the Next Thirty-three Years.* New York: The Macmillan Company, 1967. This is a brilliant series of projections on the near future by one of America's most distinguished proponents of planning "alternative strategies" for the contingencies of an uncertain future.

Morison, Robert S. "Where Is Biology Taking Us?" *Science* 155 (1967): 429–33. This is a clear analysis of the declining prestige and power of the family as a result of better formal education, especially in biology and the problems of overpopulation, genetics, and eugenics.

Moskin, Robert I. "Year 2018." *Look,* 28 May 1968, pp. 110ff. *Look's* Foreign Editor summarizes a collection of fourteen papers sponsored by the Foreign Policy Association, attempting to forecast "how the world will look 50 years from now." It is to be published as a book: *Toward the year 2018.*

Platt, John R. "Changing Human Nature." *Science* 152 (1966): 1573. Platt speculates on the future uses to which superior teaching methods ought to be put.

President's Commission on Law Enforcement and Administration of Justice. *Drunkenness.* Task Force Report on Drunkenness for the President's Commission on Law Enforcement and Administration of Justice, Washington, 1967.

Williams, Roger J. *Biochemical Individuality.* New York: John Wiley & Sons, Inc., 1963. This presents persuasive evidence that individual human beings have much more distinctive genetic constitutions than is generally recognized.

Chapter 7: The Machine Model of Man

Adler, Mortimer J. *The Difference of Man and the Difference It Makes.* New York: Holt, Rinehart & Winston, Inc., 1967. This massive display of erudition on the problem of man's uniqueness is written with great clarity but apparent dedication to the idea that there is some way to eat meat without fretting about having to kill in order to do so.

Allen, John M. *Molecular Organization and Biological Function.* New York: Harper & Row, Publishers, 1966. Allen holds that biological systems are "more" than their chemicals or the unorganized versions of their cells.

Bertalanffy, Ludwig Von. *Robots, Men and Minds: Psychology in the Modern World.* New York: George Braziller, Inc., 1967. This is an appeal to the humanist (antimechanist) conception of man and an attack on behavioristic psychology from the organicist viewpoint in biology.

Eccles, John C., ed. *Brain and Conscious Experience.* New York: Springer-Verlag New York Inc., 1966. This presents papers given at the 1964 Vatican conference called by the late Pope John XXIII.

Koestler, Arthur. *The Ghost in the Machine: The Urge to Self-Destruction—A Psychological and Evolutionary Study of Modern Man's Predicament.* New York: The Macmillan Company, 1967.

Langer, Susanne K. *Mind: An Essay on Human Feelings.* Baltimore: The Johns Hopkins Press, 1967. A distinguished philosopher and language scholar attacks both behaviorism and computer models of man and seeks a new resolution to the problem of dualism and a new theory of mind based on man's symbolic abilities.

Miller, George. *The Psychology of Communication.* New York: Basic Books, Inc., Publishers, 1967. This contains seven essays on man as an information processing machine by an outstanding student of psychology of language and computer paradigms of human behavior.

Neumann, John Von. *Theory of Self-Reproducing Automata.* Edited by Arthur W. Burks. Urbana: University of Illinois Press, 1966. This is a posthumously completed work of the great mathematician, and his last major contribution to the development of computers.

Reiner, John M. *The Organism as an Adaptive Control System.* Englewood Cliffs, N.J.: Prentice-Hall, Inc., 1968. This presents the mechanistic view at its most sophisticated, describing the properties of live machinery.

Wiener, Norbert. *God and Golem, Inc.: A Comment on Certain Points Where Cybernetics Impinges on Religion.* Cambridge, Mass.: MIT Press, 1964. The father of cybernetics extends his discussion of the moral and social implications of control technology, begun in *The Human Use of Human Beings.* Boston: Houghton Mifflin Company, 1950.

Chapter 8: The Ethics of Behavior Control

Fleisher, Frederick. *The New Sweden: The Challenge of a Disciplined Democracy*. New York: David McKay Co., Inc., 1967. Fleisher emphasizes that education and communication rather than coercion play the most important role as agencies of social enforcement in modern Sweden.

Freund, Paul A. "Is the Law Ready for Human Experimentation?" *American Psychologist* 22:5 (1967): 394–399. A Harvard Law School professor discusses legal conservatism as designed largely to protect human integrity and life. It includes discussion of New York doctors case and Nuremberg defense argument that "we are moving into a new era of experimentation when . . . advancement of social ends must override delicacy and squeamishness about particular individuals."

Hoffer, Eric. "What Strategy for the War with Nature." *Saturday Review,* 5 February 1966, p. 27. The fourth in a series of *Saturday Review* essays by "distinguished contemporaries." It argues that nature at close quarters is a brute, and man has gotten where he has in spite of her.

Jones, Ernest. "Free Will and Determinism." No. 7 in *Essays in Applied Psychoanalysis*. 2 vols. pp. 178–189. New York: International Universities Press, Inc., 1964. In a fascinating essay on psychological factors in the belief in free will or determinism, one of Freud's most famous students traces beliefs in one or the other throughout history and concludes that neither belief has significantly affected behavior in any civilization.

Lear, John. "Do We Need New Rules for Experiments on People?" *Saturday Review,* 5 February 1966, p. 61ff. A science editor reviews coercive-control technology and New York doctors case, summarizing problem of misuse with particular reference to the Nuremberg code.

Mumford, L. *The Transformations of Man*. New York: Harper & Row, Publishers, 1956. A speculative essay on human nature, from man's animal origins to the present. Mumford argues that the development of tenderness in higher mammals was one of the main factors differentiating them from lower species.

Skinner, B. F. "Freedom and the Control of Men." *The American Scholar* 25 (Winter 1955–56): 47–65. Attempts to resolve conflict of democracy with science. Skinner also fights off objections to planned cultural improvement and to frequent refusal of intellectuals to recognize scientific truth.

Chapter 8: The Limits of Behavior Control

Index

About the Author

Perry London is currently Professor of Psychology and Psychiatry at the University of Southern California.

He has served as a clinical psychologist at the Madigan Army Hospital and was formerly on the psychology faculties at the University of Illinois and Stanford University.

Dr. London received his B.A. from Yeshiva University and his M.A. and Ph.D. from Columbia University. He is now a Research Science Development Fellow of the National Institute of Mental Health.